architecture

works projects writings
TOYO ITO
edited by andrea maffei

Electaarchitecture

Editor
Giovanna Crespi

Copy Editor
Gail Swerling

Translation
Christopher Evans

Distributed by Phaidon Press
ISBN 1-904313-45-0
ISBN 978-1-904313-45-8

www.phaidon.com

www.electaweb.it

First published in English 2002
Reprinted in paperback 2006

Printed in Hong Kong

I would like to express my deep gratitude to Toyo Ito and the whole of his studio for their cooperation and the time and energy they devoted to me during the preparation of this book. In particular, I would like to thank Nozomi Tarao and Mariko Nishimura, of Toyo Ito & Associates, for their constant assistance and collaboration.
Special thanks go to Electa publishing house and to Francesco Dal Co for his attention and advice.
A.M.

Contents

Selected Writings by Toyo Ito

Appendices

Toyo Ito, the Works

Andrea Maffei

The work of Toyo Ito can be considered one of the most significant interpretations of the complexity of the Japanese world. It is difficult to make his architecture fit into a precise and consistent current of thought, and the fact is that it is not Ito's primary intention to pursue a single line of research or create a formal "style" of his own that can be applied everywhere. His research starts out from an attentive observation of Japanese consumer society and an interpretation of its social context.

While in the West cities and their streets have a design and the context has precise points of reference, cities like Tokyo appear to be undifferentiated systems with neutral and ever changing urban characteristics, which could be extended endlessly in any direction. Buildings are quickly demolished and replaced by others, with new forms and functions, over a time-span of around twenty years, so that the image of the city is always being modified without ever changing its basic concept: a neutral and fragmentary system, lacking precise points of reference except systems of transport and communication. These cities have no real and lasting substance like European cities. Instead, they retain the impermanence and precariousness of a macro-infrastructure. If we look at the Japanese tradition, buildings were constructed out of wood, never stone or brick, owing to the constant threat of earthquakes, and thus were habitually rebuilt after a short time as the materials wore out. In Japanese culture the idea of solid and substantial architecture, designed to last, does not exist.

Toyo Ito has developed the idea of an ephemeral architecture as the best way of reflecting these metropolitan non-contexts. The material consistency of his buildings is pared to the bone. He exploits technology to reduce the dimensions of structures and details to the point where they almost vanish, making extensive use of glass to abstract the buildings from their materiality and to lend them a fragility similar to that of temporary installations. Since everything in the Japanese urban context changes rapidly and nothing has lasting substance, his works seek to avoid any kind of solidity and present an evanescent, fragile and mutable appearance.

We can talk about a realistic interpretation of Japanese cities. Paradoxically the attention that Ito pays to the context, or rather to the non-context of his works, appears to be an approach to design that has a great deal in common with certain traditional and conservative Western attitudes. In fact anyone who has the chance to see Ito's actual buildings in cities like Tokyo or Yokohama will receive a quite different impression from the one produced by photographs of the same works in a magazine. To Western eyes such dynamic and light structures may look futuristic or imaginary, because they picture them in a European urban context, but when seen in their own setting the impression changes. Just as in Europe some architects pay a great deal of attention to pre-existing historic buildings and the traditional materials used in their construction, Toyo Ito starts out from an objective analysis of the conditions of Japanese society and its *modus vivendi* and goes on to devise a solution of his own. Even though the formal results are almost the complete opposite where the use of materials and the architectural solutions are concerned, there is not much difference in methodology of approach between the two positions. While more "Western" works, like the classicist ones of Tadao Ando or Arata Isozaki, look more transgressive and provocative to the Japanese—precisely because of their remoteness from the local culture and their tectonic solidity—Ito's works by contrast are light and elegant interpretations of the existing non-context.

Neutrality

Ito's production can be split into two main periods. At the beginning of his career most of his designs were for residential buildings or offices, culminating in the one for his own house, Silver Hut (1984). This marked the point of transition to the second phase, when he started to receive his first public commissions and to construct on a large scale.

The architectural concepts that Ito develops in his projects react to different aspects of the complexity that surrounds them, each in a different way. In comparison with the "chaos" of Kazuo Shinohara, always mutable whatever the direction, his buildings reflect the concepts and distinct characteristics of such a system. They do not criticize or reject them, but take up and "order" individual aspects in clear and simple design solutions. While some architects respond to the same problem with complex and chaotic forms, Ito spurns a purely formal line of research and seeks a simplicity that permits a limpid clarity of expression.

White U, Tokyo.

Some of the buildings can be seen as prototypes that Ito has used to try out his solutions, and thus allow us to comprehend the phases, recapitulations and evolutions in his research.

After the early works, which still showed signs of a certain formalism and the influence of architectural styles, Ito began to react to urban complexity in a negative way, developing an idea of neutrality. Continuing a formal line of research would only have allowed him to add new pieces of different materials and colours to an already complex system, while the negation of form permitted him to condense and at the same time eliminate the infinite solutions possible.

In his early works, the materials and forms were still left visible and clearly legible. In Aluminium House (1971) he used aluminium to enrich the form of the wooden building and create a metallic image. In the PMT Building at Nagoya (1978) he still applied a plastic *divertissement* that made the main front ripple to create a graphic and formal effect. The White U (1974), a house he built for his sister, a musicologist, marks instead the beginning of his attempt to rise above any formal constraint and move toward the neutrality of a homogeneous space, without an end or a beginning. The architectural solution bends the building back on itself, without any windows opening onto the street, but only onto an internal courtyard, so that the city cannot be seen. Reacting to the complexity of the urban context and its fragmentary character, the space is isolated and interiorized in the non-representational character of an absolutely white volume: all contact is lost with the outside, leading to an immaterial abstraction of the building. The constant fluidity of movement and change in the big city is synthesized in a choice of continuous and formless space. The negation of form frees the building from the succession of distinct parts and permits the creation of a single fluid system. With this project, Ito started to make use of a geometric form: its simple surfaces covered with white plaster cancel out any material weight and only the windows onto the inner courtyard and a few skylights interpret and modify the simplicity of the space with the weightlessness of light. The inner courtyard is covered with beaten earth, as if it were a natural desert without any vegetation to compromise its decorative form. Ito sometimes speaks of it as a "garden of light" created between two U-shaped walls.

The negation of form is a return to the underlying neutral system on which Japanese cities are based, and in which all architectural solutions can be applied and modified at the same time. It becomes a means of releasing the building from an unambiguous interpretation and opening it up to a similar and ambiguous multiplicity of readings. If it were to maintain a solidity and the

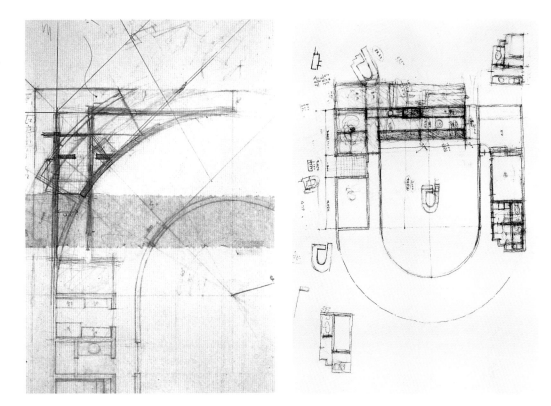

heaviness of a concrete materiality, the building would be too complete and lasting a solution. The choice of a neutral form instead sets the project in the indifferent urban fluidity that surrounds it, without diversifying it in any particular direction. The fact that the White U was demolished in 1998 seems an almost theatrical epilogue, confirming the symbolic quality of its relationship with the rapid changes of the city. The neutrality also permits Ito to propose his designs not as definite and complete solutions, but only as moments of transition in a broader process of design.

De-Composition

In his early buildings we still find a compositional order. In spite of the first moves toward neutral forms, the volumes remained compact and the parts of the building were fused together, creating a single, solid body. In some projects there was still a hierarchy of composition that bound the parts to a preestablished "order".
Silver Hut (1984), the project for his own house, was the first design in which Ito used the technique of de-composition, a means that he was often to adopt in subsequent buildings in order to

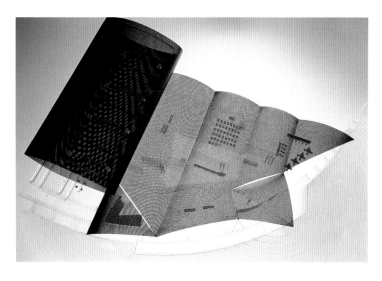

Yatsushiro Museum, model.

overcome the constraints of a definite volume. This was not a deconstruction of the design, but a fragmentation of it into separate and distinct elements of composition. Whereas deconstruction starts out from an *a priori* form and destroys it in order to give emotional expression to a deformed complexity, the sole objective of Ito's process of de-composition is a simple abstraction and dematerialization of the result. The idea of a work of architecture is fragmented into the individual elements of which it is made up in order to transfer it into an abstract and evanescent dimension.

In the Silver Hut, the overall volume is broken down into a series of vaulted roofs formed by a light reticular structure of steel, always left visible. The result is a building with no general consistency of volume, but fragmented into elements of light roofing that are either solid or transparent as in the inner courtyard. The courtyard-garden and the distribution of the volumes ambiguously compromise any distinction between interiors and exteriors and create a single and constant fluid space, rendered dynamic by the series of roofing vaults.

When Ito applies his process of de-composition it is not justified by any clear demarcation between distinct functions or different parts, merely by the freedom of the ephemeral. However, it is interesting to note that he does not abandon the use of logic to control the result. Deconstructivism deforms the volumes, structures and walls into irregular and completely irrational shapes, verging on a decorative fortuitousness. The freedom of composition, on the other hand, does not distort the regularity and geometry of the volumes, but maintains their structural or modular logic. We might call this "geometric anarchy" of composition. In this process of liberation, even the idea of a main façade is progressively abandoned and his buildings are also set free from the limitation of the hierarchy of fronts.

De-composition leaves the structural or mechanical elements open to view, abandoning any decorative form. The structure is utilized to define the primary image of the building and the reason

for its reduction to minimal dimensions is to make it lighter. These are not technological acrobatics that might escape the control of the designer, as they do in the majority of high-tech buildings, imposing themselves as the primary intention of the composition. Ito always keeps control of the techniques that he uses to reduce the material consistency of the building. Even the structures are no longer solid but broken down into modular elements that lighten them and lend them a linear, graphic appearance. In the Silver Hut, the structure of the roofing is decomposed into a triangular mesh that underlines the elements, liberating them from a heavily mechanical

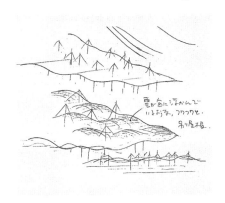

connotation. Windows, doors and walls vanish and only the lines of the structures design an almost graphic and homogeneously fluid system. In the Yatsushiro Museum (1991) and the Gallery U at Yugawara (1991) the same compositional and structural solution is reworked to overcome the limits of a regular perimeter and open up the volumes to the surrounding context.

De-composition is applied by Ito in two different ways: it can affect the whole disposition of masses in the project, as with the Silver Hut, or just the definition of the elements. In the Sendai Mediathèque (2000) the overall volume remains in one piece, but the elements of which it is made up are clearly differentiated. The structures, façades and walls are constructed with precisely distinguished materials and forms that make no formal or plastic compromise. Operating on these elements leads to a more complex and less direct result than does the decomposition of the volumes, but contributes equally to the ephemeral abstraction of the design. In this form of de-composition graphic design has an important role: it eliminates all material depth from the façades and leads us to perceive them as two-dimensional surfaces. The elevations are transformed into thin sheets stuck onto the structures, without any connection with the internal functions. The structures are dematerialized into linear elements that turn them into graphic patterns and textures which serve to characterize the image of the building architecturally.

Multi-Stratification

Tokyo remains a simulated city and Ito compares it to systems of microchips, with which it shares an immaterial fluidity and the fact that it is made up of a multiplicity of layers.[1] Light transport systems, escalators and means of communication create a constant fluidity that insinuates itself into the complex articulations of the Japanese megalopolis. Ito pays particular attention to electronic devices and the media, seeing them as analogical images of the city into which he inserts his buildings. A large-scale array of microchips looks like a vectorial aerial photograph of a city. In Tokyo's large railroad stations there are no longer boundaries between buildings with different functions, but just a great and neutral system that brings together trains, commercial outlets, cinemas, golf courses and restaurants without a break. Fluidity, multi-stratification and the ephemeral. While in the centres of European cities the historical stratifications of different

Tower of Winds, Yokohama.

periods maintain a clear distinction between one building and the next, in Japanese systems nothing has historical substance and everything is mixed up in a multiple and random stratification. Ito summed up these ideas in the exhibition "Visions of Japan", held at the Victoria and Albert Museum in London in 1991. The simplicity of a bare room was transformed into a tangle of urban flows by projecting chaotic images of the metropolis on all sides. This approach to design in which a simple element is suddenly transformed into electronic chaos was applied even in his first public buildings. In the Tower of Winds at Yokohama (1986), the stratification of the city was decomposed into electronic lines that were dynamically superimposed. Ito skilfully exploited the theme of the wind as a refined metaphor for the evanescent lightness of the ephemeral. A light structure supported a perforated, semitransparent facing of aluminium. During the day the elliptical tower remained a blank volume, clad with a homogeneous, metallic material. At night, a series of lighting elements transformed the tower into an electronic stratification that underwent continual change, thanks to the fractal calculations of a computerized system. The complexity of the signs in the neighbouring streets, the commercial spaces and the automobile traffic were emphasized in the graphic decomposition of the tower into layers of lines and points of artificial light. A monolith in which the procedure of de-composition, commenced with the Silver Hut, this time became vertical and dynamically electronic.

The Egg of Winds (1991) uses the same means of composition, structures and materials to develop the preceding Pao installations in a concrete manner and to evoke the prototype of the house of the future.

The ambiguity of these simple and neutral forms which grow complex is a confirmation of his rejection of a single interpretation. The simplicity of the building's form is not intended to make it easier to understand, but to create a neutral base on which various installations produce a complex object that is continually changing. We should not see these projects as futuristic "styles" but as objective interpretations of a simulated city.

The evolution of the theme of stratification has transformed the decomposition from horizontal to vertical. In the Silver Hut the series of vaults broke down the volumes into horizontal, parallel strips starting from the plan, not from the elevation. Since the competition for the Maison de la culture du Japon in Paris (1990), the planes that are superimposed have been exposed on the outside and utilized as horizontal lines to decompose the mono-volume into distinct vertical layers, each with different functions and characteristics. The materials, colours and forms change layer by layer, and the end result looks like a set of fragments of the city. As in the tower at Yokohama, in this case too the vertical decomposition preserves a single volume from the risk of turning into a monolith and reinterprets urban multi-stratification.

References
The temporal dimension of these buildings-cum-installations is always and exclusively the present. In fact particular models of the past do not exist in Japanese cities, still less the classical models of Western culture. In his realistic interpretation of the non-context in which he finds himself acting, Ito appropriates the Japanese rejection of permanent construction and its restriction to the present. It is difficult to see such designs in terms of the force of a vision project-

ed into the future; it would burden them with a precise choice and limit their interpretation to a single direction. Their precariousness and immateriality confines them to the dimension of the present, like temporary installations or short-term fittings. It is interesting to note that Ito's projects are never presented as a finished work, but always with the fragility and intuition of an idea, like the point of transition in a longer process. We could define them as works that are incomplete or under constant dynamic construction.

This conceptual formulation is reminiscent of the buildings of Mies van der Rohe, to whom Ito refers in many of his writings. For Ito the universal space of the Barcelona Pavilion constitutes one of the best representations of a fluid space[2] and the same quest for decomposition leading to a dynamic abstraction of space can be found in many of his buildings. The paring of structures and details to the bone also recalls Mies's idea of "less is more".

Ito's architecture draws on the teachings of various masters, from Japan as well as the rest of the world. In the first place, Kiyonori Kikutake, with whom he worked for four years after graduation and from whom he learned the lessons of the Japanese Metabolism of the sixties. Arata Isozaki remains a fundamental point of reference for Ito, both for the leading role he played in the seventies and for his sophisticated theories on the contemporary city. Although it is not possible to discern the formal influence of Isozaki in his work, we do find the same critical attention to social themes. But Kazuo Shinohara was certainly the architect who had the greatest influence on his production. From his very first buildings, like the White U, to the most recent ones, like the museum at Shimosuwa (1993) or the T Hall at Taisha (1999), we can see his influence in the absoluteness of the form and the concept of a single sign informing the whole architectural object.

But the mark left by Le Corbusier and the modern on Ito's work also needs pointing out. To reflect the stratifications of the city, the planes of the modern are used as two-dimensional layers overlaid in parallel. Ito draws extensively on the concept of *plan libre* to define his neutral spaces. The modern, which surpassed precedent styles with its rational simplicity, has helped him in turn to overcome formal constraints and come up with new forms. Neutrality fits in well with modernist rationality as it permits easy adaptation to any function or dimension. Ito had drawn on Le Corbusier's Dom-ino system in some of his earliest buildings, like the house at Umegaoka (1982), as well as in the more recent T House at Yutenji (1999).

Modernist solutions are also used in his multi-layered architecture. In the Fire Station at Yatsushiro (1995), he used the model of the Villa Savoye to superimpose two layers of functions, with a plastic distinction between open and closed spaces. On the ground floor the completely open space under the building raised on pilotis houses the parking and training areas and creates a continuity between the roads and the interiors. On the second floor are located the enclosed spaces of the offices and dormitories. Ambiguous elliptical openings in the volume of the second floor house the vertical connections and create elements of what Ito defines as "opaque transparency".

Fluid Transparency
The T Building a Nakameguro (1990) was the first in a series of completely transparent buildings. The pictures that Ito chose for the publication of these projects were always taken by night,

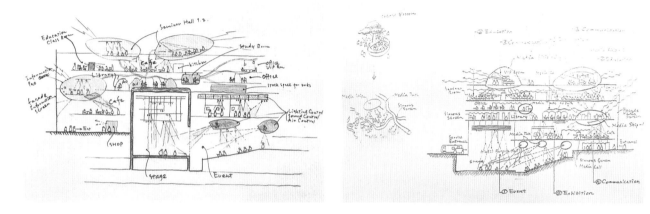

never in the daytime, as they laid bare the interiors which bestowed the insubstantiality of a circuit diagram on the buildings. The glass represents a continuation of the same design method employed with the perforated aluminium panels of the Tower of Winds: reflecting the light in the daytime, it forms the confines of a simple and elementary volume, which vanish at night. Everything becomes visible and the silk-screened parts create ambiguous translucent filters that "blur" the relations between interiors and the exteriors. The concept of using glass not as a banal high-tech material but as the ideal non-material was the first step in Ito's quest for transparency and the ephemeral.

In fact Ito was moving toward the creation of a new, fluid "material". The functions, routes and structures of his buildings were left open to view by large transparent façades that fused them into a new, fluid and dynamically homogeneous substance. Although distinguished from one

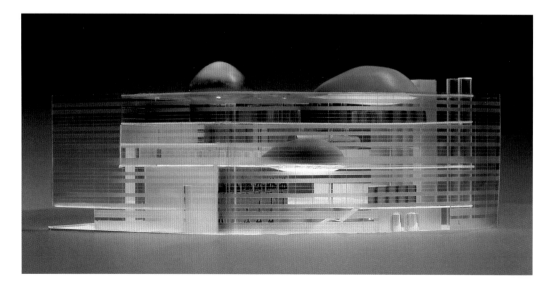

another by the form and materials adopted, the internal superimpositions are merged in the continuous transparency of the glass. The transparent mono-volumes that he started to design with the competition for the House of Japanese Culture in Paris (1990) were based on this new formula and marked the beginning of a development that was to culminate in the Sendai Mediathèque (2000): elegant glass boxes are filled with complex layers of "urban material". Ito is fascinated by the metaphor of the building-aquarium, in which another world is revealed beyond a wall of glass. He creates simple and neutral mono-volumes and immerses in them different forms or structures that characterize the architectural image. In the competition for the building in Paris, three organic volumes seem to float in empty space, on the higher levels, in a neutral context. The creation of non-neutral objects in this fluid transparency does not signify

Model of the competition project for the University of Paris Library.

a return to formal research. Ito uses them to control the limit and proportions of the neutral form. If this work had just been a mono-volume of iridescent glass, with complex computerized systems of liquid-crystal panels, it would have remained so hard to see that it would have been almost invisible. The mysterious organic volumes inside take its image onto an urban scale and are just one of the infinite possible solutions that can be immersed in this new material.

A further example of this is provided by the competition for the University of Paris Library (1992). Two layers of functions arranged in regular and rational grids create the project's overall system of organization, while two elliptical spaces of double height become the exceptions that define its architectural image. Here too the glass façades render the interiors completely visible from the outside, creating a continuous space between the city and the building. The transparency cancels out the limit of a regular perimeter and the rectangular shape appears to have neither end nor beginning.

The Mediathèque in Sendai represents a succinct epilogue to the same themes. Like the organic volumes or the elliptical halls, the structures of the reticular columns create the principal image of the building, lending substance to the neutrality of a mono-volume of plate glass. Returning to his metaphor of the aquarium, Ito imagines reticular columns waving like seaweed. To obtain this fluid transparency, he sets the device of de-composition to work on a solid volume, breaking it down into planes, façades and reticular columns and lightening it, so that all the parts of the

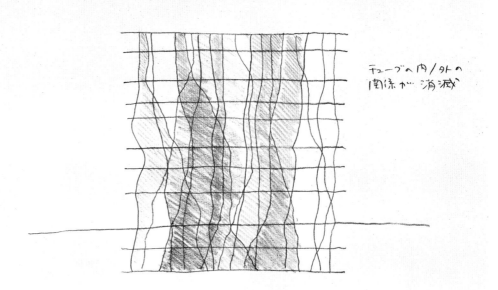

building are plainly distinguished. The succession of planes is accentuated: they are thin square sheets suspended in empty space at variable heights whose functions are clearly differentiated, without a trace of compromise. Each floor, entrusted to a different designer, has different colours, forms and materials. This vertical de-composition creates genuine layers of different "materials" that are fused into a single volume, but one that is still transparent and fluid. They are superimposed fragments of city. Transparency is also to be found in the dematerialization of the columns. Initially Ito imagined them solid and white in colour but then, fascinated by Mutsuro Sasaki's designs, decided to use reticular structures that would give the columns the appearance of interlaced lines. The new artificial and transparent organisms contain the systems of circulation, which evoke the fluidity of dynamic movement.

The system of distribution is influenced by Le Corbusier's rationalistic approach. The arrangement of the columns is always regular and the plans are open, without any formal constraint, so they can be adapted to any solution. This modernist base might raise some doubts about the motivation for certain organic forms and the multiplicity of materials and forms used. Yet there is nothing formalistic about this. Rather it is a mark of his continual search for a way of characterizing and reinforcing the neutral system which he takes as his base. The chaos of forms and materials that Ito creates is an objective reinterpretation of the random nature of metropolitan non-contexts and the multiplicity of readings to which they lend themselves. The corners of the Mediathèque are the point where these intentions are most clearly revealed: the tension that is created between the two completely different skins demonstrates the impossibility of reducing the project to the level of mere formal research, showing instead that it is a quest for the freedom of the ephemeral.

[1] T. Ito, "Architecture in a Simulated City", in *Kenchiku Bunka*, December 1991.

[2] T. Ito, "Three Transparencies", in *Suké Suké*, Tokyo 1997.

Architecture is No Longer "Architecture"
Water Cube – Sendai Mediathèque and Beyond

Koji Taki

After decades of friendship and notwithstanding the fact that I have written numerous reviews of his work, I have to admit that I have never succeeded in pinning down what Toyo Ito was trying to do in words. What I wrote always remained on the threshold of my intuition. Thinking it over now, perhaps he was staring into the distance when he designed each of his works, but without precisely grasping the significance of the path he was taking. As a philosopher, I have approached architecture from the phenomenological viewpoint and have always argued that architectural experience entails a wide variety of factors and that architecture cannot exist without them. I felt that Ito too was aware that he could not conceive an architectural work exclusively on the basis of his own thinking. He knew, I was certain, that architecture is inseparable from the experiences of the people who live in it and that it cannot be understood solely in terms of visual styles. In this connection, Walter Benjamin's view of the reception of architectural experiences is interesting: "Buildings are appropriated in a twofold manner: by use and by perception—or rather, by touch and sight. … Tactile appropriation is accomplished not so much by attention as by habit. As regards architecture, habit determines to a large extent even optical reception".[1]

The term "tactile", introduced for the first time by Alois Riegl, does not refer to touching things with your hand. Rather, it concerns a multidimensional perception of experiences processed over time and mediated by thought. It is from this perception that we can embark on our reflections on architectural production. In fact Benjamin does not just tackle the question of reception, but goes right to the heart of the problem of architectural production. And while it is true that in some of his early works Ito seemed to indulge in a highly subjective style, from the outset I found that he was very sensitive to other factors connected with the genesis of every work of architecture. He was one of the few architects capable of understanding that architecture is born out of the experiences of a society connected with the technologies on which it depends, and that the architect is the person who has the ability to translate these multiple elements into new spatial images.

Although the designs of his works are always clear and simple, at the time he was working on the Sendai Mediathèque Ito began to use the English word "blurring" to explain his architectural ideas. By this he meant his desire to let the architecture be penetrated by the multiple factors of society. He is alluding to the fact that it is necessary to redefine the sense of the architecture, an architecture capable of responding to uncontrollable penetrations by numerous social factors undergoing continual change. And for an architect aware of this situation, the question is what position to take? And what method to apply? Borrowing the words of Italo Calvino, we could say that today's architects, unlike those of the past, have to approach architecture in a radically different way, with "another perspective, another logic, other methods of investigation and verification". And if the architecture of today ought to have the capacity to anticipate the architecture of the new century, it is this new approach that will allow it to do so. Ito (and I with him) began to acquire this perspective very slowly through the long and laborious experience of the Mediathèque in Sendai, the competition for which Ito won in 1995.

Architecture in the Virtual World

Many Italian readers will undoubtedly be familiar with a marvellous book by Italo Calvino, *Lezioni americane*.[2] And Calvino and Ito, in spite of the fact that they have completely different roles (one a writer and the other an architect), use different means (words and physical space), and come from two very distant cultures, both display an almost identical faith in their own field: Calvino argued that whatever fate awaited books in the age of the computer, his faith in literature remained intact, while Ito is confident that architecture will preserve its meaning however much the world may change in the future. In addition, the five words that form the titles of the five chapters of *Lezioni americane* (Lightness, Rapidity, Precision, Visibility, Multiplicity) are strikingly reminiscent of the terms that Ito uses to describe his own research.

If Calvino sought quality of language so that literature could assume a "rarefied consistency" under any conditions, Ito for his part investigates the possibility of spaces that can still be called "architectural" in the midst of a complex environment where the architecture runs the risk of being submerged. Although I do not wish to push the analogy between the two men too far, I cannot help but notice certain correspondences between them. Calvino begins his *Lezioni americane* with a chapter devoted to "lightness"; Ito, while completely unaware of the existence of this book, has for some time been obsessed with "lightness". In the same book, moreover, Calvino refers to "rapidity", and Ito has recently shown considerable interest in this dynamic (and above all hydrodynamic) quality. In one of his articles, for example, Ito discusses the fluidity of lines in Paul Klee's drawings.[3]

The terms used—by Ito himself and, favourably or unfavourably, by the critics—to define his works, are: "lightness", "dynamism", "impermanence", etc. Ito has always shown a propensity for lightweight constructions, so light that they almost seem temporary. It is my view that Ito cannot bear the weight and rigidity of the stone with which architecture goes on crushing life while the world is steeped in ever greater fluidity. And that he feels a certain repulsion for the architects of the previous generation who, insisting exclusively on self-expression, denied the flexibility of life with their vision of architecture.

Ito's architecture is often praised for its aesthetic qualities of "delicacy" or "elegance". As far back as the seventies Kenneth Frampton, in the catalogue to an exhibition presenting the "New Wave" of Japanese architecture of that time, wrote that it was wrong to see Ito as a populist and that instead we should appreciate the delicate sensibility expressed in his works.[4]

Nomad Restaurant, Tokyo.

Frampton's assessment is correct, and yet it is still superficial. Humanity has to find a way to adapt mentally and physically to the changes in a technologically based society brought about by the development of the computer. In addition, it is also obliged to deal with the grotesque world of politics, with the many threats of conflict that stem from the globalization of capital. And in the middle of all this, human beings have to maintain their vitality. In the same way architects, today, must develop a clear idea of the changes taking place in the world in which they have to design buildings and reflect seriously on possible responses. Otherwise architecture is in danger not only of becoming an anachronism, but of losing its capacity to intensify human vitality. Contemporary human beings live in the midst of a glut of objects and information, and their bodies are now submerged by the electronic media that have transformed the world into an infinite series of images. People's daily lives are pervaded by objects and information translated into fleeting images. In this rapidly changing society, Ito has tried to find out how architecture can respond to the fact that humanity has begun to transmute its mental as well as physical nature. There can be no doubt that architecture has to respond to these transitions, but fundamentally, when it is not imaginary, it has a physical duration and cannot therefore vanish instantaneously to make room for another work of architecture in the midst of this maelstrom of objects and information.

The Paradox of Lightness and Fluidity
It is impossible to understand the approach taken by Ito, who pursues a lightness so extreme that it almost disappears, outside the context of opposition to the old concept of architecture. He has chosen a very difficult way—with his quest for rarefaction that in the end becomes "ephemeral" —to paradoxically seek the concrete meaning of a work of architecture and, with it, a new form of relationship between architecture and human beings. Thus his "lightness" or "delicacy", so valued by the critics, are actually the means he adopts for this search, and are not related solely to the fascination of a stylistic sensibility as Frampton suggested. Moreover, Ito uses another metaphor to define his work: the metaphor of fluidity, of a substance as fluid as water. But it is also the opposite of the usual concept of the work of architecture, seen as something solid and lasting. Fluidity, by contrast, is life itself.
Ito has questioned the potential of both modern architecture, which tackled social themes, and the architecture (known as post-modern) that instead sought to use stylistic games to achieve other architectural possibilities while forgetting about social responsibilities. He has understood that it no longer makes sense to repeat the approaches of the architectural movements of the past, but that architecture has to have "another perspective, another logic, other methods of investigation and verification". It is true that real architecture does not appear to have anything to do with literature, inasmuch as it certainly cannot be pure fiction like a novel. But at the conceptual level their visions of the world can be very similar. Impregnated by the media that are transforming the world into an endless series of images, the body has split into the real, human one and the virtual, infinitely mutable one. And we can attribute to this virtual body all three of the qualities that Calvino found in the poetry of Guido Cavalcanti: it is 1. light; 2. in movement; 3. a vector of information. But Ito too could very well use the same terms to explain his works.
How can these concepts be brought into play in the real design of architecture? Now we come to the subject of this article. What I want to do here is not to analyse the architectural style of the Mediathèque in Sendai or illustrate its effects, but to identify what is going on in Ito's imagination when he is at work on a design: a method for establishing a relationship between the real and the virtual.

Simulations
I once asked Ito this question: "What is the original face, the initial state of your architectural creation?" He answered: "It is a sort of spiral, that is what my architecture stems from". I was not surprised by his answer. There are so many complex factors involved in the creation of architecture nowadays that it is easy to see the process as a spiral.

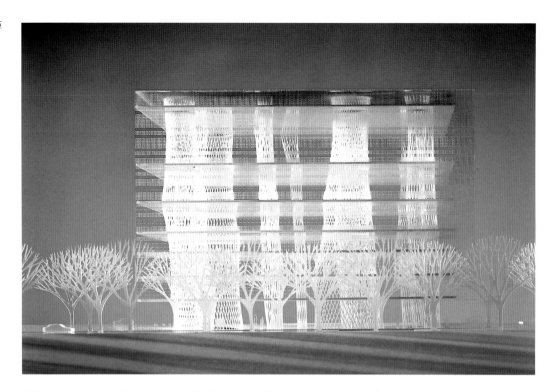

Of course, as soon the genetic spiral appears, Ito attempts to translate this amorphous image by means of the architectural vocabulary he considers most on the table. This is the process he calls "simulation". The best way to illustrate this phase of creation is to take the Mediathèque in Sendai as an example.

To identify the form of a still completely indistinct image, Ito starts out from a series of simulations for which he provisionally adopts some existing terms. In the case of the Mediathèque in Sendai, given the activities that this building was more or less expected to house, it was legitimate to imagine a superimposition of several planes and it is plain to all that Ito has borrowed Le Corbusier's Dom-ino module to initiate the simulation. Thus he has arrived at a stratification of large floors (50 × 50 metres) with no differences in level.

The principal misunderstanding to have arisen over this project has been to see it as a return to modern architecture through the Dom-ino. In reality, it is not even a rediscovery of the Dom-ino as a prototype for the architecture of the coming century. For Ito, the Dom-ino is nothing but a starting point. And since it is a schematic style that has already been applied for around a hundred years, it is also legitimate to start the simulation from it. But how is the simulation developed?

It is true that his first sketches clearly show a stratification of seven floors in the Dom-ino manner, but the gaps between the floors are not identical, creating a variation in the rhythm. We should not overlook the fluid vibration generated by the differences in the height of each floor. In addition, the pillars that connect and support the various floors begin to twist as they rise from the base. Ito had noted on the drawing: "Pillars that look like seaweeds". His objective was to completely deconstruct the Dom-ino with floating elements. In fact he has set out to transform Le Corbusier's geometric and mechanical Dom-ino into a sort of "Water Cube". Even the "seaweeds" are just one of the elements that evoke the metaphor of water.

Refusing to introduce a solid structure into contemporary society, Ito has imagined a soft structure, resembling a fluid. Judging by his own words,[5] he wanted to create a floating architecture that would follow the traces of the flow of water or air, although starting out from a solid and mechanical module. And while the design was still at the stage of a sketch what came to him were the rhythmic vibrations of the lines of the floors, and images of pillars waving like seaweeds.

Of course the architecture itself does not move, even if in the sixties, at the time of the Archigram group, there was much speculation about the possibility of works of architecture that would actually be mobile. The imagination of the time was still steeped in visions of machines. On the contrary, Ito insists today on the "importance of visualising images of electronic technologies that control mechanical dynamism, rather than expressing themselves directly in mechanical metaphors (as the architecture of the machine age tried to do) such as the car or the plane".

Making Visible the Invisible
Taking something invisible like air and turning it into a building: this is Ito's architectural response to the society of the electronic era. And "something invisible" also means life.
In subsequent phases of the simulation, the pillars inspired by seaweed begin to take on more feasible forms. Architectural elements appear: the structure of wire mesh and the surface of plate glass. These thirteen tubular pillars are positioned at random, each performing a different function: at times they serve as a staircase, at others as a structure for the lift and at yet others they become a passage for the ventilation duct. And in the end, they look not so much like seaweeds as the Caucasian elm trees that surround the building. Looking from the inside out, I realized that an involuntary continuity had been created between the pillars and the trees. And this has perhaps made it lose its original fluid vitality, leading at the same time to a series of misinterpretations. In any case, the operation that Ito calls "simulation" did not just start out from Le Corbusier's Dom-ino. Even the result looks quite similar to Le Corbusier's. At the same time, however, there are important differences between Le Corbusier's Dom-ino and the architectural forms of this building.
In the first place, while the former was a prototype, the latter can in no way be regarded as one. Anyone hoping to find a possible prototype that could be reused in different circumstances in Ito's Dom-ino (?) will be disappointed, but it is the search itself that makes no sense. What has been created here is inimitable. How is that?
The advent of Le Corbusier's Dom-ino signified that new technology had for the first time made possible the production of prototypes, freeing the architecture from the structure of walls that

Sketch.

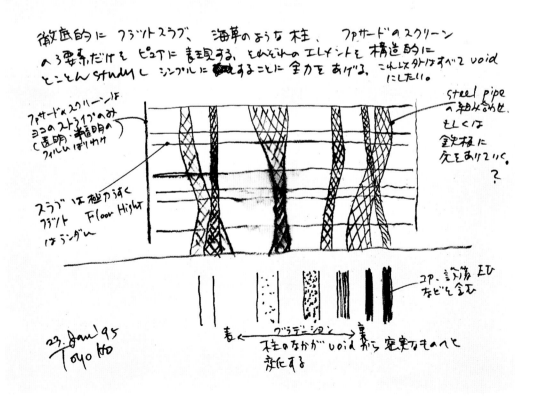

had hitherto been indispensable. Today's architecture, however, is no longer in that technological phase. Thanks to developments in non-linear mathematics and its application to structural engineering, any architectural form can now be resolved dynamically. As a consequence, there are no longer either decisive or prototypical forms. The disappearance of the prototype signifies the end of the era in which spatial solutions were found through analogical forms. All that is left at the heart of the creative act is a principle, that of making visible the invisible.

Blurring – Nature of the Boundaries

It would be too hasty a conclusion to claim that the development of electronic media has brought the era of books to an end. In spite of everything, language survives. Neither literature nor philosophy, both of them constructed out of language, will ever lose their potentiality. Literature and philosophy are in fact something invisible, and the book is only their vector. The emotion they produce in the mind does not depend on the qualities of the binding, however good or bad. Although they are dealing with a completely different world, the electronic media are just another means, another instrument. Even though the electronic media should provide us with new modes of expression, this ought not to trespass on the field of literary values. Instead the two fields should help to underline each other's independence. In other words, each field conditions other systems, and at the same time is conditioned by other systems.

But what about architecture? During the work on the Mediathèque in Sendai, Ito became painfully aware of the anachronism of an architecture that has always tried to remain isolated from the world outside. Whence his doubts about this still common attitude: "'Blur' means to smudge, obscure, make fuzzy. So 'Blurring Architecture' means 'architecture with smudged boundaries'". It is an architecture with wavy outlines like shapes seen through moving water. I am not talking about the formal questions of architecture; it does not matter here whether the forms are geometric or organic with a multitude of folds. The ambiguity of outline which I want to discuss comes in reality from my doubts about architectural boundaries that separate the inside from the outside, and about the ontology of an architecture that is too autonomous and self-sufficient".[6]

In these words I hear an echo of the same question as is raised by his "lightness" and "fluidity". But where Ito used to express these contents with the help of sensorial metaphors, here he seeks to derive a theory of design: if the media have progressively transformed the daily lives of human beings, it is no longer suitable to apply, as in the theories of the past, a typological method like that of reducing every human activity to a list of "functions" that are now habitual, or architecturally institutionalized, and coordinating these "functions" with a standardized architectural vocabulary. On each of the Mediathèque's 50×50-metre floors, Ito has created conditions that seem to make it possible for anything to happen, as if on a stage without scenery, bare and therefore rich in potential. Ito challenges the old method by which strictly defined functions are assigned to the space. And when I saw the building finished, even before its inauguration, I noted a positive sense of emptiness, a sensation that was not just one of great flexibility but also one of waiting for something.

For me, the qualities of the space created an impression similar to that of the virtual images that Ito frequently presents in his exhibitions. Personally, I was not very happy with the idea of representing contemporary society in this manner. In my view, insisting too much on virtuality runs the risk of losing sight of the real conditions of human existence (including political factors, and life and death). That way, life and death themselves would become nothing but virtual images. Today, objects have lost their solidity while remaining objects, now rarefied or almost virtual, destined solely for consumption. But if architecture too were to be reduced to this state, it would lose its suitability for human life and threaten to eliminate it. Ito, however, wants to restore architecture's capacity to exalt human life while coexisting with the advent of the virtual dimension rather than rejecting it.

Having closely followed his reflections during the design of the Sendai Mediathèque, I am now able to understand why he insists on "an architecture in which we see, as in a theatre, a continual shifting of scenes without the physical structures moving". Everything is fluid, everything is mutable. The place no longer has a fixed role. At this point, it is no longer just a question of architectural methods but (although Ito may not be aware of it) assumes a political dimension as well.

A Place for Information

With the Mediathèque in Sendai, Ito had to tackle a complex subject, connected with media technologies. And over the fairly long period he worked on it he acquired a degree of confidence in a new approach to architecture, discovering "another perspective, another logic, other methods of investigation and verification".

After the conquest of this new and very free perspective, Ito went on to produce a series of increasingly light and fluid designs that, in spite of their variety, create the impression of a new order of thinking. Among the most interesting are the Trade Fair Centre at Hiroshima, the Municipal Cultural Hall at Matsumoto and the project for the Cognaq-Jay Hospital in Paris. Work has not yet commenced on the realization of these projects and I do not intend to speak of them here, but I would just like to point out that at bottom these projects, which apparently bear no resemblance to the Sendai Mediathèque, breathe the same sense of freedom that he achieved during the design of the latter.

Right from the moment it was submitted to the competition, the project for the Mediathèque in Sendai has attracted a great deal of attention, but even in Japan there are not many who fully understand it. In the initial phase of the work, many elements were still not very clear to Ito himself. This is why I have chosen to describe the evolution of his vision over the course of the design here.

But this building is not yet a *fait accompli*. The architectural design also involves all the activities that will go on in this space in the future. What will be designed there? What type of information will be transmitted from this place? The architecture undergoes endless evolution. It is a place of production, like a theatre that produces theatrical messages every evening. Indeed, it is a sort of theatre that receives information emitted by the world and transmits other information in turn.

Since the theme of the competition was linked to new technologies (as a place intended for the study and development of the electronic media), attention has tended to focus on this area. In reality, however, Ito's true theme in this project was the redefinition of the concept of architecture as a place (or theatre) for information in contemporary society, and of the position of the architect, no longer seen as an omnipotent figure. Notwithstanding the difficulties—and the strains—that are sometimes involved in dealing with local administrations, Ito has been able to come up with an important response to this difficult theme.

[1] W. Benjamin, *Das Kunstwerk im Zeitalter seiner technischen Reproduktiertbarkeit* (1936), Surkamp, GSI-3, 1974; English trans. *The Work of Art in the Age of Mechanical Reproduction*.
[2] I. Calvino, *Lezioni americane*, Mondadori, Milan 1993
[3] T. Ito, "Generating Form of Paul Klee", in *Asahi Museum Weekly*, no. 2, 1995.
[4] K. Frampton, *The New Wave of Japanese Architecture*, catalogue of the exhibition at the Institute for Architecture and Urban Studies, 1978.
[5] T. Ito, "Tarzans in the Media Forest", in *2G*, no. 2, Barcelona, May 1997.
[6] T. Ito, "Changing the Concept of Boundaries", in *Shinkenchiku*, January 2000

Works and Projects

Aluminium House
Fujisawa-shi, Kanagawa
1970–71

opposite
*Ground and
first-floor plans,
legend:
1 entrance
2 living-room
3 bedroom
4 kitchen
5 storeroom
6 void.*

Exterior view.

This house, Toyo Ito's first project, is built of wood. It is located in a suburb of Tokyo. Beams, set perpendicularly to two sturdy octagonal columns, form the two main areas. Roofs of polyhedral shape cover these two spaces, which are illuminated from above. The bedrooms and other private sections are laid out around these centres. A well of light is created by the two central columns, allowing sunlight to pass through to the ground floor. Stairs, constructed in the form of ladders, are set in this well and lead to the first floor. The huge wooden frame of this building and the steep stairs reflect the traditional Japanese house, but the outside walls, clad with sheets of aluminium, resist this interpretation. This was Ito's first experiment with metallic materials, a theme he was to develop in later projects.

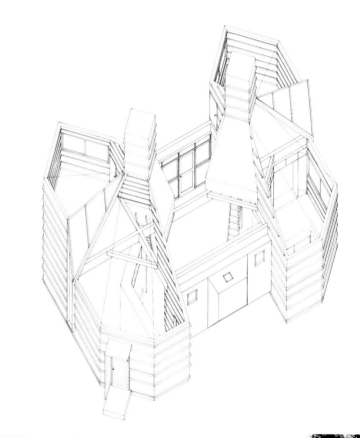

*General
axonometric
projection, view
from the outside.*

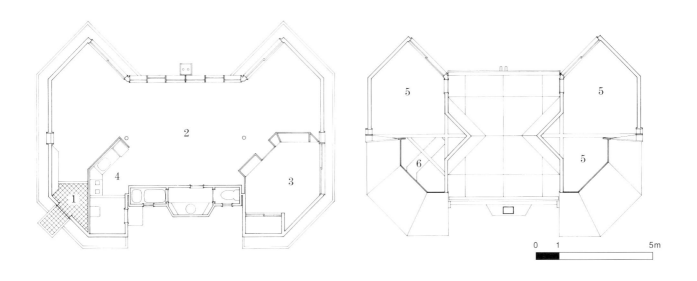

White U
Nakano-ku, Tokyo
1975–76

White U is located in a residential area of midtown Tokyo and looks out onto the nearby Shinjuku skyscrapers. The locality is a mix of wooden houses, blocks of flats and small and medium-sized apartments. A reinforced-concrete structure made up of two parallel walls encloses a horseshoe-shaped central courtyard covering about 75 square metres. Inside is a ring-like space, where a penthouse roof slab slopes towards the centre. The tubular interior extends around the building, which is finished in pure white, with daylight entering from above and the sides. The gradation of the lighting lends a soft nuance to the space inside, making a noteworthy contrast with the courtyard, itself encapsulated by concrete walls.

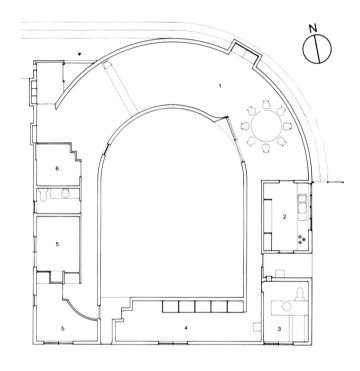

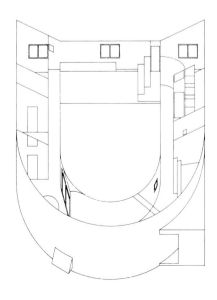

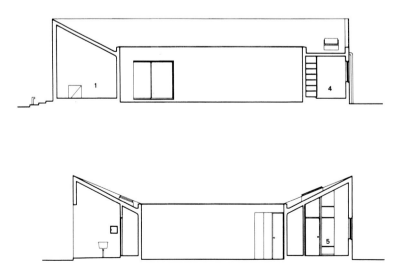

The house in its
urban setting.

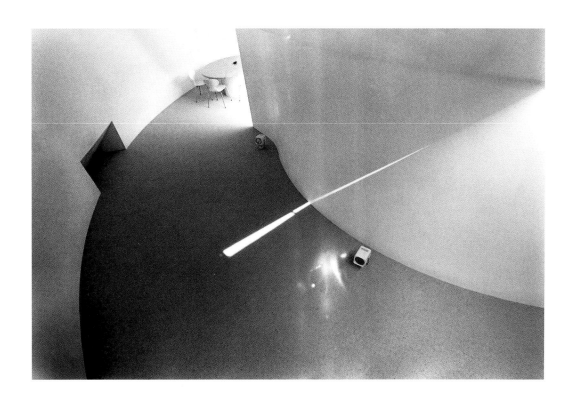

PMT Building
Nagoya-shi, Aichi
1976–78

This four-storey building was designed for a printing-machine importer/dealer in Nagoya. The ground floor is used as a showroom large enough for the display and demonstration of several large printing machines as well as a repair shop. The showroom is two storeys high and the section for commercial activities is located on the mezzanine overlooking the display area. The two upper floors are used for offices.

RC Rahmen (rigid frames) are employed as the main structure. Various walls, stairways and other elements extend across the concrete frames.

The building is characterized by an aluminium façade which is attached to one of the frames as if it were a mask. The façade undulates gently along the curved line that connects the two slightly staggered masses, i.e. the volume comprising the ground and first floors and the one containing the second and third floors. The decision to stagger the axes of the two volumes gives the façade a manneristic instability and vibration. The façade looks as if it were a piece of paper dancing in the wind.

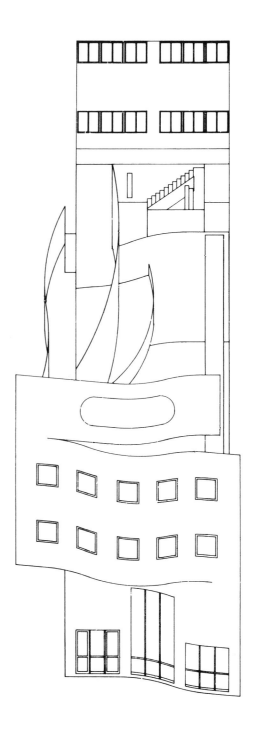

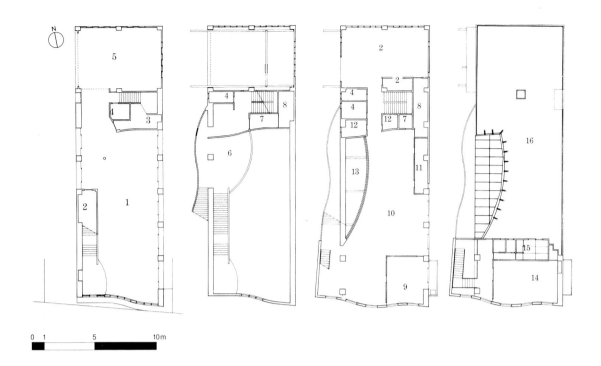

0 1   5   10m

opposite
*Ground, first,
second, and third-
floor plans, legend:*
1 showroom
2 storeroom
3 toilets
4 services
5 machine shop
6 waiting room
*7 water supply
system*
*8 air-conditioning
plant*
9 reception
10 office spaces
11 study
12 changing room
13 void
14 meeting room
15 restroom.
16 attic.

View of exterior.

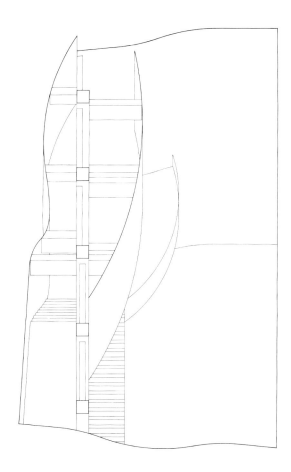

*Access to the upper
floor.*

*Axonometric
section.*

House in Kasama
Kasama-shi, Ibaragi
1980–81

This is a wooden house of about 290 square metres built on a module of 2×4. As the T-shaped structure is situated on a part of the site that slopes towards the south, the south wing has two storeys while the north wing only has one. Two ridges are connected at an angle with the entrance located at the intersection. All the outer walls are clad with asbestos-cement panels whose only finishing is a waterproofing treatment. The client was an artist working with ceramics. The house is roughly divided into three sections with different functions: a small gallery under the north gable roof directly connected with the entrance, a studio and bedroom on the ground floor of the south wing and the living space on the first floor.

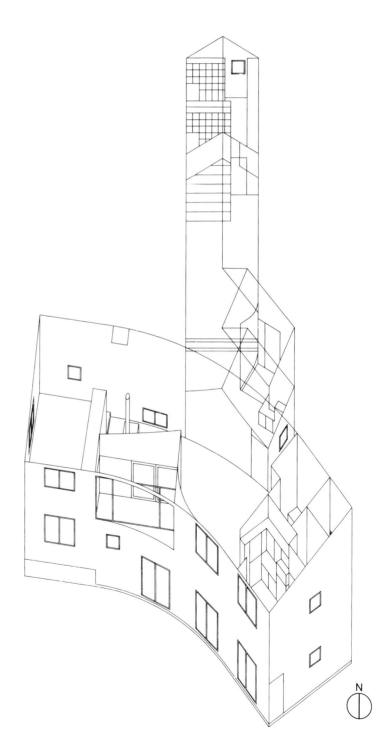

*Elevations
and sections*

opposite
*Basement and
ground-floor plans,
legend:*
1 entrance
2 living-room
3 gallery
4 study
5 solarium
6 storeroom
7 kitchen
8 services
9 studio
10 bedroom
11 airing cupboard
12 bathroom
13 toilet facilities.

Views of interior:

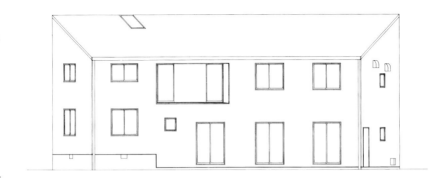

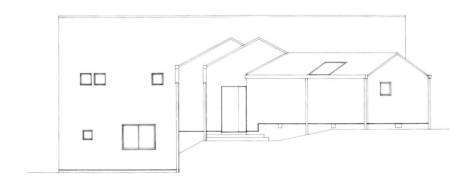

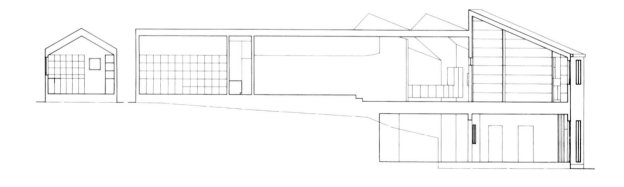

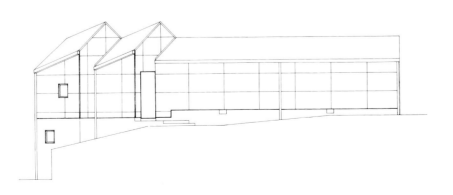

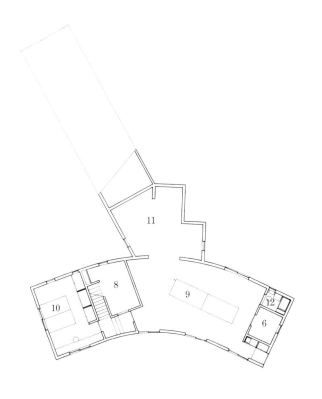

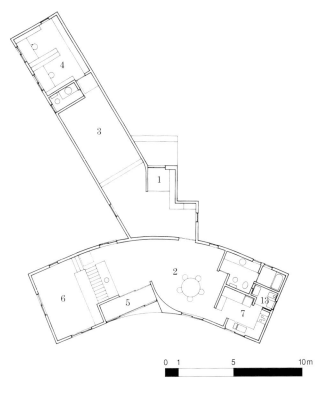

0 1   5   10m

41

Silver Hut
Nakano-ku, Tokyo
1982–84

General plan of the Silver Hut alongside the White U designed earlier for the architect's sister. Note that the project is not an extension of the adjacent building but has been developed along completely different lines.

Exterior view.

Silver Hut is Toyo Ito's own house and is located in a residential area in the centre of Tokyo, just fifteen minutes by train from Shinjuku. It consists of a flat floor, concrete posts erected at 3.6-metre intervals and a roof constructed out of a steel frame with seven shallow vaults positioned over the posts. The gable runs from south to north. A courtyard is set in the middle of the south side and covered by a movable tent, permitting easy control of ventilation and sunlight. The courtyard is an almost external space that can be used for a variety of functions, depending on the season and weather. On the western side are set the utility room, kitchen and bedroom in the form of a concrete box half-buried underground, and a child's room on a mezzanine above. The north side houses the dining area and living-room, while there is a study and a Japanese room on the east side, each covered by separate vaults. Minimal walls, furniture or screens are used to separate the rooms. The furniture is DIY or fashioned out of old car parts. The fixtures emphasize practical functions throughout.

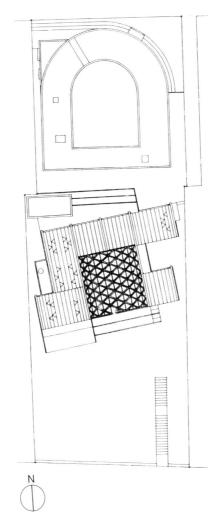

N

*Axonometric
projection.*

*Ground-floor plan,
legend:
1 courtyard-garden
2 living-room
3 kitchen
4 tatami room
5 studio
6 his daughter's
room.*

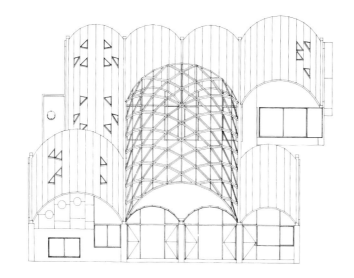

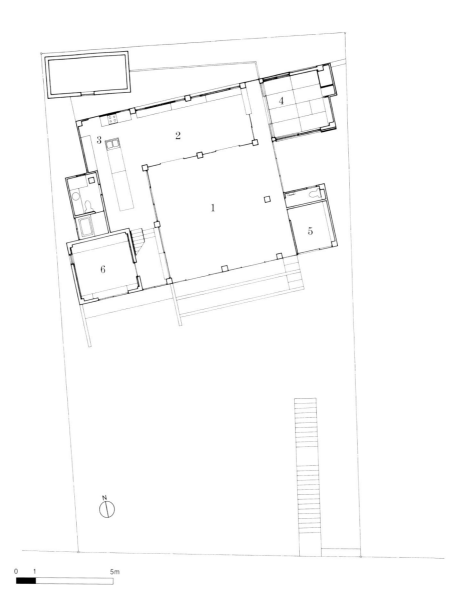

0 1   5m

Courtyard-garden.

*Longitudinal
section.*

*View of his
daughter's bedroom.*

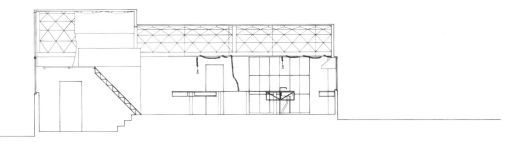

Kitchen.

South elevation.
Cross-sections.

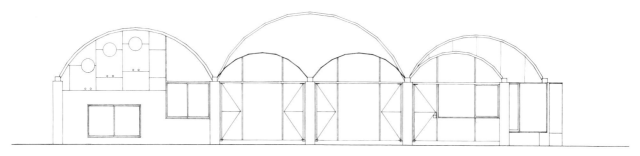

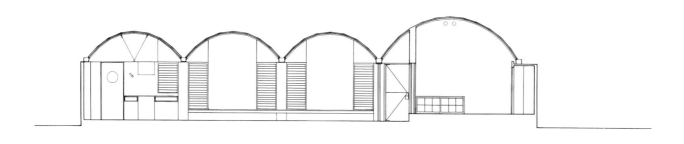

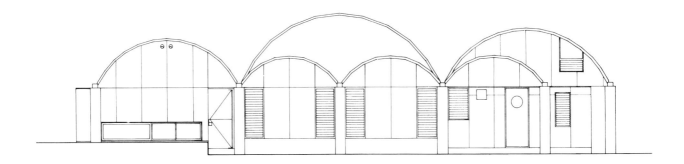

Tatami room.

Pao I, Installation for "Pao:
A Dwelling for Tokyo Nomad Women"
Seibu Department Store, Tokyo
1985

This is a project for an installation in a Tokyo department store. An enormous amount of new information is produced and digested in Tokyo every day. The heroine of the project is a girl who drifts airily through this city of information and consumption as if she were a nomad. The *pao*, or nomad's tent, was created as an abode for her.

1. Pre-furniture for styling

A combination of a dresser and a wardrobe. She grooms her hair, makes up her face, tries on a new outfit and gazes into the mirror. Styling, or transforming, brings her into her own dreaming space.

2. Pre-furniture for intelligence

A combination of a chair and a desk equipped with a variety of media for information. A bookshelf stocked with fashion magazines, gourmet guidebooks, etc., implements for cutting out and filing articles, a cassette recorder with a dubbing system, a walkman and a telephone to receive input from her friends: these are her means of subsistence, without which she cannot plan for collages in the future or join in the "dream-talk" that goes on outside.

3. Pre-furniture for snacking

A combination of a petite tea table, a minimal set of dishes and other dining and cooking utensils and a shelf to keep them on. She drinks a cup of coffee and eats fast food before or after the collage of dreaming. In this dwelling she takes only light meals, a plate of spaghetti at the most.

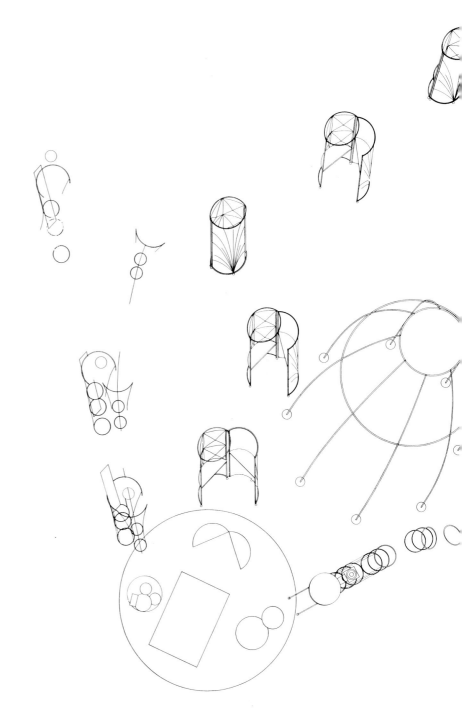

Sections of the nomad's house.

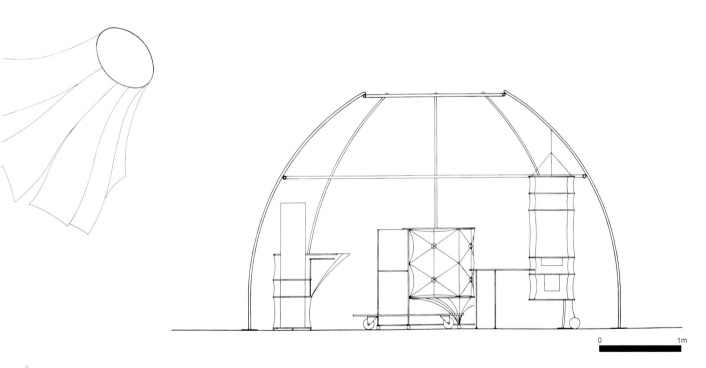

0   1m

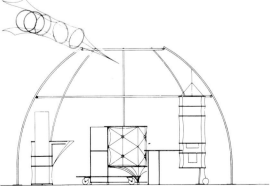

51

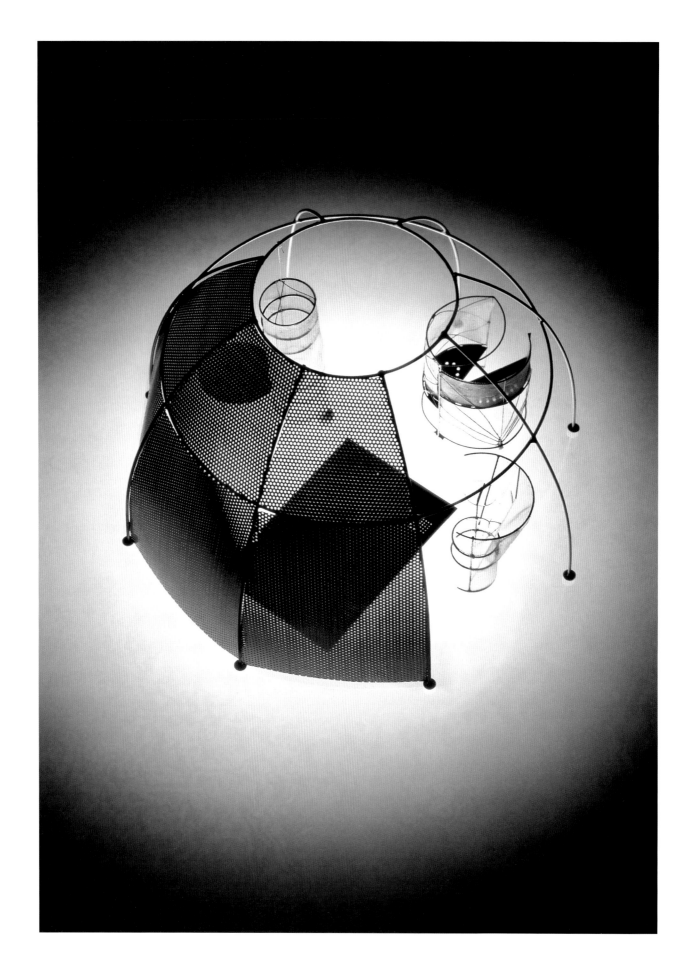

*Prototype of
compact facilities
for the nomadic
woman.*

House in Magomezawa
Funabashi-shi, Chiba
1985–86

A residential area close to the city of Funabashi, Magomezawa is approximately one hour by train from Tokyo. The house is constructed from reinforced concrete and steel. The bottom floor, sunk just below ground level, has concrete walls, finished on the inside and out with mortar laid on with a trowel. It forms a concrete box enclosed by two vaults assembled out of steel frames. A small bedroom (approximately 20 square metres) below these vaults is partitioned by sashes. The construction allows light and wind to pass freely through the bedroom, in contrast to the kitchen and living-room on the ground floor. These are enclosed by concrete walls but form two very different spaces, linked by a utility room and a terrace. Galvanised steel panels are used for the façade and form skin-like membranes which let in daylight and fresh air. The panels are similar to those used on building sites to temporarily close off areas to public access.

View of east façade.

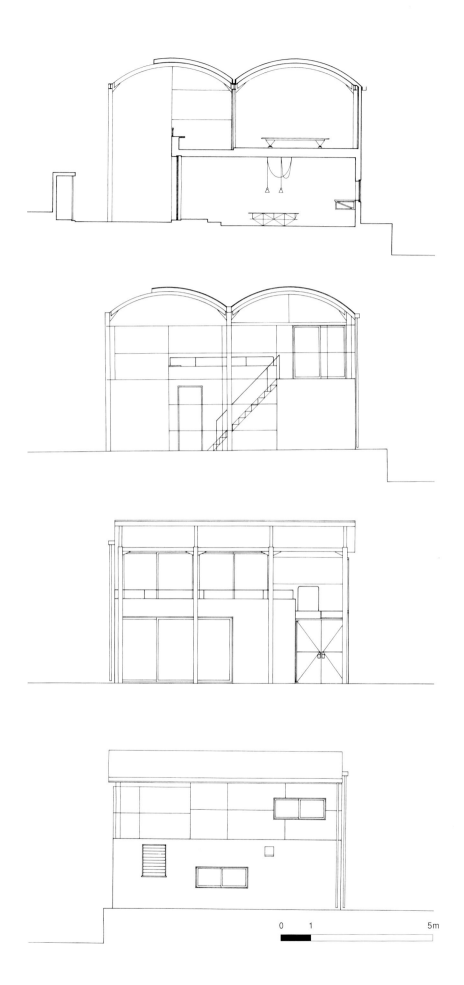

0   1   5m

opposite
Partial view of east front.

Ground-level and first-floor plans, legend:
1 hallway
2 daytime zone
3 night-time zone

4 bathroom
5 storeroom
6 office
7 terrace.

Interiors in the daytime and night-time zones on the first floor.

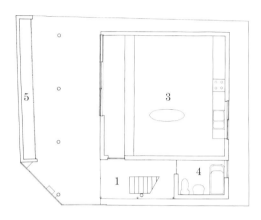

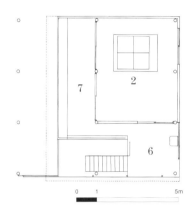

0   1   5m

57

Project for the Exhibition:
"Furniture for Tokyo Nomad Women"
Tokyo
1986

This project was carried out for an exhibition sponsored by a leading Japanese furniture manufacturer that makes use of moulded-plywood technology. The suite of furniture comprises a large, multipurpose round table (1.5 metres in diameter) with cut-out portions, simple dining chairs (with and without arms) for use at the table and expanded-steel lounge chairs. The furniture was designed with the aim of drawing attention solely to the tabletop and the seats of the chairs, so that they all appear to float lightly in space.

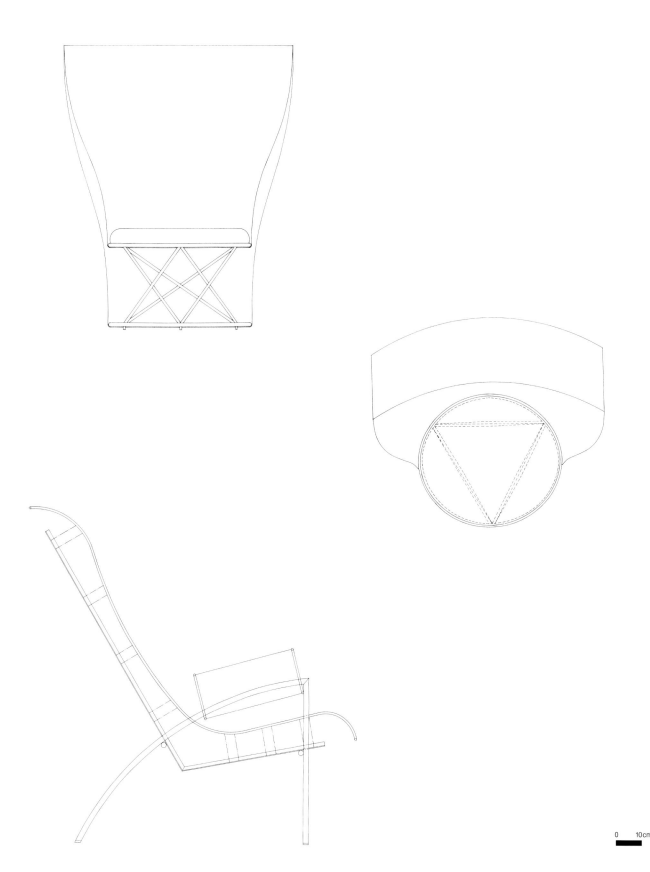

0   10cm

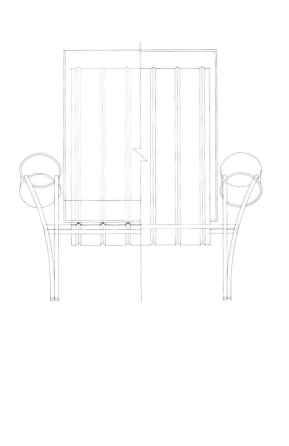

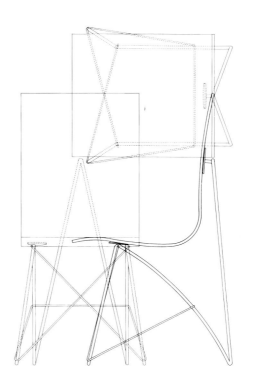

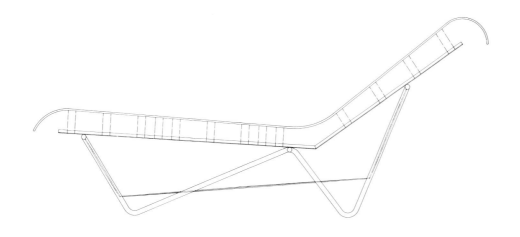

61

Nomad Restaurant
Minato-ku, Tokyo
1986

Designed as a temporary structure to solve a problem caused by a delay in the granting of planning permission, the Nomad restaurant and bar are located in Tokyo's most popular entertainment district, Roppongi. The atmosphere inside is reminiscent of the theatre: everything looks staged, from the entrance hall, fixtures and menu to the waiters' uniforms and the background music. The simple act of eating a meal and chatting with friends is transformed into a fictional and surreal affair. Taking the form of an enormous tent, the Nomad is an oasis for travellers in the desert of Tokyo, as well as for people who live their lives on a whim. They are drawn in by the restaurant's bright neon lights. A steel-frame structure ensures that the maximum of volume and height are obtained within the limits permitted by the planning regulations and budget restraints. Inside this frame float the main construction materials: fabric and perforated aluminium, which create the tent-like environment. Resolutely, there is no architectural form—the tent-like building defies a consistent, determined design. The interior is enlivened by a wide variety of finishes and furnishings, creating an illusory architectural quality. The diners appear to have been turned into nomads, seated at tables benath metallic clouds that flutter in the artificial breeze.

Interior.

*Mezzanine and
ground-floor plans,
legend:*
1 entrance
2 restaurant
3 kitchen
4 toilets

Cross-section.

following pages
*The interior from
above.*

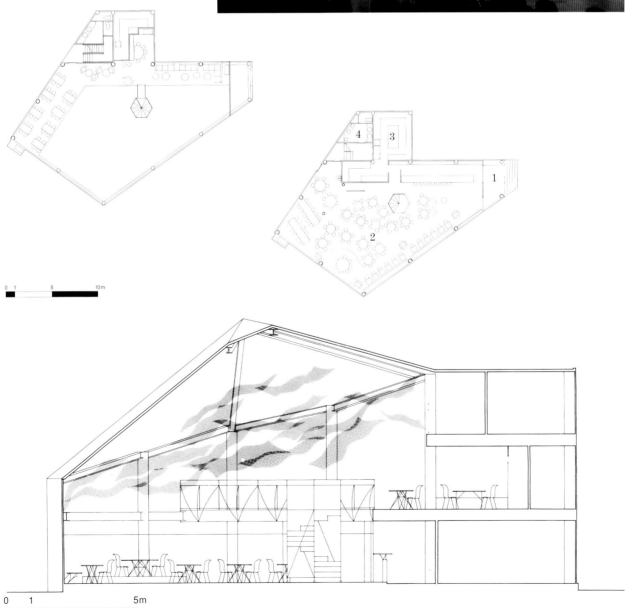

Tower of the Winds
Yokohama-shi, Kanagawa
1986

Site plan.

*Section and plan
of the tower.*

opposite
Daytime view.

following pages
Night-time views.

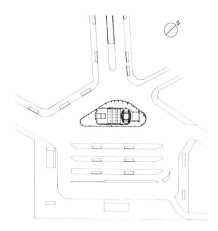

A twenty-one-metre tower at the centre of a roundabout near Yokohama train station was covered with synthetic mirrored plates and encased in an oval aluminium cylinder. When lit, floodlights positioned between these two layers give the tower the appearance of a giant kaleidoscope. The reflective properties of the aluminium panels emphasize the tower's simple metallic shape during the day. At night, the "kaleidoscope" is switched on, presenting a brilliant display of reflection on reflection. The tower contains 1280 mini-lamps and twelve bright white neon rings, arranged vertically. Thirty computer-controlled floodlights (twenty-four on the inside, the others on the outside) make patterns of light within the tower, varying with the time of day. Natural elements such as noise and the speed and direction of the wind affect the intensity of the floodlights: the result is a controlled "natural" phenomenon. The panels sometimes appear to be a translucent film, while at others they seem to float to the surface.

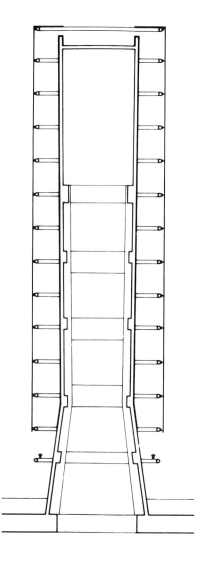

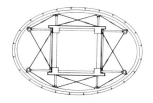

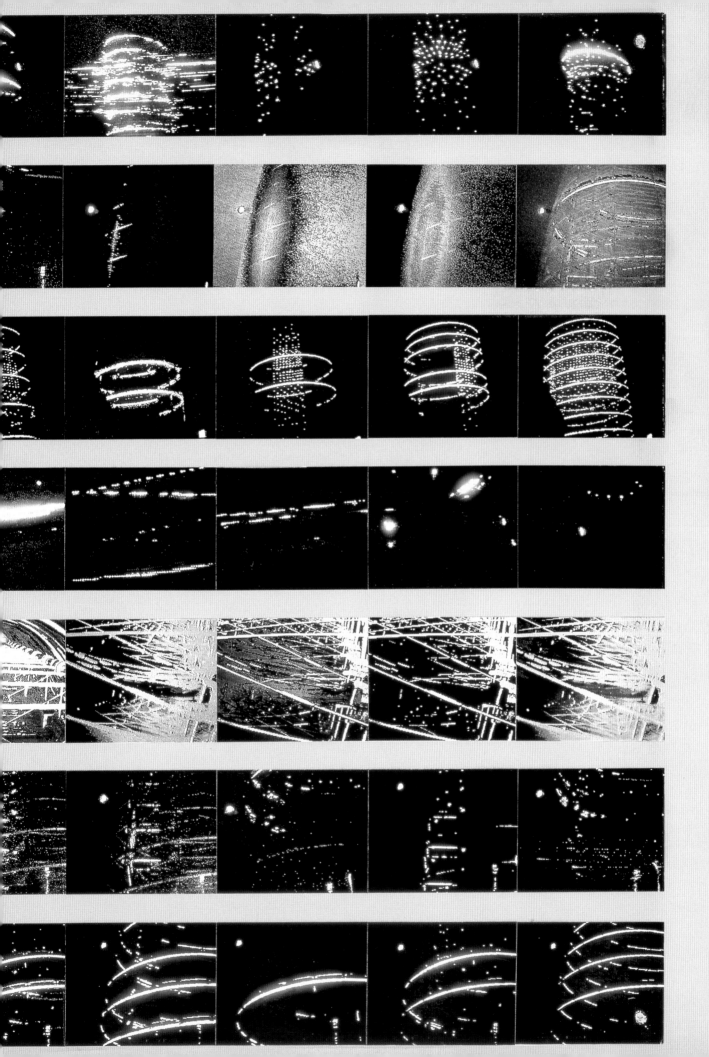

*Night-time views
with electronic
transformations
based on fractal
calculations.*

Yatsushiro Municipal Museum
Yatsushiro-shi, Kumamoto
1988–91

Yatsushiro Municipal Museum was one of the first major projects for the Art Polis programme organized by the Kumamoto Prefecture. The programme, which was drawn up by the Kumamoto Prefecture in collaboration with Arata Isozaki, aimed to co-ordinate the efforts of architects to turn the prefecture into a cultural and architectural centre. As a result, the city of Yatsushiro decided to build a new museum to house its many historical artefacts, previously stored in different locations, under one roof, something that would help to make Yatsushiro one of the main cultural centres of Kyushu. Different structural systems were used to meet the requirements of the purpose for which each space was intended. The ceiling height of the ground floor is the minimum possible in order to save space. The extremely thin roof is divided into triangular pieces of different heights that face in different directions. These pieces impart a rhythmic lightness to the scene, looking as if they were dancing in the air. Glass walls are set between the roof and the artificial mound constructed next to the main approach, creating an open façade and emphasizing the lightness of the roof. This open façade reduces the enclosed and oppressive atmosphere that museums are prone to produce. Metallic cylinders rising above the vaulted roof are used for storage. A steel-frame, multi-vaulted roof covers the first floor in order to let in natural light. The rear of the building consists of a rigid, reinforced-concrete, frame structure. By combining these different structures and spaces, an attempt was made to create a museum in which people would be able to enjoy not just the exhibits but also the building itself.

on these pages
*Preparatory
sketch.*

Main front.

雲が宙に浮かんで
いるように、フワフワと・
吊り屋根.

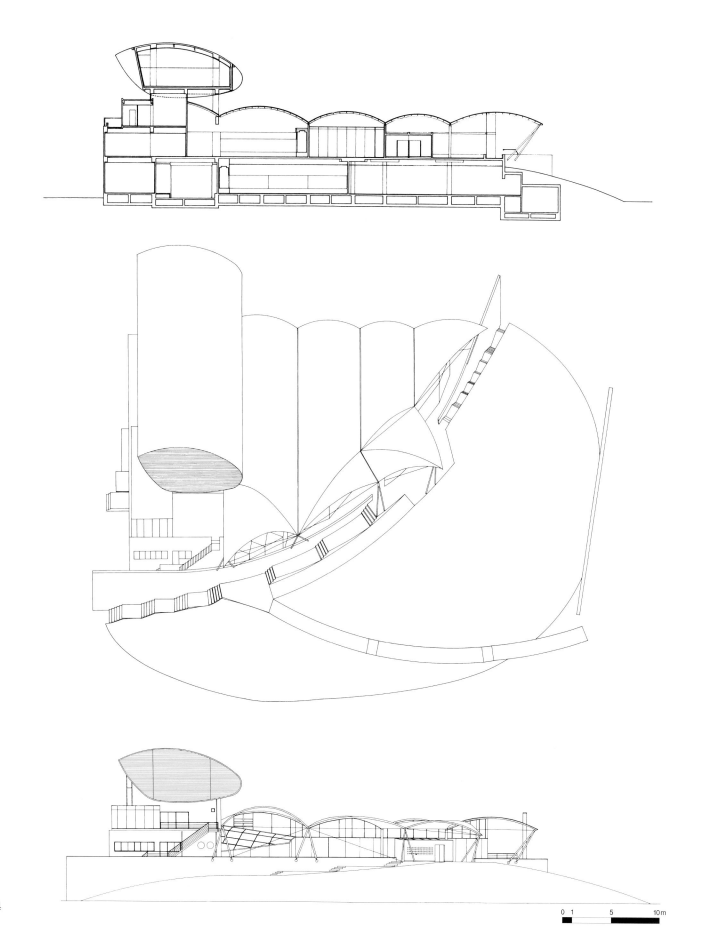

74

0 1   5   10m

opposite
*Cross-section,
general
axonometric
projection and
main elevation.*

*Exterior view
of the reticular
structures of the
vaulted roofing.*

opposite
View from above.

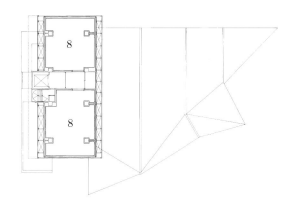

*Plans of various
levels, legend:
1 entrance
2 reception
3 cafeteria
4 gallery
5 conference room
6 offices
7 loading-
unloading bay
8 storehouse
9 studio
10 workshop
11 terrace
12 technical areas
13 void.*

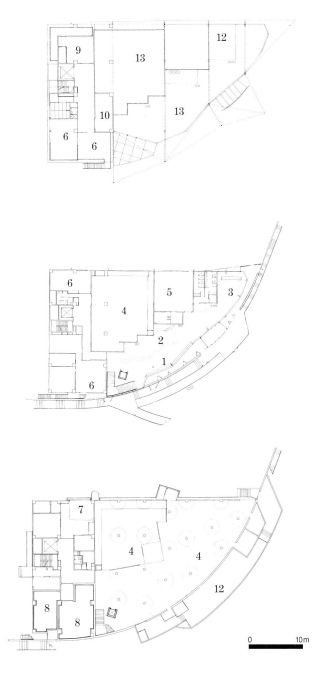

0   10m

The museum's
main entrance
and bar.

The gallery
in the museum's
basement.

Pao II, Exhibition Project for "Pao:
A Dwelling for Tokyo Nomad Women"
Brussels, Belgium
1989

For the exhibition in Brussels Ito constructed the prototype of his electronic
home for the nomadic Japanese woman.
In the Japanese megalopolis the house
has lost almost all value apart from that
of being a place for women. Social life
now goes on out and about, in work-
places, restaurants and places of entertainment. So Ito hypothesized a precar-
ious structure covered with canvas, a
sort of nomad tent to be set up amidst
the skyscrapers of the metropolis. No
longer a fixed abode, but a self-sufficient micro-system that can be moved
at will. A polyhedral steel frame covered with fabric contains a bed to sleep
on, a table to eat at and a space to fresh-
en up. The outer envelope prevents the
identification of a finished solution, con-
serving the choice of an electronically
nomadic existence.

Imaginary view of Tokyo showing the electronic camps of nomadic women.

Model of the "electronic tent" at the exhibition in Brussels.

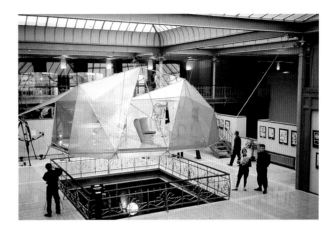

The "electronic
tent" and drawings
for the model.

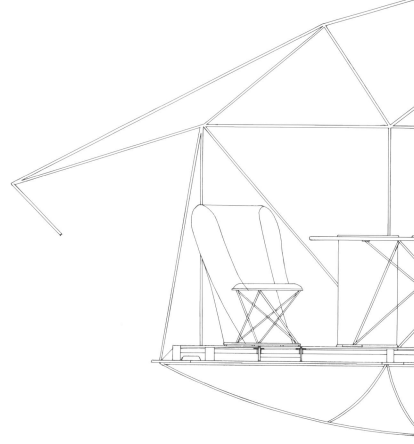

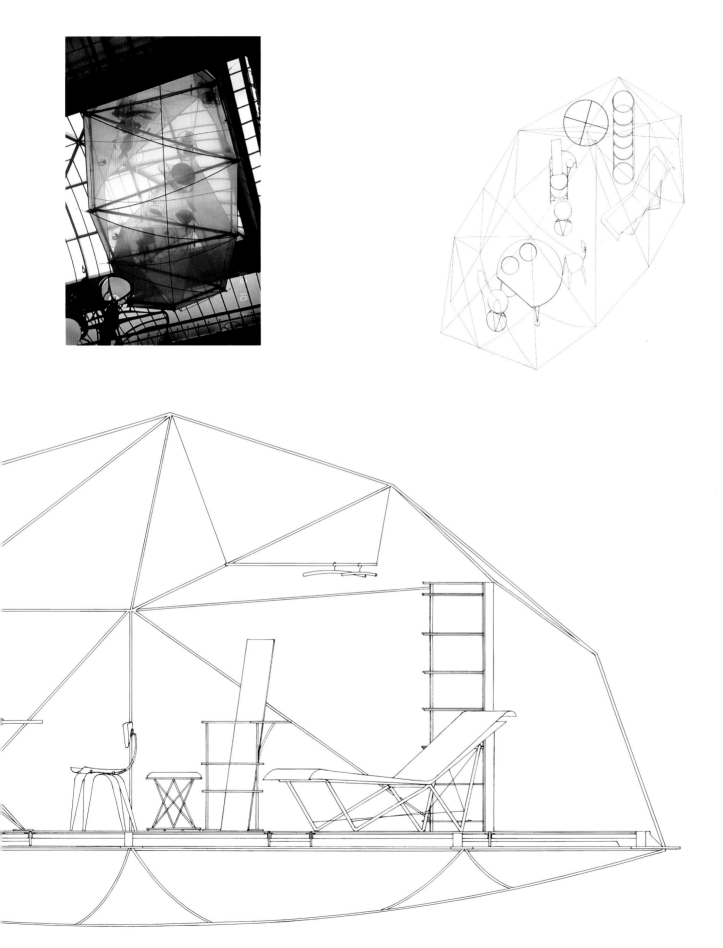

T Building in Nakameguro
Meguro-ku, Tokyo
1989–90

Surrounded by commercial, industrial and residential areas, this project stands among tall buildings and family houses. Along the boundary with the street runs a "skin" made of a milky and filmy substance attached to a long screen. The areas designated for offices are concentrated in one section, so that they can easily be adapted for various purposes when necessary. Between this area and the screen lies a "void", three storeys high, housing "hovering" services: toilet cabins are suspended from the ceiling, as are the stairs, deck slabs and glazed-steel lift shaft. People only spend a short time here, and so it is filled with a sense of constant flux. The screen blurs the concept of inside and outside: one permeates the other. At times this void seems an integral part of the building, but at others it appears to be completely separate. It illustrates the illusion of "reality" in the same way as an aquarium presents us with a "natural" environment. The building harmonises the perceptions of architecture and landscape. The lightness of the structure represents an evanescence amidst the constant fluidity and chaos of the city.

View of the outside at night.

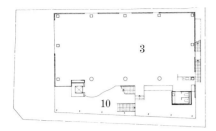

*Basement,
ground, first and
second floor plans,
legend:
1 car park
2 technical plant
and storeroom
3 offices
4 storeroom
5 lobby
6 meeting room
7 toilets
8 conference hall
9 president's office
10 void.*

*Cross-section
and elevations.*

opposite
*Detail of the
façade.*

*Double-height
internal volume
with accesses
to the upper floors.*

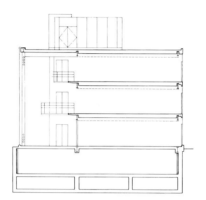

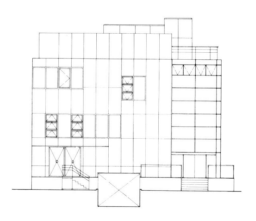

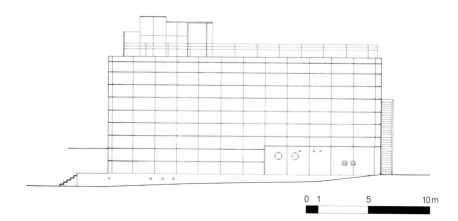

0 1   5   10m

Gallery U in Yugawara
Yugawara-cho, Kanagawa
1989–91

This gallery of contemporary art, open only at the weekends, is situated in a resort about 100 kilometres west of Tokyo. The gallery is fairly private in character and the owner's weekend home is located on its grounds. It is made up of two volumes of extremely simple shape: one is a box-like structure of concrete walls and slabs, used for storage, and the other houses the exhibition space, under a vault of steel frames. The enclosed form of the storage space and the openness of the vaulted roofs make a vivid contrast.

The project dates from more or less the same time as the Yatsushiro Municipal Museum (1991), and this prompted the adoption of the same truss system of flat steel bars as was used for the vaults of the museum's roof. The system permits the use of materials of minimal thickness and imparts an air of lightness to the building.

The resort to inorganic and monotone materials such as the steel-frame truss and concrete walls creates a space with the unadorned simplicity of a loft.

*Axonometric
projection.*

opposite
*Entrance
to the covered space
of the gallery.*

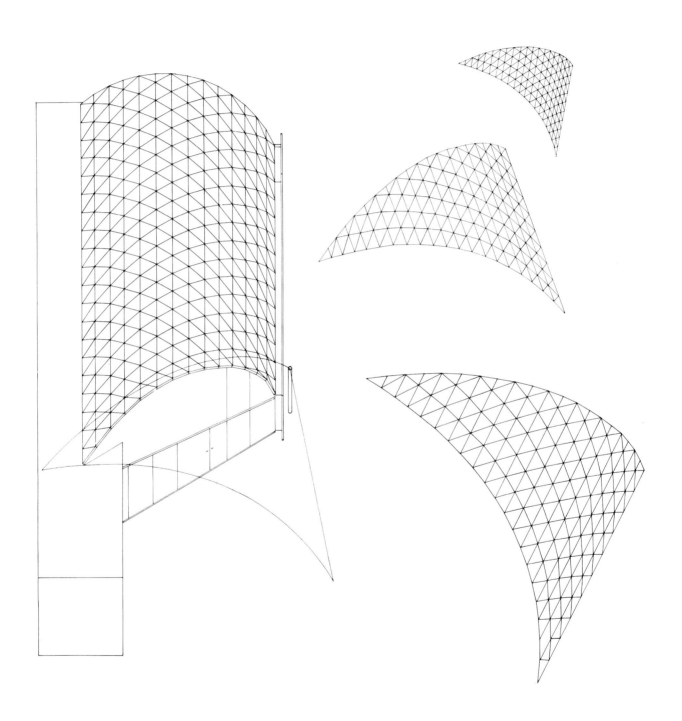

89

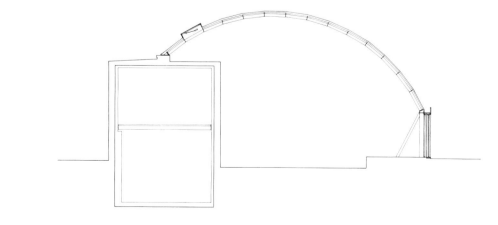

Interior exhibition
space, cross-section
and longitudinal
section.

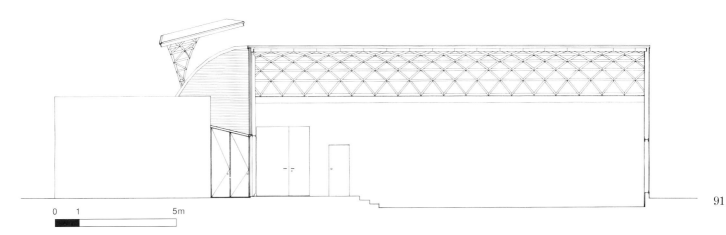

0   1   5m

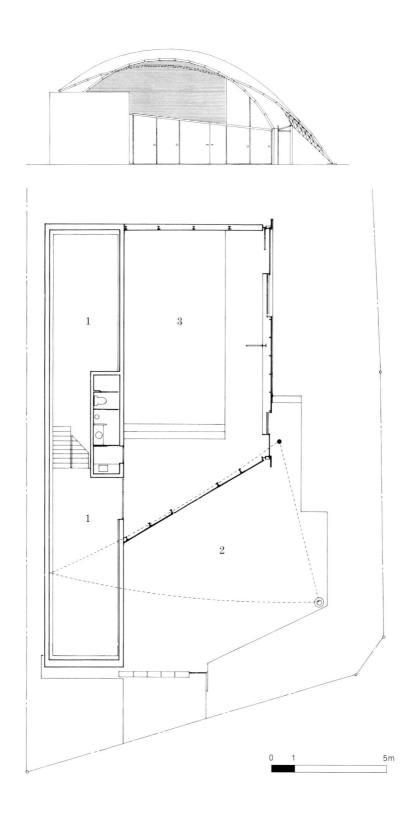

Elevation and plan, legend:
1 storeroom
2 terrace
3 gallery.

1

3

1

2

0   1   5m

*Details of the
reticular structures
and triangular
mesh.*

.

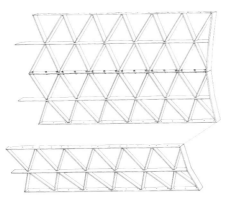

93

Project for the Maison de la culture du Japon
Paris, France
1990

Designed for the competition for the Maison de la culture du Japon in Paris, this project—entitled "Media Ships Floating on the Seine"—was intended for a site by the Seine not far from the Eiffel Tower, in an area characterized by traditional Parisian terraced houses and contemporary buildings. The design was influenced by the image of a spaceship drifting in from Tokyo with a cargo of information and culture. This is expressed in its skin-like façade made of glass embedded with liquid crystals, behind which float many different functional spaces and facilities. Beyond this "skin" lie three "bubble" shapes that are wrapped in turn in a permeable skin like the nuclei of cells. They have particular functions related to such

human needs as learning, talking, socialising and eating, and are situated in the academic area of this building. One is an information "control room" which hovers in the library space, while the other two bubbles—the VIP room and a restaurant—hover near the roof, commanding panoramic views over the city. A variety of images can be reflected off the restaurant's glass façade, thereby turning it into a theatrical space. Like a skin or screen, the floors and walls are indicators. All the spaces are temporary, having originated from the information emitted. This project shows how a unique form of architecture is able to evolve, by engaging individualized symbols with a soft and transparent entity.

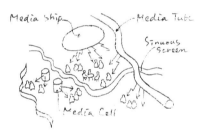

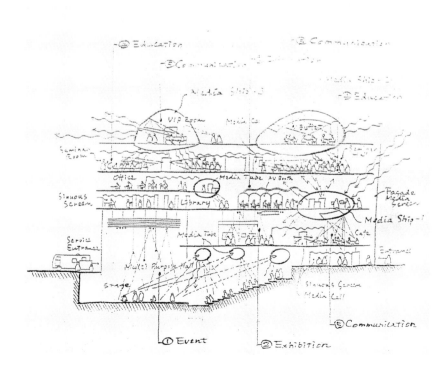

Design sketches.

opposite
Continuous façade of liquid-crystal glass that changes according to internal needs: views of the model and elevations.

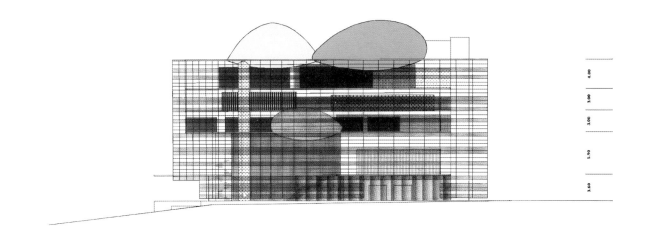

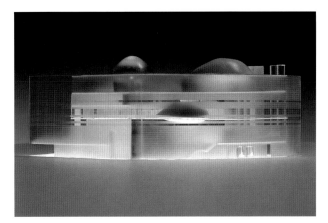 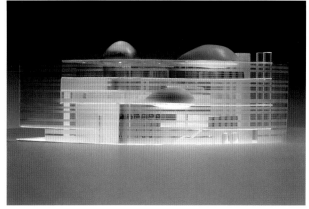

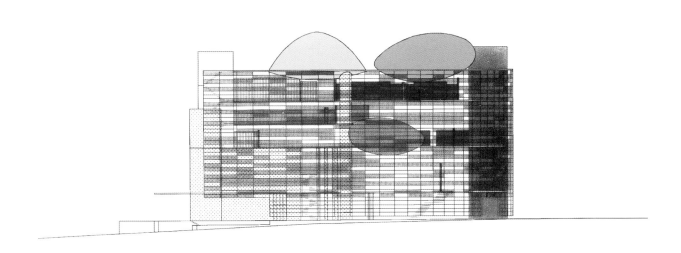

*Sections of the
building.*

opposite
*The model showing
its location in the
surroundings.*

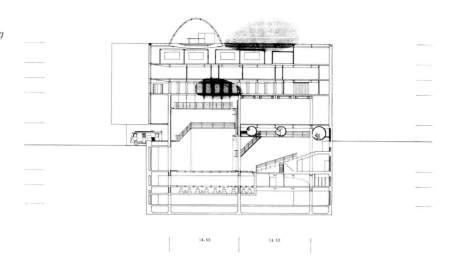

14.50   14.50

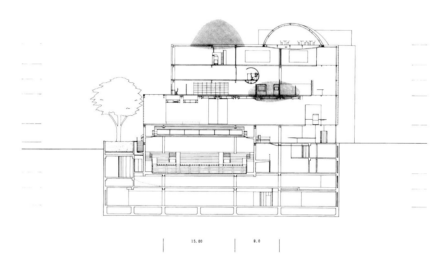

15.00   0.0

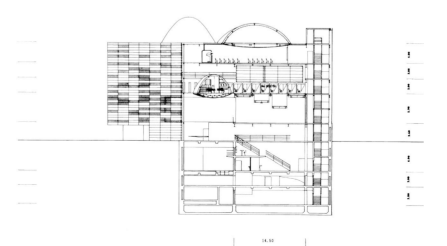

14.50

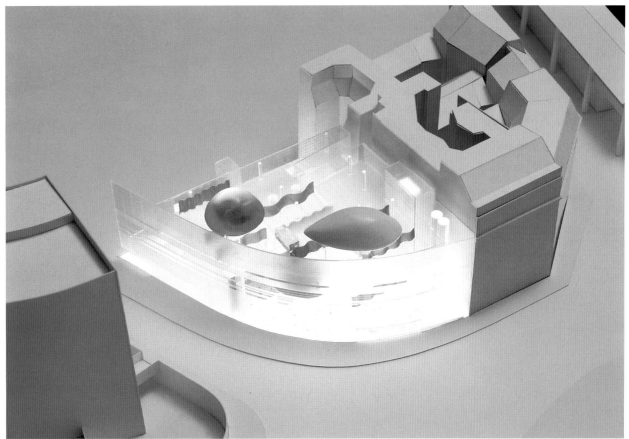

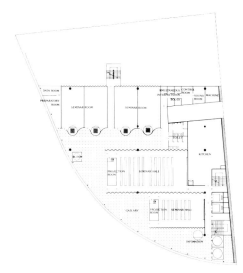

5th floor

4th floor

Plans.

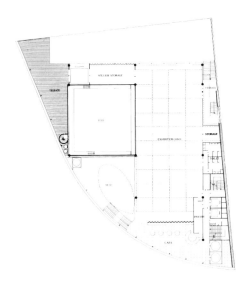

1st floor

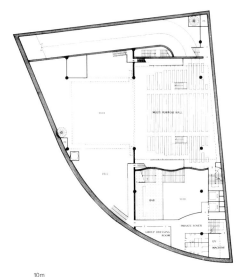

0   10m

mezzanine

1st basement

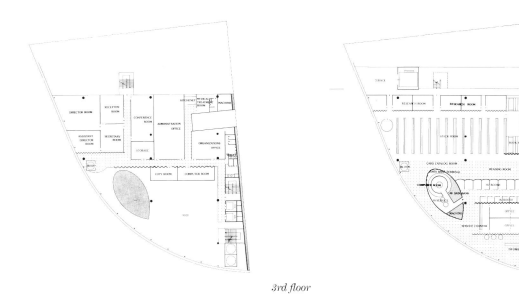

3rd floor

2nd floor

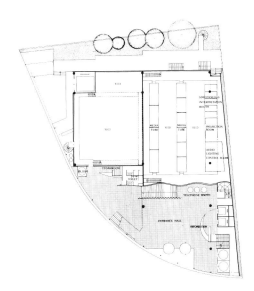

ground floor

2nd basement

3rd basement

Gate of Okawabata River City 21 ("Egg of Winds")
Chuo-ku, Tokyo
1990–91

This rotating oval (16 metres along its major axis and 8 along the minor one) floats 4 metres above the ground on top of the entrance to a parking lot of the Okawabata River City 21 residential complex.

Encased in 248 panels, sixty of them made out of punched aluminium, it looks like a flying saucer or unidentified flying object when it reflects the sunlight with a dull silver sheen. At dusk, however, when people are coming home from work, the built-in liquid-crystal projector and lighting start to operate and silently turn the "Egg of Winds" into an object that emits its own light. The five liquid-crystal projectors set inside the egg project pictures onto two screens at the rear and the punched panel facing. The projection of the pictures is controlled by a computer that operates three kinds of light source and is capable of combining five different sources of images. Acting as a light source, the liquid-crystal projector enables the "Egg of Winds" itself to send out information and images and represents a new type of exhibition space for video artists as well as a way for residents to exchange information.

Close-up and panoramic views of the Egg of Winds in its context.

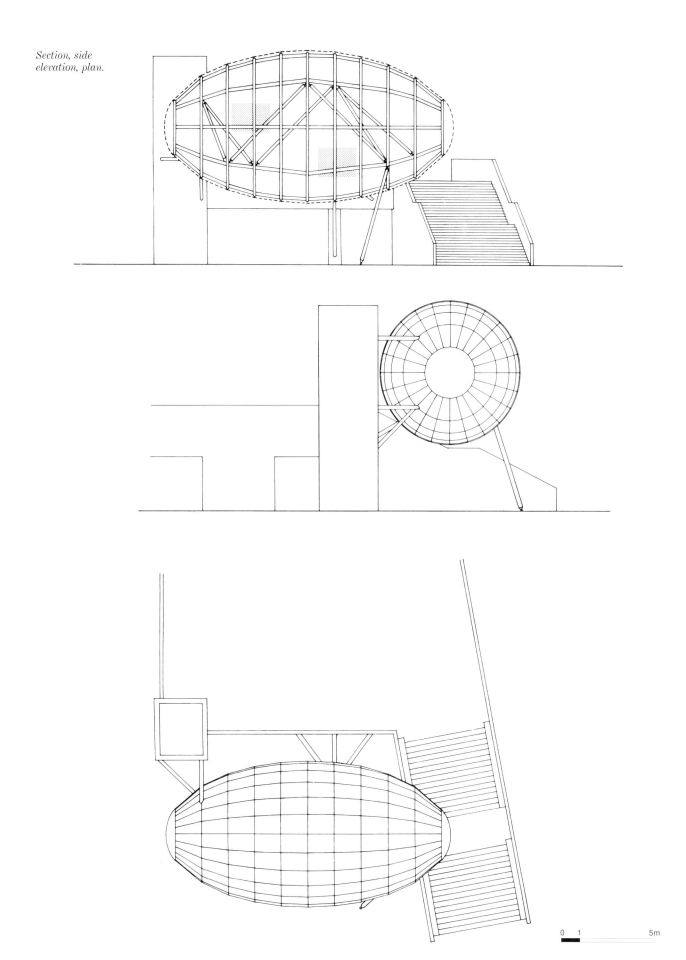

*Section, side
elevation, plan.*

0   1   5m

Image at night.

Shimosuwa Municipal Museum
Shimosuwa-cho, Nagano
1990–93

To commemorate the centennial of Shimosuwa, a city at the centre of the Nagano Prefecture, the decision was taken to rebuild the municipal museum on the shores of Lake Suwa. The design was selected in a competition held in June 1990. The new museum had to house two permanent collections: materials and artefacts related to the history and natural environment of Lake Suwa and a collection of mementos of the famous local poet Akahiko Shimagi. There are two volumes: the permanent exhibits are housed in a linear structure on the lakeside while the northern storage room is set on the mountainside. The walls, which run along the curve of the site, are covered with steel frames set every three metres, drawing the structure in an arc towards the lake. A three-dimensional membrane emerges, forming more arcs in elevation and section, to cover the space. The single most distinctive element is the aluminium panelling covering the front of the building, giving it the appearance of an upturned ship floating on the Suwa lake. This curved surface resembles the hull of a ship cutting through the surface of the water. The covering is particularly welcome in the cold climate and provides a double layer of waterproofing. As in the Yatsushiro Municipal Museum and the Tower of Winds, open-jointed panels are attached directly to the steel frame, forming part of the structural configuration. The indoor lighting fixtures and air-conditioning plant are concealed in recesses in the ceilings and walls. The floor is heated by water from the nearby hot springs, which enhances the impression of a controlled environment. The scenery of the lake is projected onto a glass screen and reflected by a shallow sheet of water in the courtyard, creating an illusion of ripples on the outside.

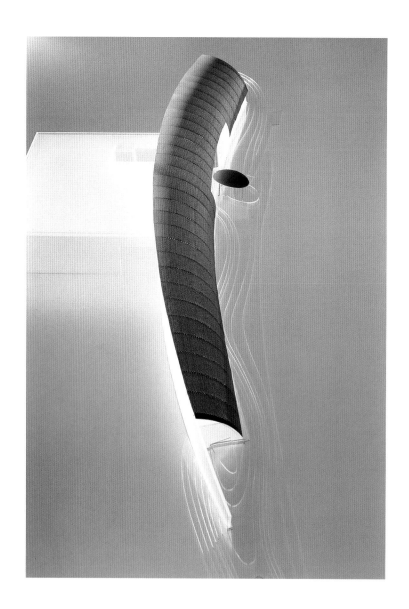

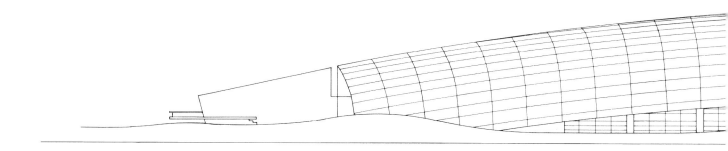

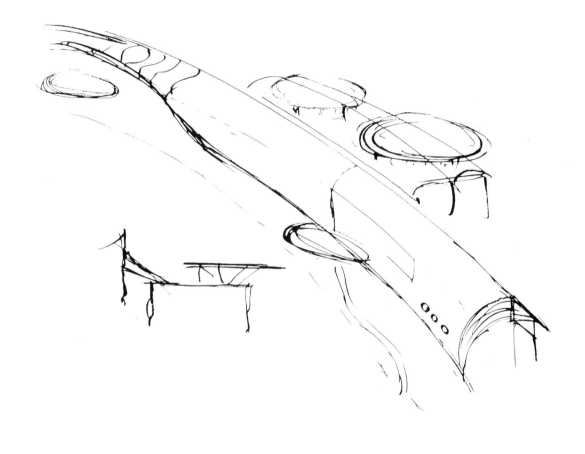

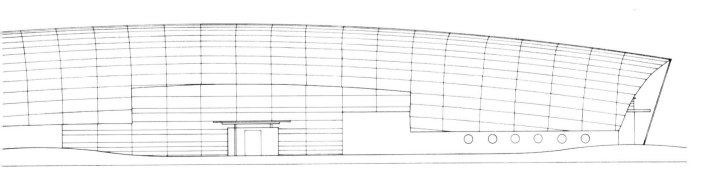

0   1   5m

opposite
*Side view, detail of
the main entrance
with its canopy.*

*Plans of the three
levels, legend:*
1 entrance
2 exhibition gallery
3 conference hall
4 offices
5 Akahiko wing
6 cafeteria
7 storerooms
8 void.

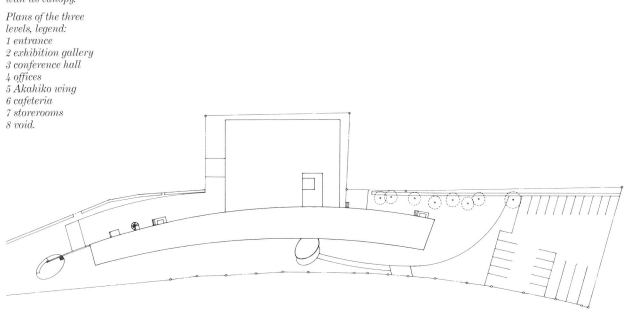

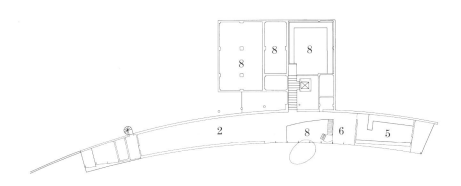

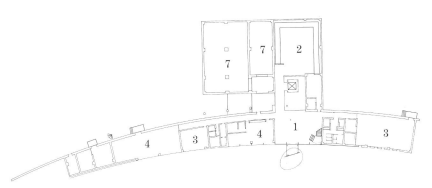

0   10m

Cross-section,
space providing
access to the first
floor; exhibition
gallery on the first
floor.

opposite
The foyer, view
of the exhibition
gallery.

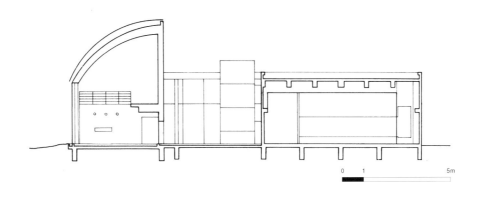

0 1   5m

111

"Visions of Japan" Exhibition
Victoria and Albert Museum, London
1991

Installation.

The room prepared by Ito was part of an exhibition on contemporary Japan organized by Arata Isozaki, who had invited a series of architects to decorate the rooms. Ito's project attempted to visualize the particles of information emitted into the city air by various media in the form of clouds or mist. It represented an opportunity to replace the atmosphere of a typically Victorian space with a beautiful and translucent one, and to create "visions" of Japan using a life-size, liquid-crystal glass façade projecting information directed at the visitors onto the walls, floor and floating devices. An undulating screen formed a media wall whose transparency could be electronically controlled: a permeable membrane of information. In its translucent state the light particles from the video projector were transmitted onto the screen while light gradually permeated the media wall and was projected onto the reflective panel opposite, or onto the surface of the visitors' clothing. Images of Tokyo city were incessantly screened at random, in the manner of a multimedia display. The light projected onto the floating floor could also be manipulated so that images floated slowly on the resinous surface as if on still water. When the light from the fluorescent tubes set under the floor increased in intensity, the room suddenly turned into the sea of "Planet Solaris": a white, soft space where all substances seemed to melt and disappear. Five media terminals—called Bambon, Hyoro, Pukupuku, Dandan and Guruguru—floated on the surface of the water. These were linked with "Tokyo City", allowing people to communicate interactively.

Section and plan.

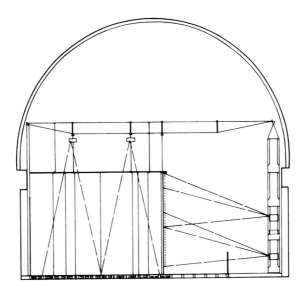

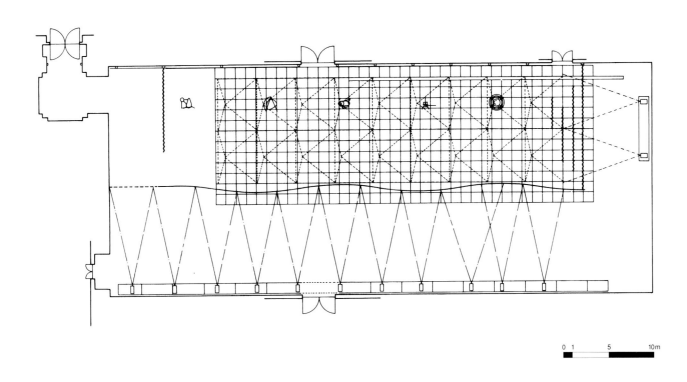

*Ever-changing
images of Tokyo
projected onto the
walls and flowing
across the floor
to convey the
electronic flow of
the great Japanese
cities.*

Hotel P
Shari-gun, Hokkaido
1991–92

General plan.

opposite
*Axonometric
projection, detail
of entrance to the
elliptical court.*

following pages
General view.

This hotel looms abruptly into sight on the vast agricultural plain of Hokkaido. Although it is on a small scale, with only twenty-six rooms and a fully equipped restaurant and meeting room, it has an authentic hotel atmosphere. The composition is a simple one: two floors with guest rooms and a floor with the restaurant and lobby, providing high-quality dining and accommodation facilities for the local population. Despite the conditions of the site, the intention from the start was to create a kind of city hotel as an extension of urban space designed for individuals.

In this sense, it represents an extremely abstract and artificial presence in the environment. Sentimentality is not the way to meet the challenge of the Hokkaido environment. Thus the site consists of bold zones marked by broad stripes, each of which turns into a green lawn, flowerbed or artificial pavement. All the guest rooms have a distant view of Mount Shari in the south-east. The oval shape of the public section, with parallel lines appearing in each of the rooms, articulating the interior and creating a sense of enclosure without defining a centre,

results in a highly transparent spatial quality. The hotel forms a wall against nature that is almost as solid as concrete. The winding wall surrounds the inner space, as if protecting it from the grandeur of Hokkaido. This forms an urban air bubble that appears to float on the green meadow in the summer, or on the expanse of snow in the winter. The letter P stands for *poluinya*, a Russian word meaning a place in the middle of a glacier where water collects without turning into ice.

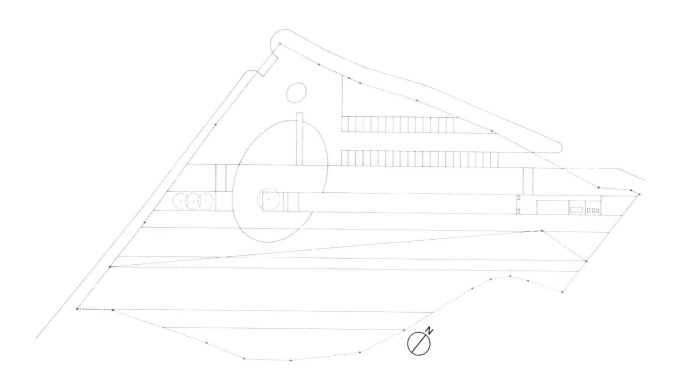

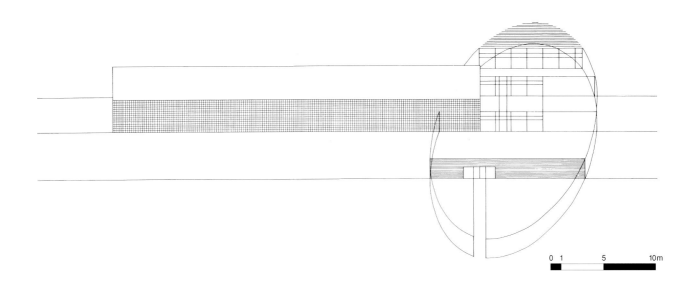

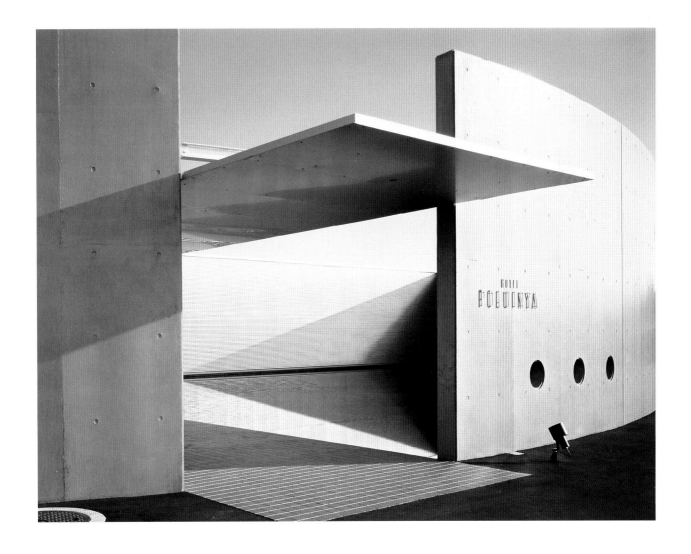

117

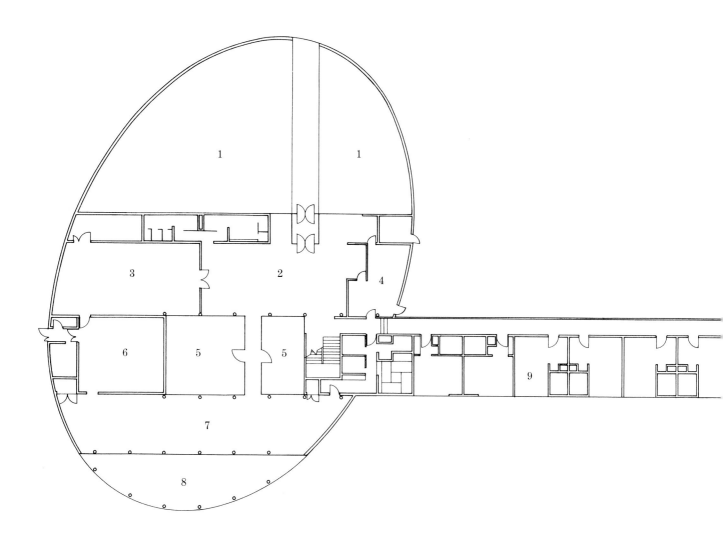

*Plans of the two
levels, legend:
1 pool of water
2 entrance
3 conference hall
4 offices
5 internal garden
6 kitchen
7 restaurant
8 terrace
9 bedrooms.*

*Detail of the
elliptical court.*

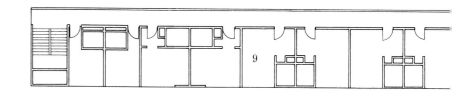

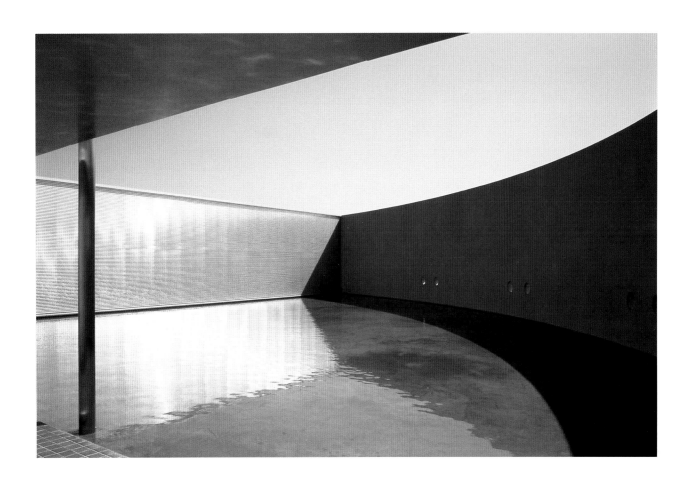

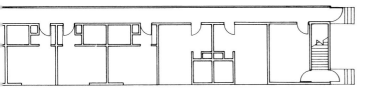

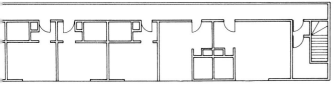

0 1   5   10m

following pages
*Longitudinal
section, view
of the rectilinear
volume of glass
and concrete with
the hotel rooms,
elevation.*

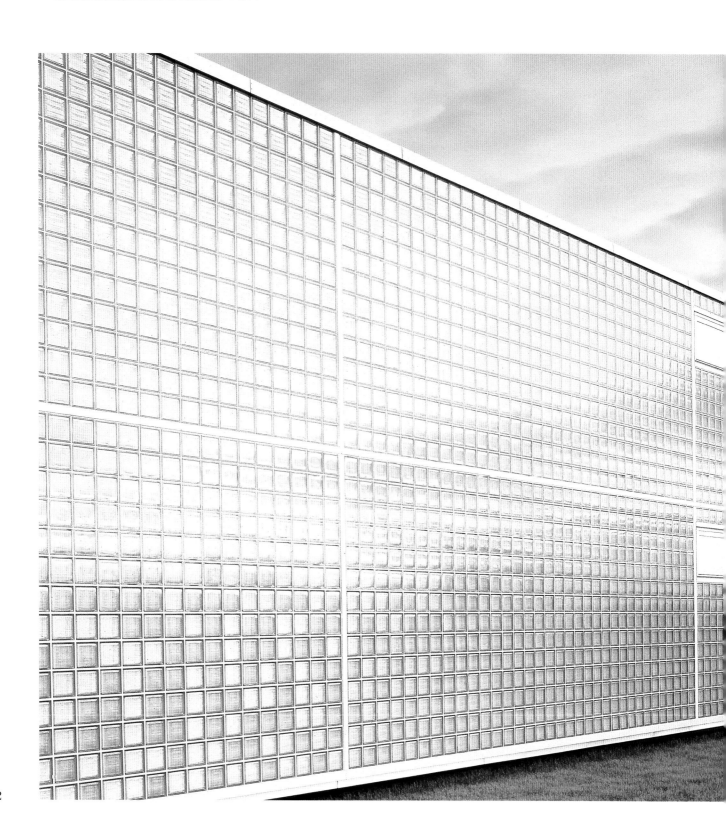

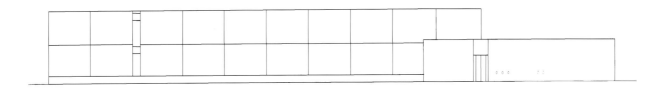

Detail of the pool of water reflecting the glass-and-concrete volume.

The straight corridor providing access to the hotel rooms.

opposite
Access to the main entrance from the elliptical court.

View of the external terrace at the rear of the hotel.

ITM Building in Matsuyama
Matsuyama-shi, Ehime
1991–93

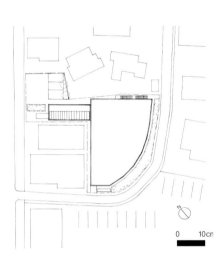

0   10cn

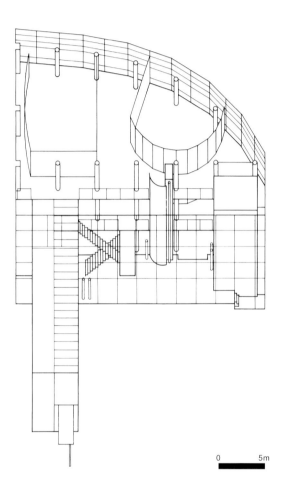

0   5m

The building houses the head offices of the associated companies of the long-established confectioner Ichiroku. The site is in a residential district on the southern edge of Matsuyama. A dedicated office facility like the T Building constructed in Nakameguro in 1990, it is classified under the Japanese Building Standards Act as an intermediate structure: something between the totally fire-resistant building and the ordinary wooden one. The 1500-square-metre site has a three-storey-high "void" containing stairways, small kitchen areas, toilets and other open-plan functions. This "void" is a space animated by the presence of people and objects. It constitutes a new kind of "location for communication" where working people can meet and chat in a relaxed atmosphere. Offices are scattered around the core, which itself houses the ground-floor rectangular entrance hall and the first-floor recreation rooms. Daylight enters each functional area from different directions and the result is a building filled with light. The three-storey-high void consists of a huge glass screen integrated with the structural columns. The glass is completely covered with a milky film that possesses a high interference factor, limiting the passage of ultraviolet light and softening the intensity of the afternoon sun. During the day, light for the offices comes through the multifaceted aluminium curtain wall shaped to fit the site. Skylights are set in the ceiling of the recreation rooms, allowing light to pass through the glass floor to the entrance hall underneath. The ITM is an open-plan building: there are very few walls dividing up the space. For this reason the indirect light that enters individual areas is dispersed, giving the interior of the building a homogeneous quality. In addition, this light reflects off the aluminium, glass, white ceramic tiling and other surfaces used, breaking down fixed conceptions of floor, wall and ceiling. The subdued light given off by these surfaces interferes with people's sense of direction: the interior of the building is suffused with a floating impression as if it were utterly weightless.

View of the glass-walled volume at night.

*Main façade,
cross-section
and longitudinal
section.*

opposite
*Plans of the three
levels, legend:
1 meeting room
2 boardroom
3 recreation room
4 offices
5 computer room
6 entrance hall.*

*View of the double-
height volume
of the entrance
to the upper floors.*

An office area.

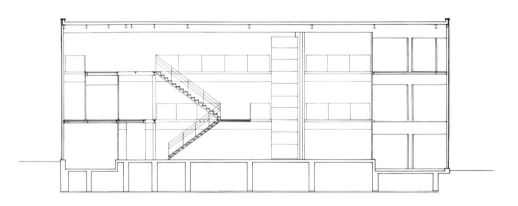

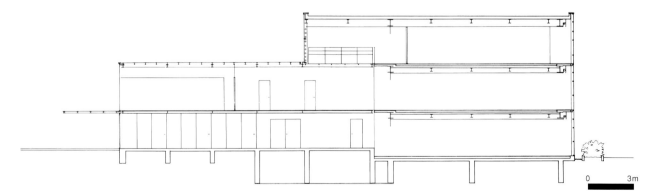

0   3m

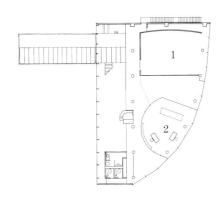

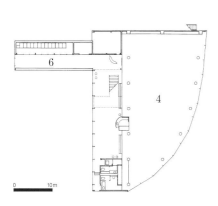

0   10m

Planning and Urban Design for Luijazui Central Area
Shanghai, China
1992

The Chinese city of Shanghai has been undergoing rapid change since the beginning of the 1990s as a consequence of the investment of foreign capital. The Pudon district in particular has been the target of a large-scale rejuvenation project designed to turn it into something comparable to the Parisian district of La Défense, a scheme promoted by the Chinese government as a symbol of the "New China". The part of the Pudon district called the Bund is located on the other side of the river from the quay and is characterized by a group of beautiful buildings constructed in the 1930s.

Ito's firm was involved in the project for the rejuvenation of Luijazui Central Area, covering 170 hectares right at the heart of the Pudon district. The proposed master plan encompasses office buildings, hotels, conference halls, leisure and commercial facilities and housing, covering a total floor area of almost four million square metres. Envisaging future development of the city toward the south along the river, the proposal divides the site into strips of land running in a north-south direction and provides for zones with different functions. Starting from the riverside, these include the leisure/cultural area, the central commerce/business area, sports facilities and a buffer green belt, convention facilities and housing developments. Networks of various transport systems will be superimposed on the district, irrespective of the zoning. The multi-layer transport networks consist of underground railway systems, tunnels beneath the river, underground arterial roads, a network of former creeks that will be uncovered, footpaths and subsurface motorway systems set at shallow depths, like moats. Office buildings, hotels and housing constitute the vertical elements that penetrate these layers of horizontal grids.

Like the rejuvenation plan for Antwerp, the surface level is open to the public and forms a spacious park. The method of superimposing different networks in such a way that transparent interactions are created among them is a result of efforts to learn from the chaotic and yet vigorous reality of the city and to reconstruct it in the light of an innovative concept.

General plan.

opposite
Model.

following pages
Illustrations to the competition project with perspectives.

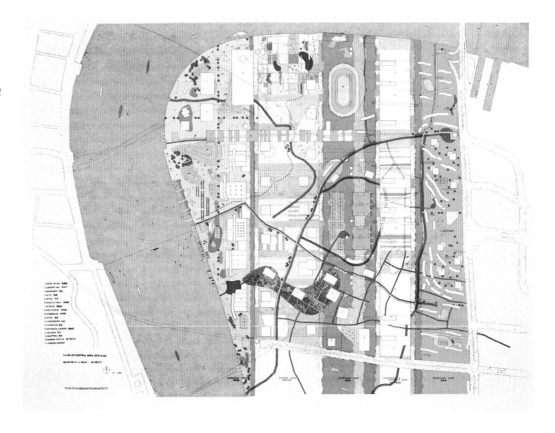

131

ELEVATION WEST

SECTIONAL ELEVATION SOUTH

TOYO ITO & ASSOCIATES ARCHITECTS

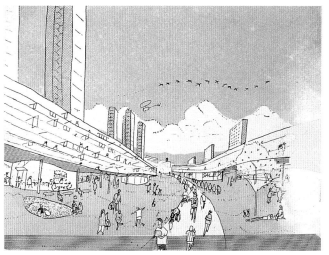

Old People's Home in Yatsushiro
Yatsushiro-shi, Kumamoto
1992–94

The building is located on an area of land reclaimed from the sea beside the fishing harbour in Hinagu, on the coast of the Shiranui Sea, and houses a small community of fifty senior citizens. It is a hundred metres long, with a corridor running the length of a single line of rooms, a layout designed to maximize exposure to sunlight. On the other side of the corridor, the dining-room, bathrooms, meeting rooms and other communal facilities are positioned on the basis of their frequency of use and in such a way as to keep walking distances within acceptable limits. The elements under the roof are distributed seemingly without design, to such an extent that they create an impression of fracture. Features such as the courtyard and rooftop garden are extremely artificial, looking almost like stage props, and offer distinct views. The spaces of the building are loosely arranged so as to achieve a soft blending of areas. The structure operates as both a medical and an educational facility, and can be thought of as a large residence for a family of fifty, or as a long-term residential hotel with fifty rooms. One of the main aims of the design was to produce a simple solution for a building type whose typical architectural programme tends to be very complex. This building is an illustration of how to strike a balance with efficiency, in order to give the closed configuration of a nursing home the loosest possible arrangement. It has a relaxed atmosphere that will tempt even non-residents to drop in as they pass by. The meeting rooms open onto a broad expanse of greenery which can be used for a wide range of activities, such as croquet matches, a film festival in the spring, firework displays in the summer, a harvest festival in the autumn and kite flying in the winter. Ideally, a facility that tends to be isolated from the outside world so as to make life easy for its managers should be open to the town in which it is located and function as a meeting place for its inhabitants.

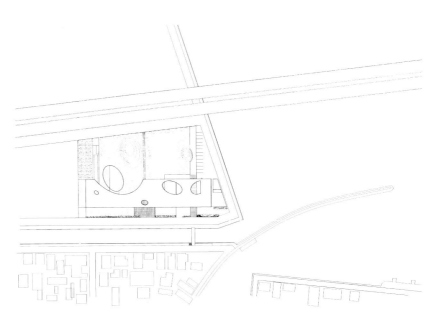

Access to the entrance across footbridge.

General plan.

Exterior views.

Plans of the two
levels, legend:
1 entrance
2 workshop
3 roof garden
4 internal
courtyard
5 loggia
6 meeting room
7 dining-hall
8 kitchens

9 offices
10 installations
room
11 conference hall
12 medical
consulting room
13 bedrooms for the
elderly with tatami
14 bedrooms for the
elderly without
tatami.

opposite
Exterior views
showing the loggias
and covered
meeting places.

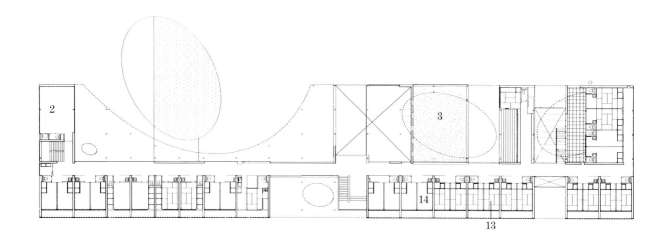

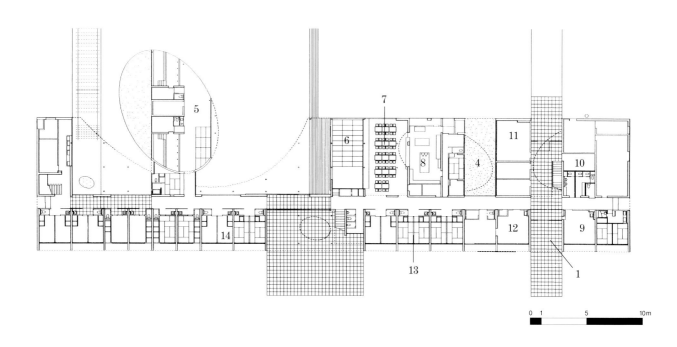

138

*Longitudinal
section and
elevation.*

*Glimpses of daily
life at the old
people's home.*

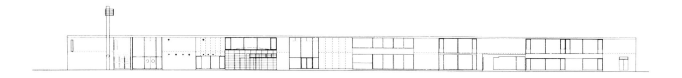

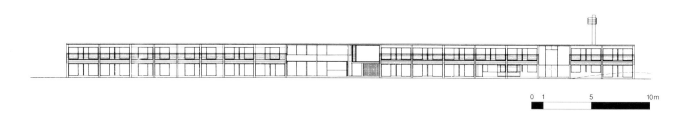

*Communal
dining-hall.*

*Elevations and
cross-sections.*

Yatsushiro Fire Station
Yatsushiro-shi, Kumamoto
1992–95

The fire station is a complex that comprises the Yatsushiro Regional Fire Service Headquarters, with operational control over seven fire stations in the region, and the Yatsushiro Fire Station, a base for firefighting and emergency services in the centre of the city. The criteria for this project called for the most efficient and rational arrangement of the fire station's various functions. Another intention was to create a very open space, like a city park, suited to the surrounding environment: mostly residential with a local government centre. These requirements were processed in parallel, making it possible to co-ordinate decisions on the numerous plans. The volume containing the offices, the sleeping quarters for the personnel and other internal functions is raised 6 metres above the ground, and the training area is delimited by a curved boundary. Thus the internal space is an accumulation of subdivided sections, whose positions are determined by the priority of their functions in relation to the garage for emergency vehicles on the ground floor. The realization of the project depended on achieving ideal forms for two very different settings: the park-like area and a highly efficient fire station. The result is a unique combination of the two.

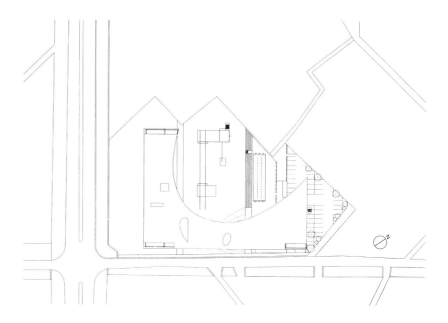

*General plan,
view of the main
front inspired
by Le Corbusier.*

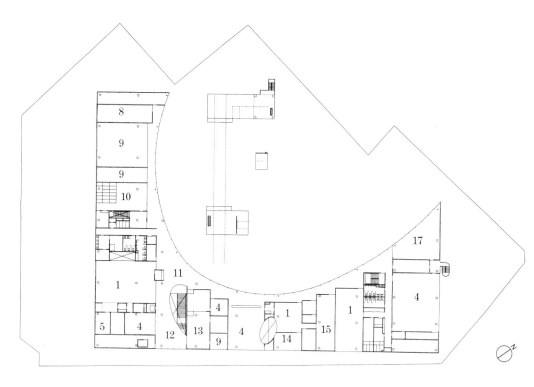

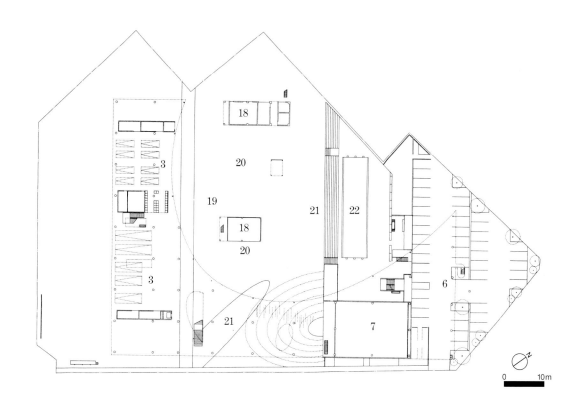

West, north,
east and south
elevations.

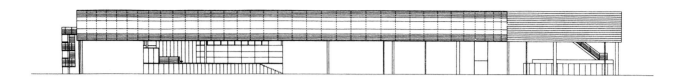

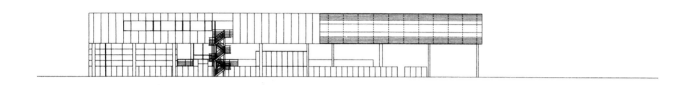

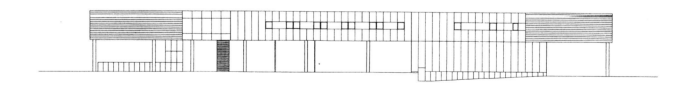

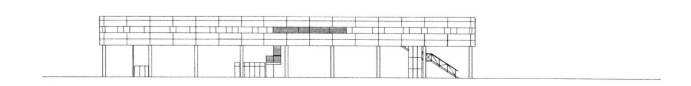

0   10m

Longitudinal section, lateral elevation.

Detail of main façade.

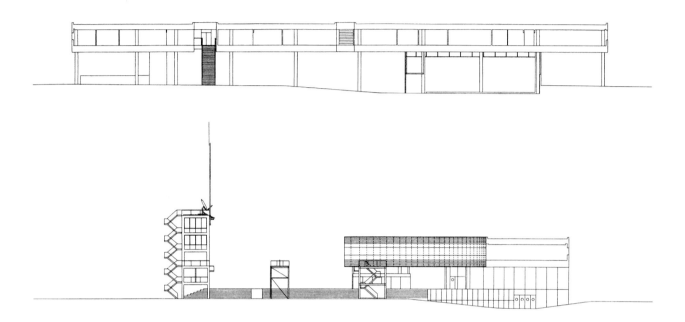

*The multicoloured
opening from the
ground floor.*

opposite
*Main entrance
and stairs leading
to the upper floor.*

148

Nagaoka Lyric Hall
Nagaoka-shi, Niigata
1993–96

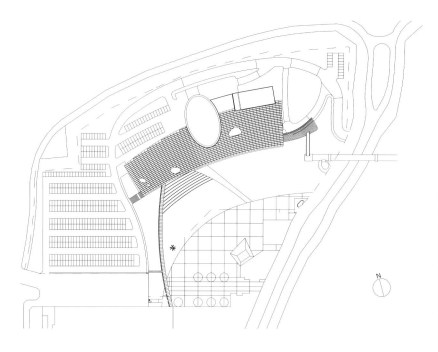

This complex includes a 700-seat concert hall, a 450-seat theatre and ten studios of various sizes. The site is located in the cultural and educational district of the city of Nagaoka, in a vast and flat landscape that in turn emphasizes the immense expanse of the sky. Since Nagaoka already has a multipurpose hall seating 1500 people, the two halls in this complex are intended exclusively for musical and theatrical performances. The concert hall and theatre are volumes with oval and rectangular plans respectively. Other sections of the complex are covered with a softly undulating vaulted roof. A gentle slope on the grass-covered mound leads to the foyer on the southern side of the complex. The corrugated glass wall enveloping the concert hall protects the interior from the noise

of the by-pass to the north of the site. At twilight, light from inside glows through the glass wall and turns the hall into a landmark. The roof seems to blend in with the surrounding mountains and the grassy mound creates a marked contrast to the two projecting volumes behind, forming a naturalistic but man-made landscape in the otherwise nondescript environment. The immense roof that covers the foyer, studios and information lounge has an RC, non-beam, plate structure. Rays of sunlight shower the complex between randomly arranged pillars, coming from the courtyard and through holes in the roof and creating an atmosphere like that of a forest. The concert hall is designed as a single-box type with an oval plan. Because of its shape and the two rows of balcony

seats on both sides of the stage, a feeling of unity between the audience and performers is created. The proscenium stage-type theatre is rectangular in plan and has as simple a spatial layout as possible so as not to impede freedom of movement on the stage. The theatre boasts a high level of technical facilities, comparable to the finest theatres in the metropolitan area. They are freely accessible to citizens equipped with magnetic cards, allowing the complex to serve as a cultural centre for the community on a daily basis. The largest of the studios is the same size as the stage of the theatre, permitting full-scale rehearsals. The complex only opened recently, but is expected to play a significant role in the community as a location for cultural activities open to the public.

*Plan of the site,
general view.*

following pages
*General view from
the grassy slope.*

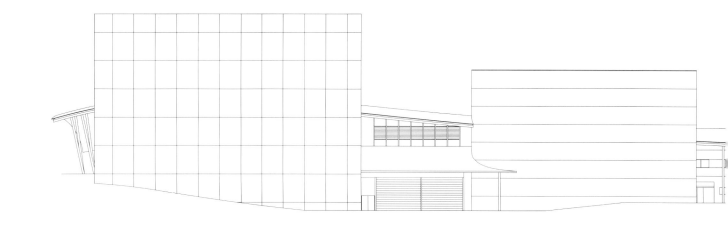

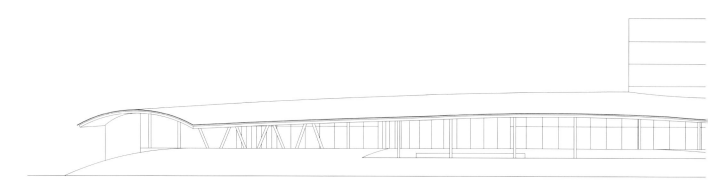

*Rear, side and
main elevations.*

*Night-time view
of the illuminated
concert hall.*

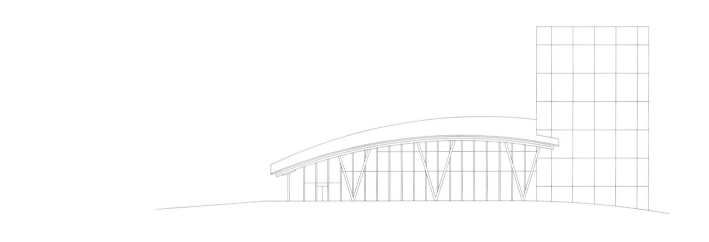

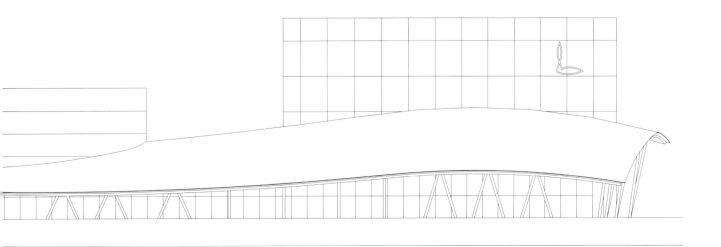

*Communal spaces
of the entrance;
the connection
between the concert
hall and theatre.*

*Gallery leading
to the car parks.*

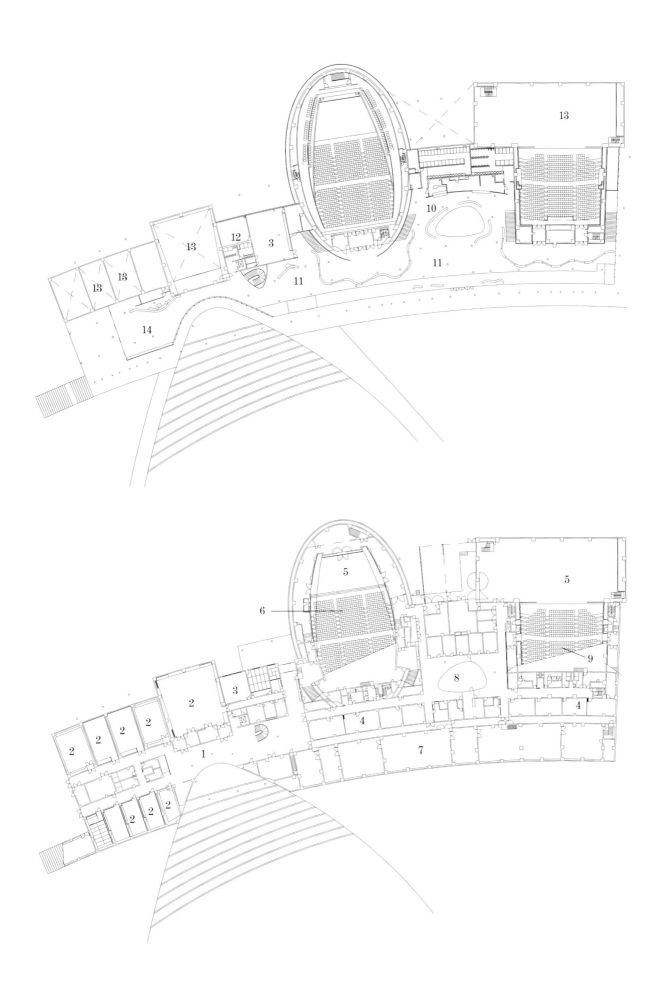

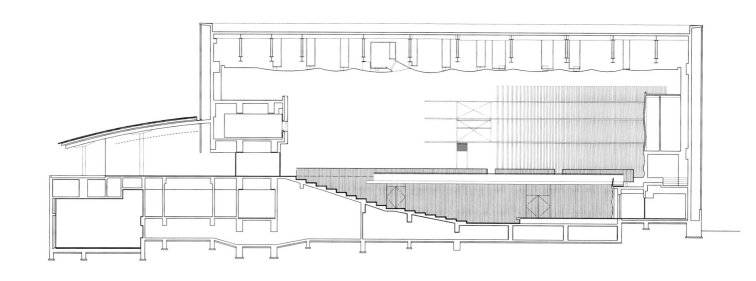

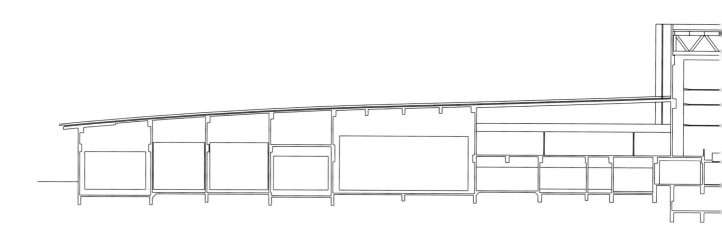

Longitudinal section of the concert hall and view of the interior.

Cross-section of the complex and of the two auditoria.

Longitudinal section of the theatre.

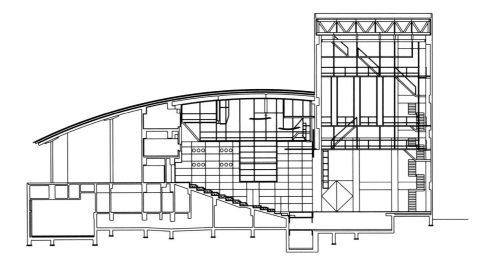

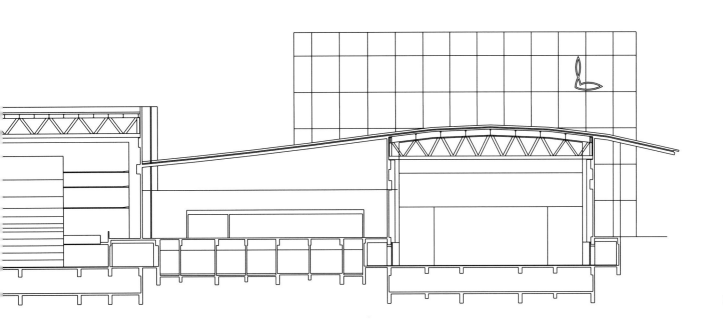

159

Dome in Odate
Odate-shi, Akita
1993–97

This multipurpose dome built in the city of Odate, in Akita Prefecture, won a two-stage competition in October 1993. Because of the extremely large scale of the structure, requiring special construction techniques, close collaboration between the architects and the contractor was essential to a comprehensive proposal covering planning, the structural system, equipment, the construction method, costs and management. In April 1994 discussions began with the governments of Akita Prefecture, the client, and the city of Odate, administrator of the dome, on the construction of an all-weather, multipurpose dome seating around 5000 people (but with a maximum capacity of 10,000). Working drawings were completed in March 1995. Odate, located in a mountainous region in the north of Akita Prefecture, is noted for its logging industry and the production of laminated timber, along with the neighbouring cities of Noshiro and Takasu on the Yoneshiro River. At an early stage it was suggested that cedar wood should be used in order to promote local industry. The site is located in a rich natural environment with a range of mountains in the background and includes a forest of broadleaf trees, but is covered with snow during the long winter. Consequently, Ito wanted the design to reflect an attitude of confronting nature. A "dome born out of nature": the configuration of the dome was determined by aerodynamic considerations, taking into account the prevailing south-westerly winds from the Yoneshiro River and the snow, as well as the trajectories taken by balls in baseball games and the flow of air inside. Bi-directional arch-trusses made of locally produced laminated cedar are used in the structure to create a sense of harmony with nature. A "dome fused with nature": the dome merges with the surroundings and appears to hover lightly above the ground. It is part of an extensive continuum that includes a pond, an athletics field, a green hill and

a broadleaf forest. A "dome that creates a natural environment": to create a natural indoor environment even during the harsh winter, a Teflon membrane is used to let sunlight in during the day. At night, the domes glows with light from the inside, floating in the air like a moon.

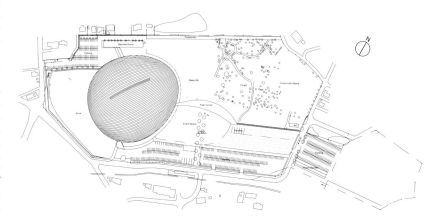

The dome
from the lake.

opposite
Aerial view
and general plan
of the site.

View at night, side elevation, detail of the lobby.

opposite
Plans, legend:
1 main entrance
2 rest area
3 storerooms
4 multipurpose hall
5 toilets
6 technical spaces
7 park centre
8 arena for sports activities
9 tiers for the spectators
10 meeting room
11 restaurant
12 kitchen
13 shop.

following pages
General view of the arena.

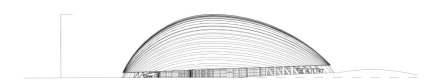

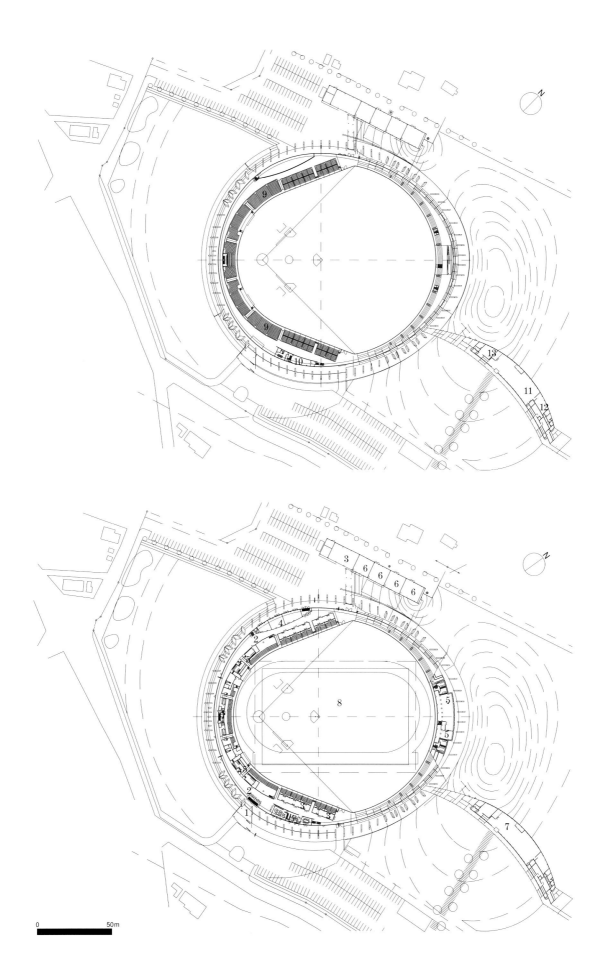

0   50m

Community and Day-care Centre in Yokohama
Yokohama-shi, Kanagawa
1994–97

This multipurpose facility, built on a rise in the city of Yokohama, consists of a community centre with a gymnasium and Care Plaza, a day-care centre for the elderly. The building is made up of two primary volumes, one set on top of the other. On the ground level, the gymnasium extends to the lobby, the courtyard and the dining and dayroom areas of the Care Plaza. The upper level is essentially a single, large open space with a ceiling height of 5 metres. The lift lobby, reading corner, volunteers' corner and multipurpose space are all set openly under this ceiling. Smaller enclosed units, such as a kitchen, meeting rooms and *tatami* room, are located along one wall, as though subject to the main space. Although the sense of community is said to be in decline everywhere, the level of usage of facilities of this type is relatively high in provincial areas. In general, what is lacking in these facilities is interaction between the users. They usually come there with a specific purpose (such as visiting a karaoke room) and leave promptly afterwards. This apathy on the part of users is in part the consequence of the arbitrary and fragmented nature of the programme requirements formulated for this type of building, and is often the outcome if these requirements are not judiciously handled in the course of the design process. This results in a building with no overall sense of a harmonious whole that would inspire user interaction.

So an attempt was made here to increase the degree of transparency throughout the interior by minimising the barriers between the various functions and their users. At the same time, natural effects like sunlight and breezes are readily perceived inside with the help of such devices as the wooden louvers and decks, skylights, plants in the courtyard, etc. The underlying intention here was not so much to bring the inside and the outside closer but to transform the internal space into a new kind of integrated environment that used natural phenomena as a catalyst.

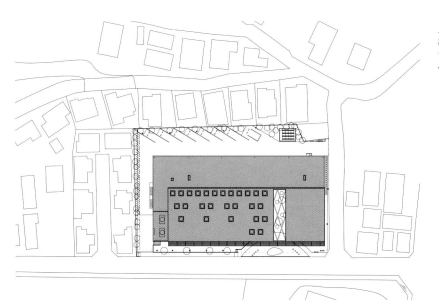

Plan setting the complex in its urban surroundings.

*Front with the
main entrance.*

Plan of the second
level and general
plan, legend:
1 main entrance
2 courtyard
3 restaurant
4 common room
5 rest area
6 changing room
7 bathrooms
8 kitchen
9 toilets
10 offices
11 consulting room
12 multipurpose
room

13 showers
14 technical spaces
15 gymnasium
16 information
17 library
18 space for
voluntary workers
19 infirmary
20 games room
21 lounge
22 workshops
23 traditional room
with tatami
24 recreational
spaces
25 void.

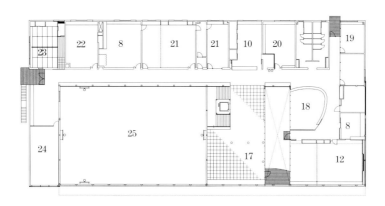

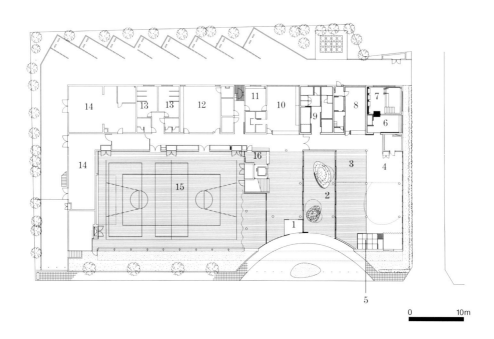

0   10m

Exterior elevations.

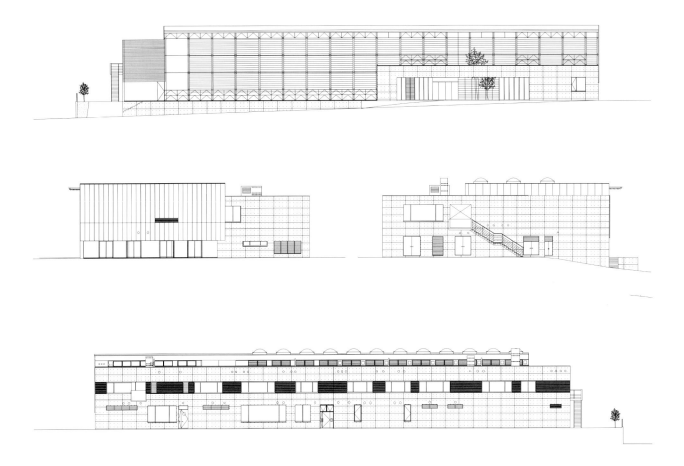

*Cross and
longitudinal
sections.*

*Partial view of the
suspended lamellar
ceiling with its
circular skylights.*

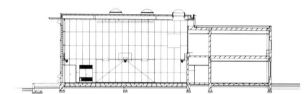

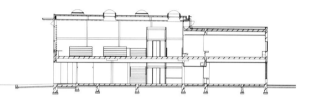

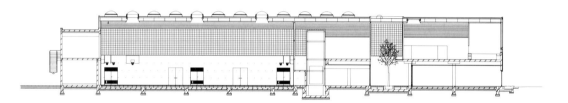

0   10m

Library on the first floor.

S House in Oguni
Oguni-cho, Kumamoto
1995–96

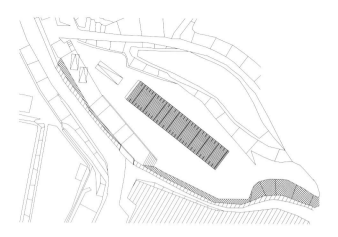

The site is located on the gently sloping side of a mountain and encircles an irrigation pond. Out of the project to build a living, work and exhibition space for two artists on this plot of land, the living quarters and studios have been completed. Cohabitation, creative artistic activities and communal activities with local residents are of equal importance to the couple. Through discussions with them, Ito came up with a house from which their activities would spontaneously diffuse into the surroundings. The various activities out of which they wove the pattern of their life were fragmented and loosely rearranged within a volume open to both the inside and outside. A corrugated roofing sheet of about 30 × 6 metres supported by flat bars on both surfaces is set on top of ten steel columns to form a lattice beam. The slab on the upper floor is subject to greater loads and supported by extra pillars. The interior has hardly any finishing and the external materials and piping are left exposed. The volume defined by a very simple skeleton and thin, mass-produced plates is sectioned into smaller volumes with different functions. The rationally subdivided spaces are contained in a large volume of air that expands and contracts with the light and wind. The very large and bare volume, clad with cold and dry materials, is remarkably austere in appearance. A new life has begun for the couple, surrounded by stone and cloth and by the natural setting of Oguni, and the people of Oguni will also find a new life with a different quality through their joint activities with the artists.

General plan.

View of the main front.

Plans, legend:
1 sculpture studio
2 terrace
3 painting and
weaving studio
4 gangway
5 meeting room
6 living-room
7 bedroom
8 toilets.

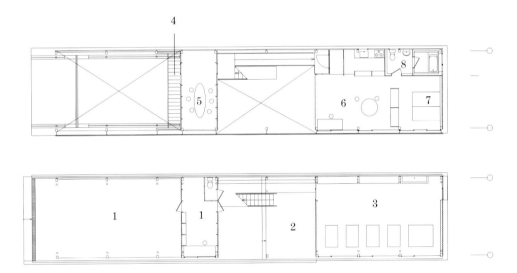

*Details of the
curtain materials.*

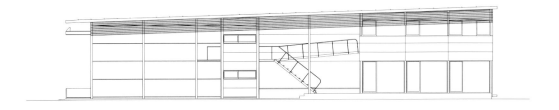

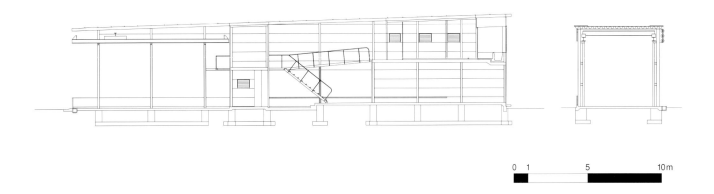

0 1   5   10m

Ota-ku Resort Complex in Nagano
Chiisagata-gun, Nagano
1995–98

*Plan of the site
and contours
of the ground.*

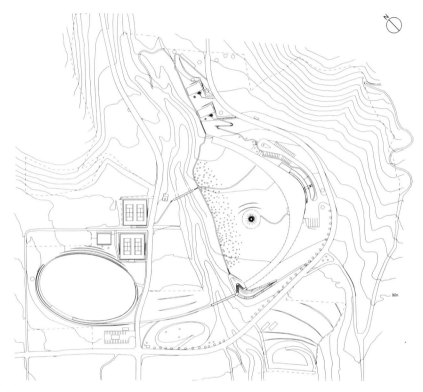

The site is located on a gentle, south-facing slope near the Chikuma River at the foot of Mount Asama in Nagano Prefecture. The resort complex for Ota-ku includes housing for its citizens and extra-curricular teaching facilities for its junior high-school pupils. The complex is shared by these two functions, but distinctions are made to facilitate its management. Work, training and recreation are separated from each other in urban life (in Ota-ku) and have lost their continuity with nature. Reintegration of this fragmented urban existence through contact with nature was the main theme of the project. The building has therefore been designed as a sensory mechanism that will help the human body—the physical body that has become so vulnerable and insensitive—to perceive nature and adapt to it. Site preparation was kept to a minimum to preserve as much as possible of the natural setting. To impart integrity to the site, which is bisected by the Kanahara River, flowing from north to south, the building, bridge, promenade and athletics field are arranged in a gently curving line. The sharply curved building stands at the foot of Mount Omuro and encircles the beautiful sloping meadow. The main facilities are situated on the east side and the rooms are arranged in a line across the descending contour lines. These two areas are to some extent interchangeable, as the boundary partition can be moved to adapt to the number of pupils that have to be accommodated. The two-storey building includes housing, located mainly on the lower floor which is built out of concrete to shield it from the cold climate and noise. The bathrooms, seminar rooms, halls, restaurants, banquet hall and convention hall on the upper floor have large openings offering beautiful views of the surroundings. The structural steel frame, in the shape of an inverted U, envelops the entire concrete section on the lower floor and the concrete acts as an auxiliary support, protecting the steel columns from buckling, earth tremors and wind pressure. As a whole, the building has the appearance of a gently curving steel tube lying on a slope and lined with concrete on the inside. The surface of the roof is warped into three dimensions to match the contour lines of the ground, and the corrugated panels follow these curves. The wall is clad mainly with metal plates on the outside, but wooden louvers are attached to the columns on the side facing the courtyard to screen out sunlight and prying eyes. They also prevent direct exposure of the glass and concrete materials, preserving the harmony between the building and its environment.

*Bird's-eye view
of the complex in
its surroundings.*

*Elevation and
partial view.*

opposite
*Views of the rear
of the building
showing the main
entrance for people
arriving by road.*

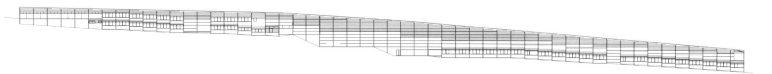

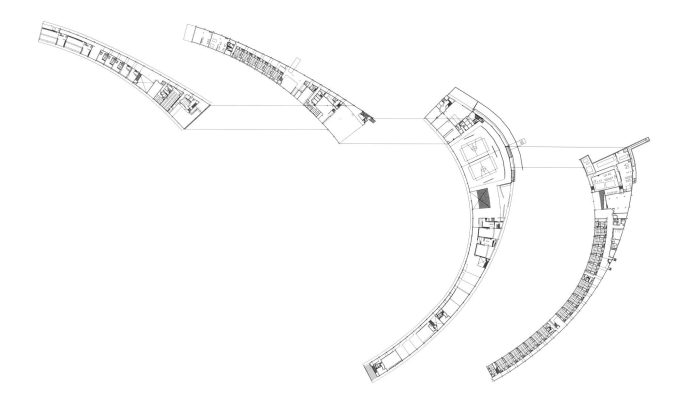

*Plans of the two
levels of the
building broken
down into two
sectors (north and
east-south wing).*

*View looking out
from the building.*

opposite
*Longitudinal
corridor of
distribution.*

*View of the
gymnasium.*

Notsuharu Town Hall
Notsuharu-machi, Oita
1996–98

When the old town hall in the centre of Notsuharu, a small settlement of 6000 people, grew too old and small, the decision was taken to build a new one and Ito was invited to take part in the competition. His proposal was selected. Two main issues were confronted in the design of the town hall. One was how to produce a construction that would be adapted to the site and in harmony with the surroundings. The other was how to convey a sense of comfort and freshness, as the town hall was in a sense an office building. Though it had to be suitable to the region, Ito did not want it to be too closely adapted to the locality. So his aim was to find an intermediate solution that would reconcile the two issues. As the site happened to be located between two highways, he set out to create an architecture of intersection, a theme he had tackled on previous occasions. It did not have to be a destination but, just like an airport or a station, a place of interchange and passage. The idea was to produce a place where the people passing by or through the building would be able to communicate with one another. The town hall consists of a single communal hall with the counters of the various services and a ramp that follows the slope of the ground. The municipal offices are arranged as closed volumes along the east side, with the lattice steel structures visible behind the facing of translucent glass, creating graphic effects that characterize the internal volume.

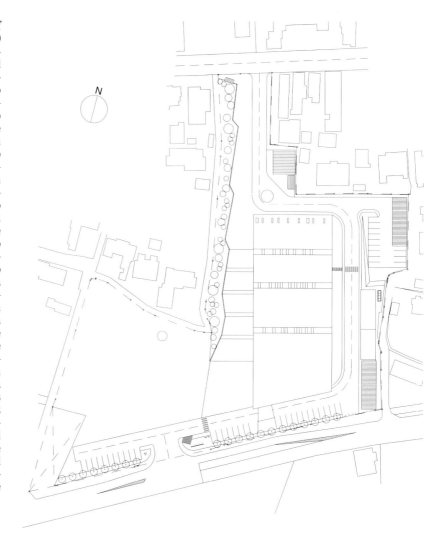

General plan.
View by night.

Plans, legend:
1 offices
2 toilets
3 information
centre
4 entrance hall
5 ramp leading
to the upper floor

6 computer room
7 library
8 archives
9 meeting room
10 changing rooms
11 winter garden
12 void
13 guest room

14 terrace
15 mayor's office
16 secretary's office
17 council chamber
18 canopy

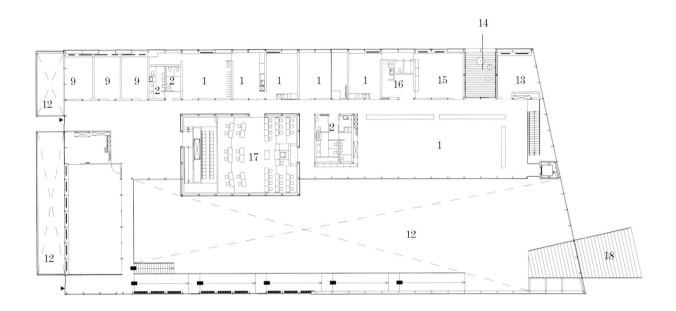

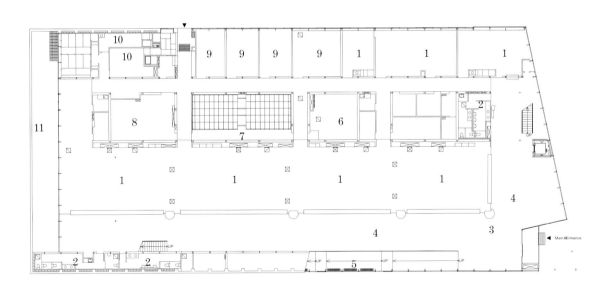

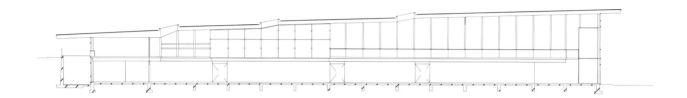

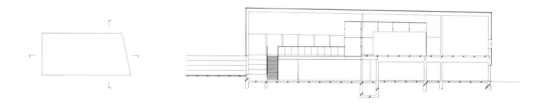

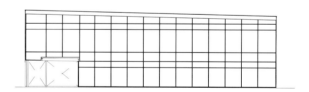

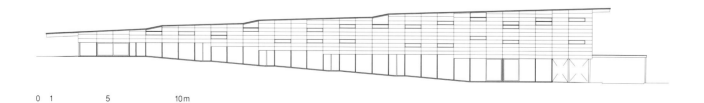

0 1   5   10m

View of the volume
of the council
chamber.

opposite
Large hall
with counters
for the public.

Interior of the
council chamber.

T Hall in Taisha
Taisha-cho, Shimane
1996–99

Taisha is a coastal town with a population of 16,000 situated in the prefecture of Shimane. The project was produced for a competition by invitation held by the public administration for a multi-functional cultural centre to house recreational and study activities. Initially, the client wanted it to be a centre for the practice of Kabuki, the traditional Japanese theatre. A library and spaces for study were added to the programme later. The aim was to rehabilitate the adjoining area as a cultural zone for the town. The site was characterized by the presence of a number of public buildings, a navigable canal linking the town to the sea and a series of detached houses. To respond to the conditions of the context, Toyo Ito conceived a building in the shape of an artificial mound, ringed by the main access route that leads to the parking lot. The main front, facing the existing public buildings, consists of a large glass wall with a curved profile that derives from a transverse cut across the mound. The only parallelepiped volume that projects from the roof contains the stage tower of the theatre. The new centre establishes a direct relationship with the public buildings: the aim was to create an urban space in which all the town's public functions could be concentrated. The entrance hall is a large space from which visitors can enter the theatre, multipurpose hall and library. The theater, with fixed seating for 600, has been constructed from prefabricated panels of reinforced concrete. The gaps created between the panels by their slight rotation have been filled with glass walls of double thickness that let in natural light. Alongside is set an open-air theatre with tiers of seating, creating a separate entrance to the center for people coming from the residential areas. The multipurpose hall, used for conferences, video screenings and performances, has a circular plan and 200 movable seats, permitting the maximum of flexibility. The curved volume next to the main entrance houses the library, containing 100,000 volumes, and is naturally illuminated by means of its two inner courtyards. In the reading room, free of structures and partitions, the distribution of functions is determined solely by the book-shelves and other items of furniture. The offices, storehouses and service spaces have been concentrated in the area alongside the library. A number of secondary entrances at the rear of the building permit a flexible use of the complex. The structure of the principal volumes—the theatre, multipurpose hall and offices—is made of reinforced concrete, while the roofs are constructed out of steel.

(A.M., from *Casabella*, no. 682, 2000)

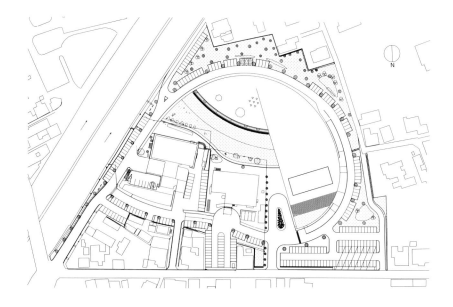

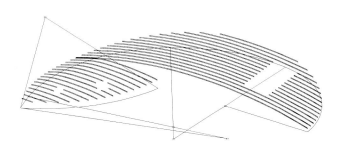

General view and
detail of the main
entrance.

East elevation.

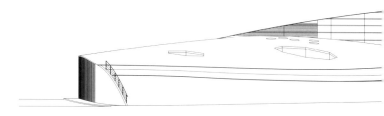

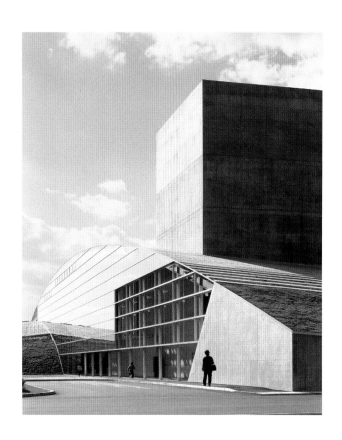

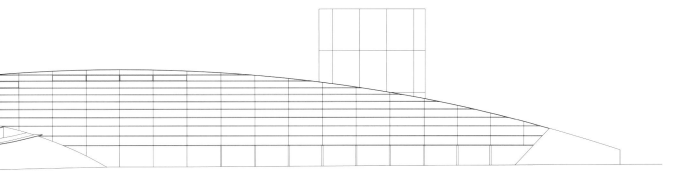

*West, south and
north elevations.*

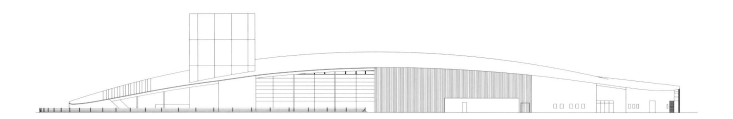

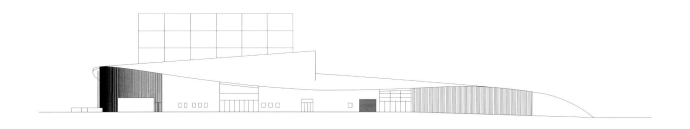

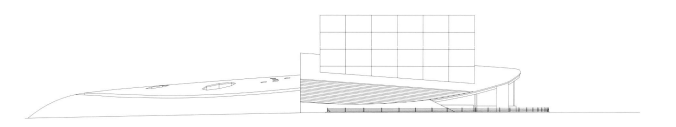

*Open-air theatre
and entrance
on the west front.*

South-east front.

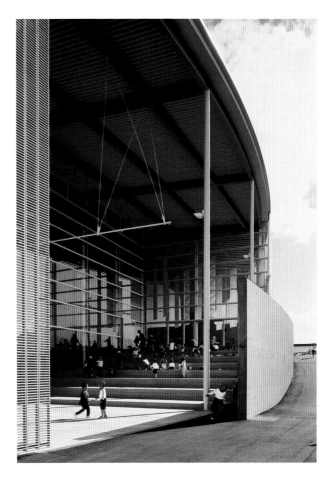

199

opposite
Entrance hall.

*Corridor serving
the offices.*

*Longitudinal
section.*

*Plan at the level
of the entrance hall,
legend:*
1 main entrance
2 foyer
3 theatre
4 stage
5 open-air theatre
6 multipurpose hall
7 toilets

8 office
9 meeting room
*10 secondary
entrance*
11 library
*12 storeroom
for books*
13 children's corner
14 internal courts
15 information
16 children's room.

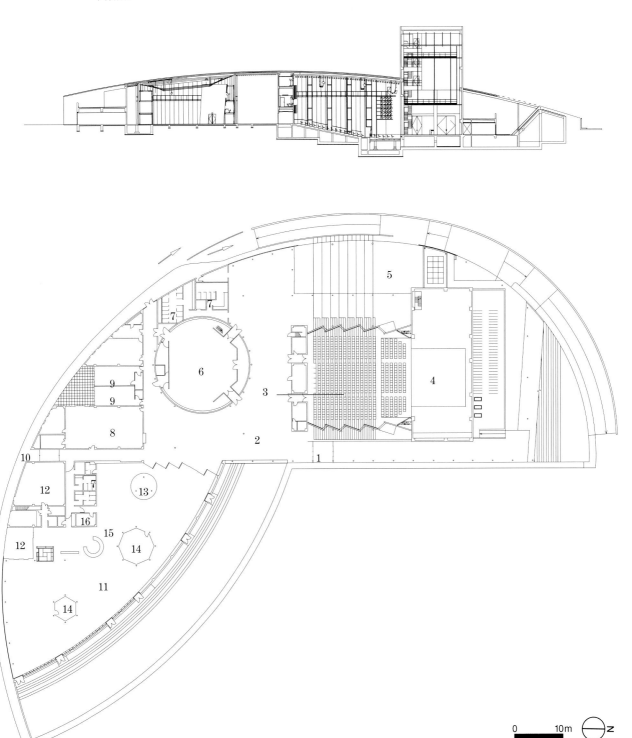

0   10m

201

*Views of the library
showing internal
courts for natural
illumination and
the reading spaces.*

The multipurpose theatre.

Glazed distribution spaces alongside the theatre at the rear of the building.

opposite
Foyer with the cafeteria and multipurpose hall.

Crystal Ballpark, Competition Project
for the Seoul Dome
Seoul, Korea
1997

The Crystal Ballpark is a Crystal Palace
of the twenty-first century.
People used to enjoy playing baseball or
soccer under the open sky. They kept on
chasing the ball even when the sun set
in the west and the moon rose. Sporting
activities have always been carried out
in a natural setting.
For people living in modern cities, the
stadium is the most exhilarating space
for recreation. It is a space where dra-
mas are staged without scenery and
where thousands of people come together and go wild with joy and excitement. It is a space that symbolizes the
largest community in a city, a role that
was played by squares in the past. Now
there are many domes in the world.
Is it impossible to build a dome where
we can enjoy the excitement of sport
while experiencing the sounds, sights
and warmth of nature, and can such an
experience be transmitted to the entire
city?
We have proposed a wholly transparent
dome. It would be more appropriate to
call the dome a ballpark in the sense
that the building allows us to feel nature even when we are inside. It will be
a brand-new symbol of the city that
sends a message of exhilaration to the
whole city.

*Computer graphic
simulating the
dome in its
surroundings.*

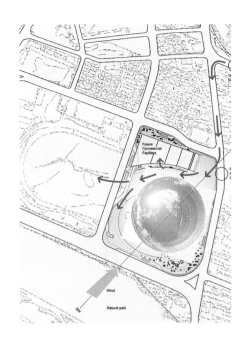

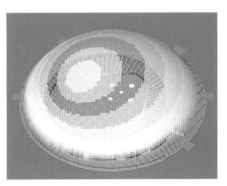

209

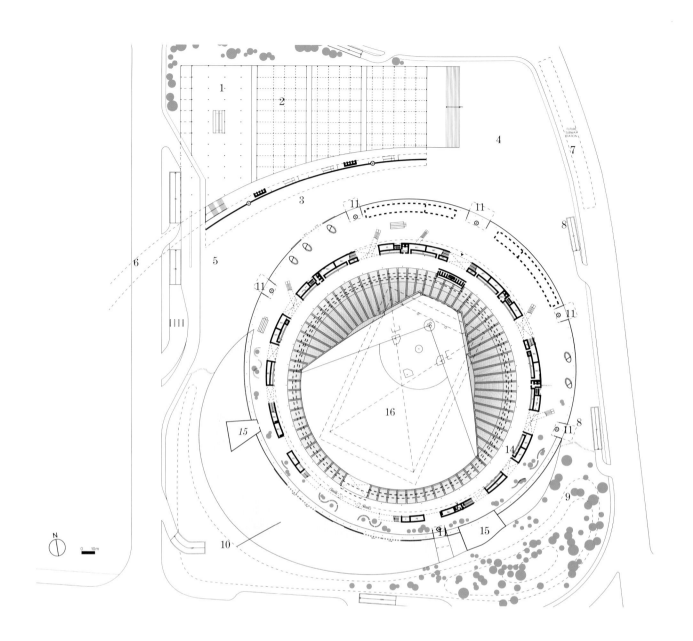

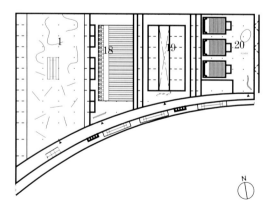

General plan
and plan of a level
of the block to the
north-east, legend:
1 department store
2 retail sales
outlets
3 market
4 plaza
5 bus stop and taxi
stand
6 footbridge
7 future
underground
railway station
8 access to the
underground car
parks

9 green area
10 pool of water
11 entrance
12 hall for
distribution
of the public
13 toilets
14 distribution
corridor
15 cafeteria
16 sports arena
17 tiers of seating
for the public
18 indoor sporting
activities
19 exhibition zone
20 multi-screen
cinema.

*Orthogonal sections
of the complex.*

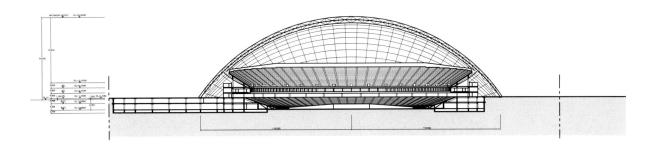

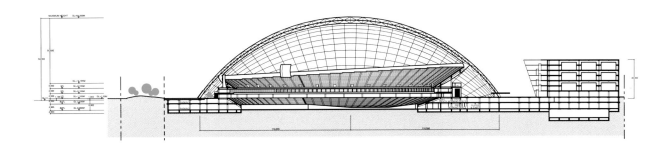

211

Possible
configurations
of the arena,
legend:
1 soccer
2 concert hall
seating 10,000
3 American football
4 basketball
5 concert hall
seating 5000–10,000
6 athletics
7 boxing
8 exhibitions.

opposite
Axonometric
exploded diagram
of vehicular
and pedestrian
circulation.

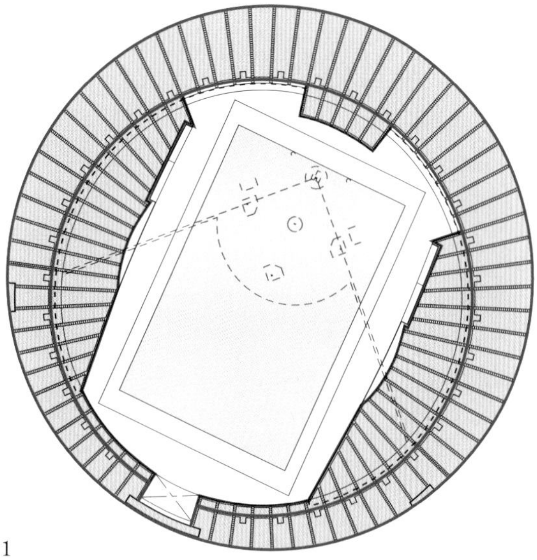

1

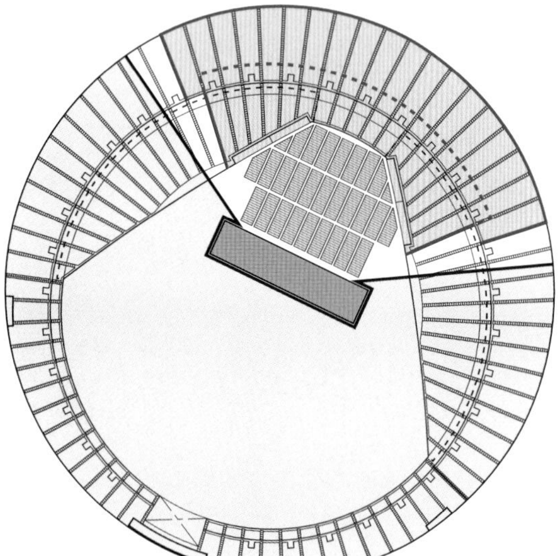

2

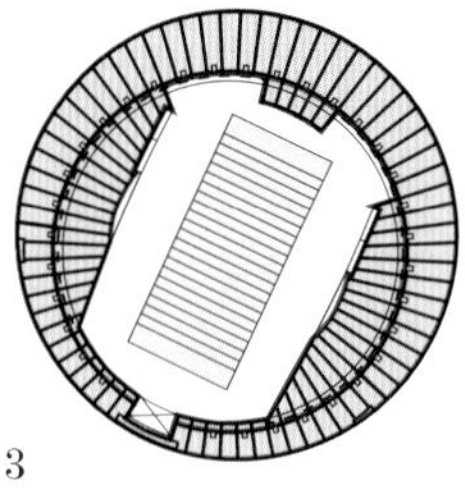

3

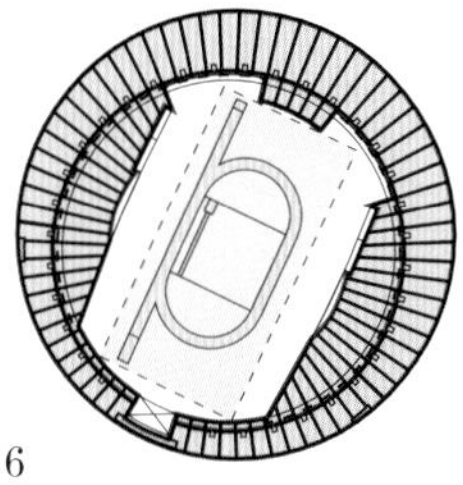

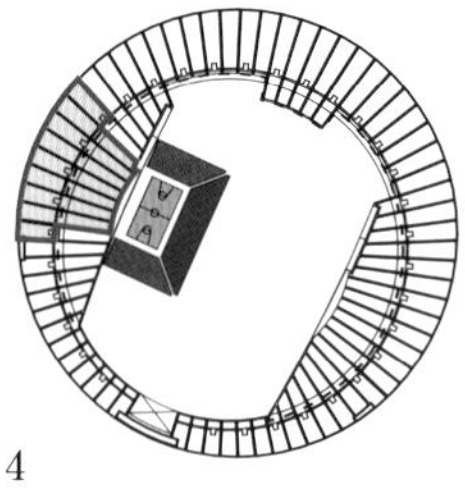

4

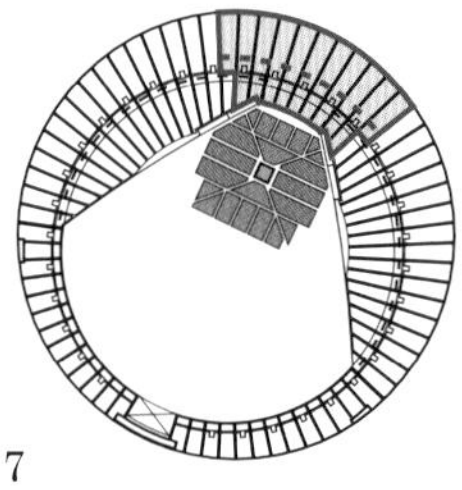

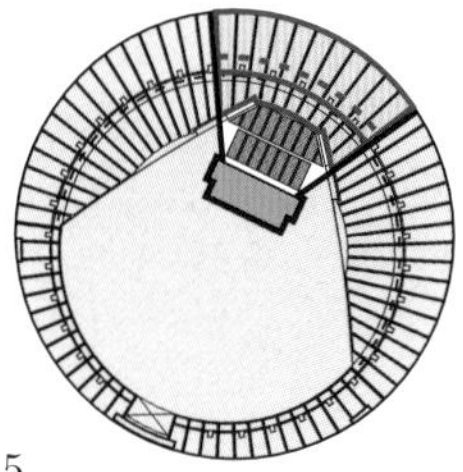

5

6

7

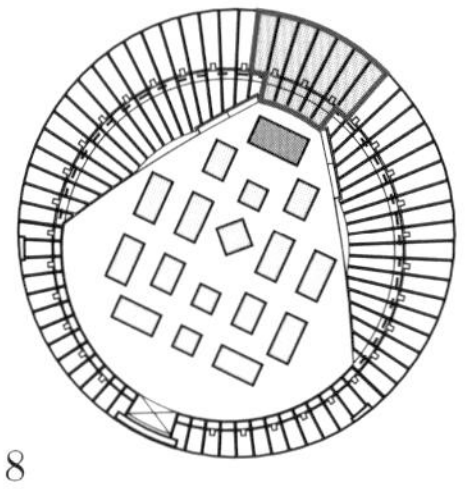

8

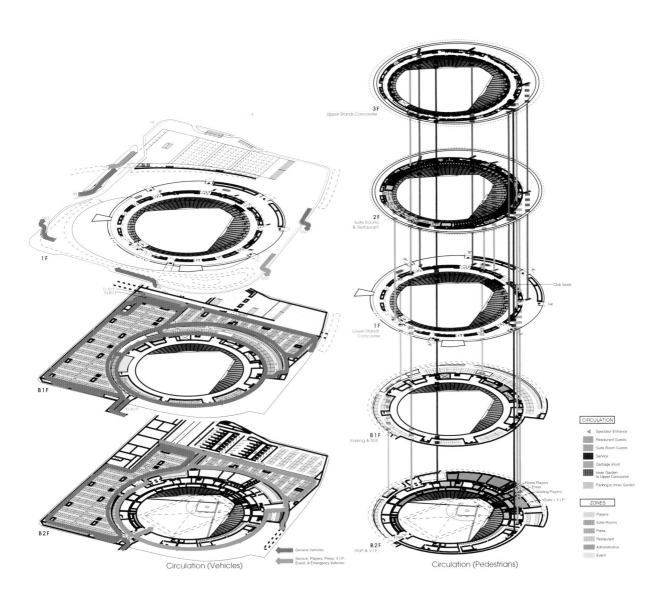

1F

B1F
To B2F
To B2F

B2F

Circulation (Vehicles)

General Vehicles

Service, Players, Press, V.I.P.,
Event, & Emergency Vehicles

3F
Upper Stands Concourse

2F
Suite Rooms
& Restaurant

1F
Lower Stands
Concourse

Club Seats

B1F
Parking & M/E

Home Players
Press
Visiting Players
Suite + V.I.P.

B2F
Staff & V.I.P.

Event

Circulation (Pedestrians)

CIRCULATION

Spectator Entrance
Restaurant Guests
Suite Room Guests
Service
Garbage shoot
Inner Garden
to Upper Concourse
Parking to Inner Garden

ZONES

Players
Suite Rooms
Press
Restaurant
Administrative
Event

213

*Computer graphics
simulating the
structures and
the systems
for the control
of natural light.*

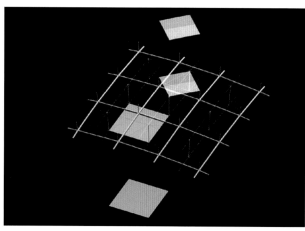

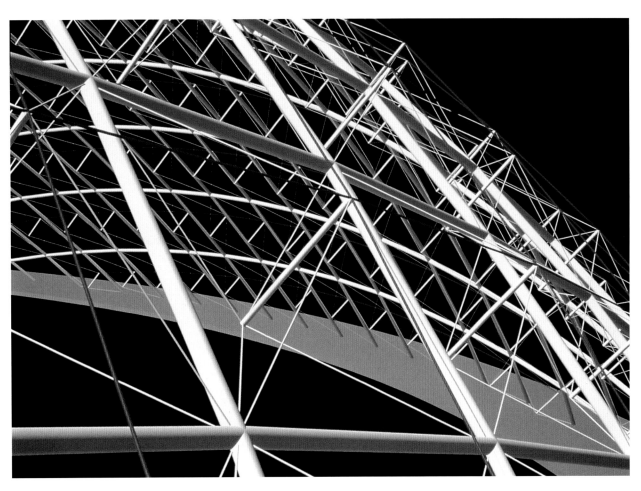

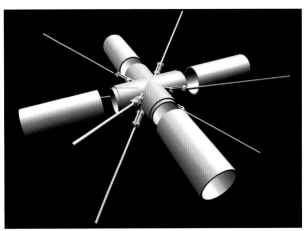

Project for Redesigning the Waterfront of Thessaloniki, Thessaloniki, Greece
1997

City in a flow: land and sea, city and nature, architecture and environment, individual and society, nation and region. Humankind has always made distinctions and attempted to build solid walls between them to clarify their identity. We justify and glory in the self-reliance of the city, of architecture, the individual ego and the nation. The boundary—as a manifestation of one's presence—is an external expedient for differentiating oneself from the surroundings. Its order is created through independence. As a consequence, it has encouraged the constant destruction of nature and the environment.

Over sixty per cent of the human body is made up of water. Humans survive by imbibing and eliminating water. So we tend to live near water, seeking its benefits. The human being is a watercourse: human bodies are linked to nature and form part of it. The modern mind, however, demands separation from nature and the independence of the ego. This is symbolized by the human figure inscribed in a geometric pattern that is complete in itself.

Likewise, architecture has been regarded as a complete model of the universe, independent of the world outside. A wall had to be constructed, making a clear distinction between inside and outside. This made it possible to obtain an internal order. Architecture and the human body are similar in the sense that neither can survive without a link to nature. Electronic media like the television, telephone and computer provide us with a link to the world, and to the most primitive notion of nature.

It is time the wall was removed. The wall of the ego, of architecture, the wall between region and city, the wall as a demarcation between the city and the sea.

Although human beings have always revered the sea, we have attempted to define the boundary between the land on which we live and the sea. Numerous works of architecture have been built facing the sea, and most of them have played the monumental role of a proud assertion of our presence.

This project sets out to blur the demarcation between land and water, through flexibility, ambiguity, fusion and mutual permeation.

The concept of the "archipelago" dismantles and diversifies the monotonous opposition of these two elements. It is based on the suggestive notion of a versatile, networking society where it is neither a single line nor the juxtaposition of centre and district that defines the entity.

A hopeful new approach to urban planning influenced by the charming islands of the Aegean Sea.

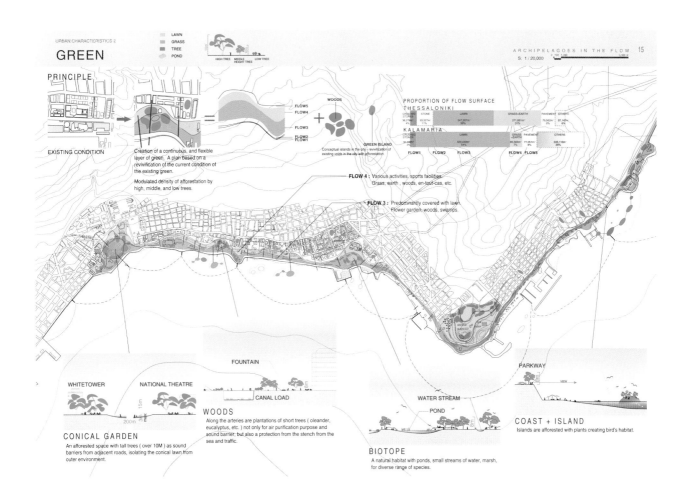

URBAN CHARACTERISTICS 2

GREEN

LAWN
GRASS
TREE
POND

HIGH TREE   MIDDLE HEIGHT TREE   LOW TREE

PRINCIPLE

EXISTING CONDITION

Creation of a continuous, and flexible layer of green. A plan based on a revivification of the current condition of the existing green.

Modulated density of afforestation by high, middle, and low trees.

FLOW5
FLOW4
FLOW3
FLOW2
FLOW1

WOODS

GREEN ISLAND

Conceptual islands in the city : revivification of existing voids in the city with afforestation.

PROPORTION OF FLOW SURFACE

THESSALONIKI

KALAMARIA

FLOW1   FLOW2   FLOW3   FLOW4   FLOW5

FLOW 4 : Various activities, sports facilities. Grass, earth , woods, en-tout-cas, etc.

FLOW 3 : Predominantly covered with lawn. Flower garden, woods, swamps.

WHITETOWER   NATIONAL THEATRE

CONICAL GARDEN

An afforested space with tall trees (over 10M) as sound barriers from adjacent roads, isolating the conical lawn from outer environment.

FOUNTAIN

CANAL LOAD

WOODS

Along the arteries are plantations of short trees (oleander, eucalyptus, etc.) not only for air purification purpose and sound barrier, but also a protection from the stench from the sea and traffic.

WATER STREAM

POND

BIOTOPE

A natural habitat with ponds, small streams of water, marsh, for diverse range of species.

PARKWAY

COAST + ISLAND

Islands are afforested with plants creating bird's habitat.

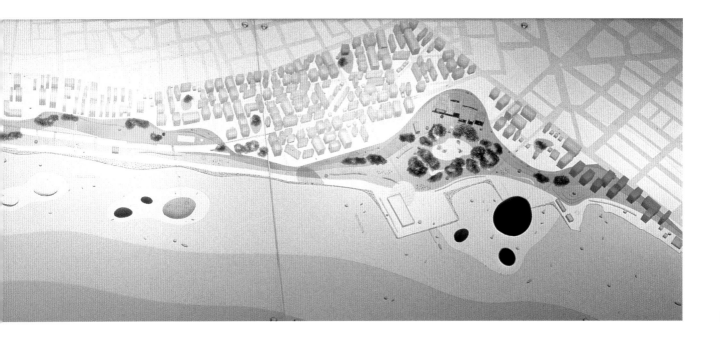

Model and competition illustrations of the functions distributed along the seafront with the aquarium and botanical garden on new, artificial islands in the sea.

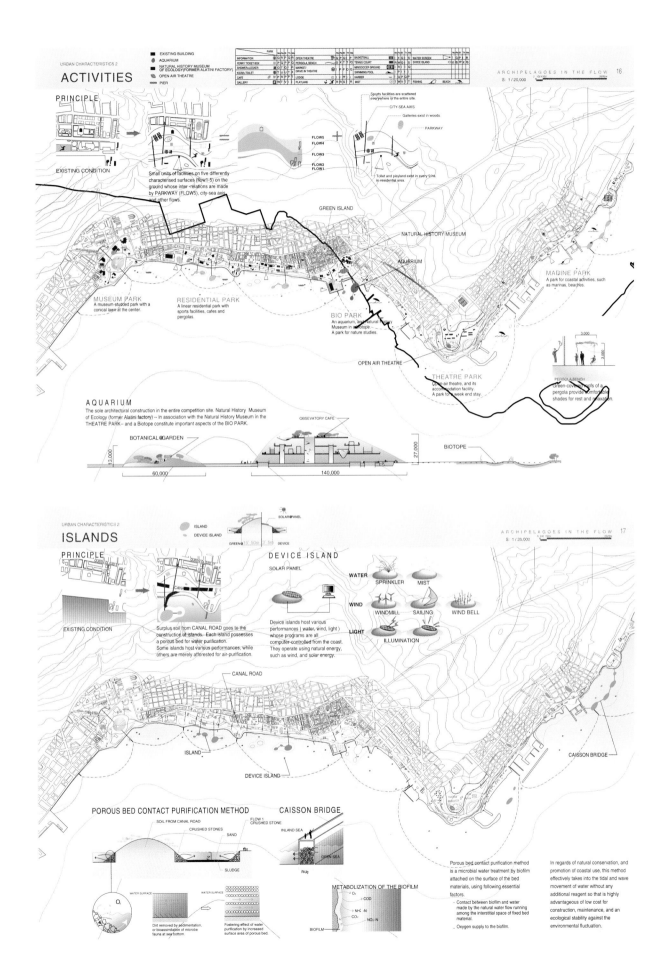

URBAN CHARACTERISTICS 2
ACTIVITIES

■ EXISTING BUILDING
◉ AQUARIUM
◆ NATURAL HISTORY MUSEUM
   OF ECOLOGY(FORMER ALATINI FACTORY)
▦ OPEN AIR THEATRE
〰 PIER

PRINCIPLE

EXISTING CONDITION

Small units of facilities on five differently
characterised surfaces (flow1-5) on the
ground whose inter-relations are made
by PARKWAY (FLOW5), city-sea axis
and other flows.

FLOW5
FLOW4
FLOW3
FLOW2
FLOW1

Sports facilities are scattered
everywhere in the entire site.

CITY-SEA AXIS

Galleries exist in woods.

PARKWAY

Toilet and playland exist in every 9 ha.
in residential area.

GREEN ISLAND

NATURAL HISTORY MUSEUM

AQUARIUM

MARINE PARK
A park for coastal activities, such
as marinas, beaches.

MUSEUM PARK
A museum-studded park with a
conical lawn at the center.

RESIDENTIAL PARK
A linear residential park with
sports facilities, cafes and
pergolas.

BIO PARK
An aquarium, large natural factory
Museum in biotope.
A park for nature studies.

OPEN AIR THEATRE

THEATRE PARK
Open-air theatre, and its
accommodation facility.
A park for week end stay.

PERGOLA BENCH
Green-covered roofs of a
pergola provide comfortable
shades for rest and relaxation.

AQUARIUM

The sole architectural construction in the entire competition site. Natural History Museum
of Ecology (former Alatini factory) -- in association with the Natural History Museum in the
THEATRE PARK -- and a Biotope constitute important aspects of the BIO PARK.

BOTANICAL GARDEN

OBSERVATORY CAFE

BIOTOPE

60,000   140,000

URBAN CHARACTERISTICS 2
ISLANDS

SOLAR PANEL

ISLAND
DEVICE ISLAND
GREEN   DEVICE

PRINCIPLE

EXISTING CONDITION

Surplus soil from CANAL ROAD goes to the
construction of islands. Each island possesses
a porous bed for water purification.
Some islands host various performances, while
others are merely afforested for air-purification.

DEVICE ISLAND

SOLAR PANEL

Device islands host various
performances (water, wind, light)
whose programs are all
computer-controlled from the coast.
They operate using natural energy,
such as wind, and solar energy.

WATER   SPRINKLER   MIST

WIND   WINDMILL   SAILING   WIND BELL

LIGHT   ILLUMINATION

CANAL ROAD

ISLAND

DEVICE ISLAND

CAISSON BRIDGE

POROUS BED CONTACT PURIFICATION METHOD

SOIL FROM CANAL ROAD
CRUSHED STONES
SAND
SLUDGE

CAISSON BRIDGE

FLOW 1
CRUSHED STONE
INLAND SEA
OPEN SEA

O_2

WATER SURFACE

WATER SURFACE

Dirt removed by sedimentation,
or bioassimilation of microbe
fauna at sea bottom.

Fostering effect of water
purification by increased
surface area of porous bed.

METABOLIZATION OF THE BIOFILM

O_2
COD
NH_4 -N
CO_2
NO_2 -N

BIOFILM

Porous bed contact purification method
is a microbial water treatment by biofilm
attached on the surface of the bed
materials, using following essential
factors.

· Contact between biofilm and water
made by the natural water flow running
among the interstitial space of fixed bed
material.
· Oxygen supply to the biofilm.

In regards of natural conservation, and
promotion of coastal use, this method
effectively takes into the tidal and wave
movement of water without any
additional reagent so that is highly
advantageous of low cost for
construction, maintenance, and an
ecological stability against the
environmental fluctuation.

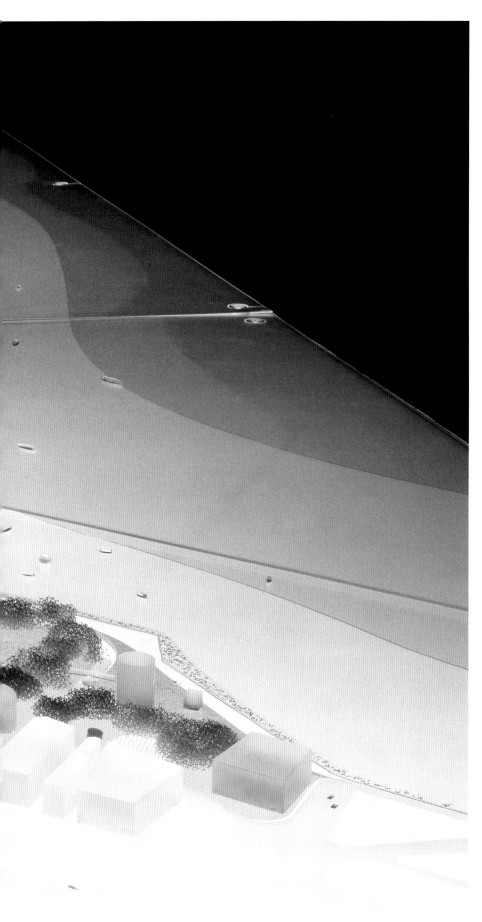

CONICAL GARDEN

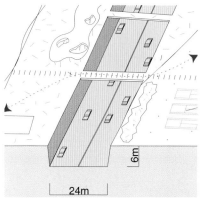

6m

24m

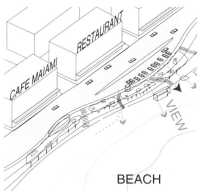

CAFE MAIAMI

RESTAURANT

VIEW

BEACH

221

T House in Yutenji
Setagaya-ku, Tokyo
1997–99

Located in a residential area quite near the centre of Tokyo, the house was designed for a husband and wife who own a graphic-design studio, and their son who is a researcher. When the rising sun is reflected off the milky white façade, it looks like a giant screen. The big cherry tree, to which everyone living in the neighbourhood is greatly attached, casts its shadow on the screen. Looking through the large window, there is an uninterrupted view of the blue sky and garden. The family spends most of its time at home, without any boundary between the activities of eating, sleeping and working. At first, we imagined a life spent walking through different kinds of rooms. Studio and living-room, the bedroom for the parents and a room for their son, utilities such as bathroom and toilet… We tried to discover the ideal volume for each room and envisaged setting them parallel to each other.

As the degree of privacy required in each room differed, we thought of using different materials for their structure. In view of a number of problems that arose, we finally settled on a thin shear wall. The structure of the house consists of three sets of pillar-walls standing side by side, two types of openings between these pillars and slabs on each floor level, producing a cylindrical interior of approximately 15 × 5 × 5.4 square metres that is partitioned by wooden panels and fittings, slicing the plan up into rectangles. The trilateral relationship between the openings in the pillar-walls, the slabs and the partitions creates a suitable sense of space in the house without destroying its overall unity.

Taking into consideration the clients' strong feelings about "living", it seems that we have designed a house that is a response to our own strong feelings about "building". The basic conditions of the surroundings and our determination to produce a refreshing and comfortable area that would satisfy the clients are the factors that shaped this very simple house.

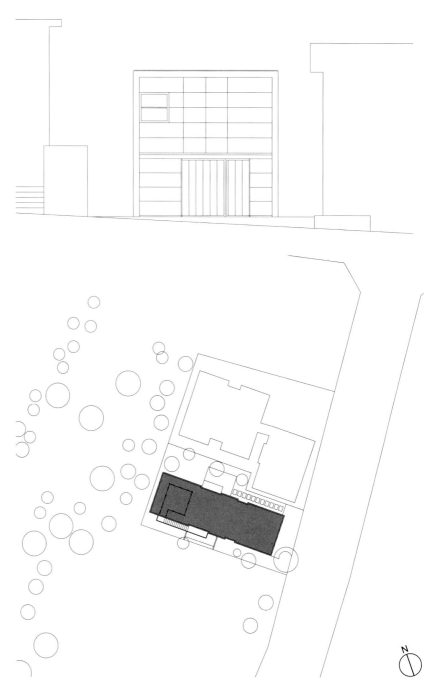

Front.

*First-floor plan
and ground-floor
plan, legend:
1 entrance hall
2 parents' room
3 son's room
4 garage
5 living-room
6 void above the
entrance hall
7 studio.*

*South elevation
and longitudinal
section.*

opposite
*Stairs and,
in the background,
the studio.*

*The studio,
the void above the
entrance hall and,
in the background,
the living space.*

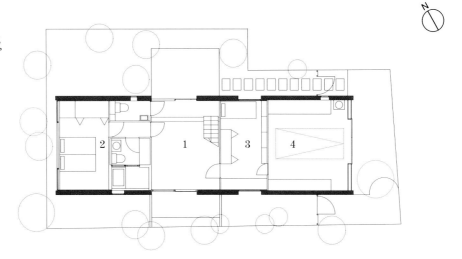

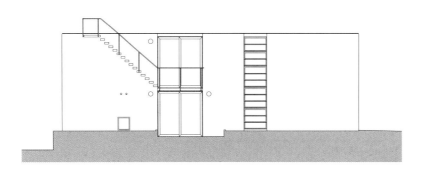

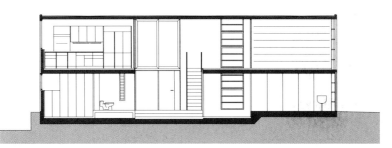

0   1   5m

Aluminium House in Sakurajosui
Setagaya-ku, Tokyo
1997–2000

This building is the home of a married couple in a quiet residential area of Setagaya-ku, Tokyo.

Aluminium has been used for all the structural components and the living spaces are meant to exude the light and pleasant atmosphere of no-fuss design. All the living spaces in daily use, including the kitchen and bathrooms, are located on the ground floor, while the top floor has a guest room and roof terrace. The special qualities of aluminium minimize the usual hierarchical distinctions between structural elements, blinds and other fixtures. This, together with the effects of the natural lighting and the breezes admitted by the two-storey-high, half-unroofed space (sunroom) at the centre of the plan creates a bright, fluid space like that of a loft.

The flat structure of ribbed aluminium panels disperses the loads, allowing the individual structural members to be very small. At the same time, the reversibility and durability of aluminium permits the use of structural panels on the outside, and the use of sash frames as columns. The result is that the structure has no more presence than the fixtures and furnishings. The distinctive soft texture of aluminium along with the impression of abstraction produced by the fineness of aluminium materials helps to downplay the presence of the structure even more.

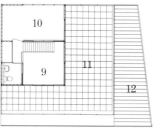
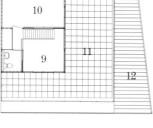
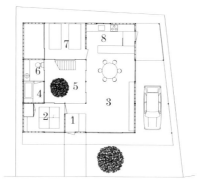

0   5m

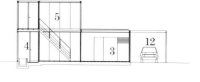

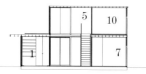

*Scheme of the
bioclimatic project
for ventilation
and internal
illumination.*

*The court-solarium
on the ground floor.*

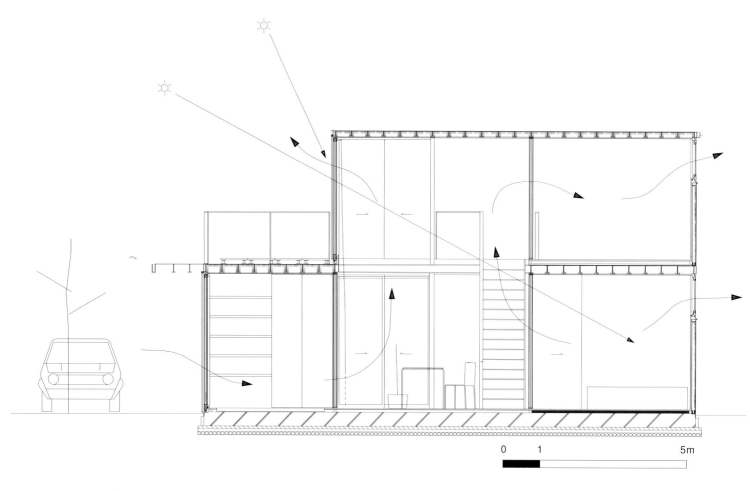

0 1   5m

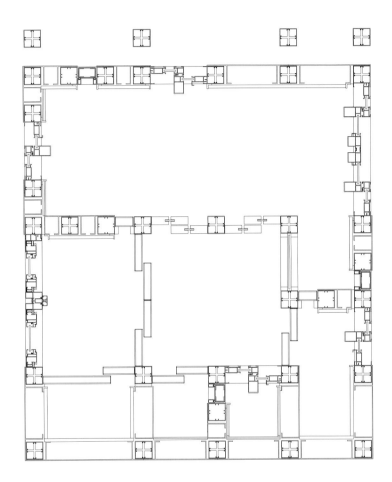

Detail of the
aluminium
supporting
structure.

Axonometric
exploded diagram
of the structural
system.

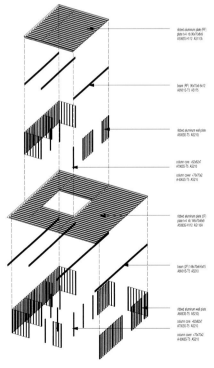

ribbed aluminum plate (RF)
plate l=4 r.b 96x70x6x6
A5083S-H112 AS110A

beam (RF) 96x72x6-6x12
A6N01S-T5 AS175

ribbed aluminum wall plate
A6063S-T5 AS210

column core +62x62x7
6700S-T5 AS210

column cover +70x70x2
A-6063S-T5 AS210

ribbed aluminum plate (2F)
plate l=4 r.b 149x70x6x9
A5083S-H112 AS110A

beam (2F) 146x70x6-6x15
A6N01S-T5 AS210

ribbed aluminum wall plate
A6063S-T5 AS210

column core +62x62x7
A700S-T5 AS210

column cover +70x70x2
A-6063S-T5 AS210

*The living-room
from the
court-solarium.*

*Details of the
beam-pillar joint.*

opposite
*View looking
inwards from
the garage.*

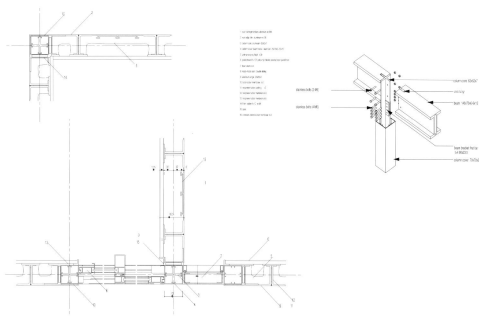

Sendai Mediathèque, Competition
Sendai-shi, Miyagi
1997–2000

Initial sketch of the structural principle made by Ito for the engineer Mutsuro Sasaki.

Sketch of the planimetric distribution.

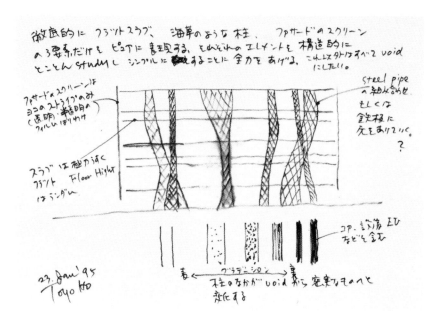

In 1994 an international competition was held for the design of a media library in the city of Sendai, in the north of Japan, about two hours by train from Tokyo. The structure was to be built on a site in the centre of the city, on one of the main streets and close to the Koto-dai Park and the most important public buildings such as the theatre and the seats of local government. The functional programme called for a library, galleries for exhibitions and multimedia spaces. The jury, chaired by Arata Isozaki, was made up of Katsuhiro Yamaguti, Yoshio Tsukio, Terunubu Fujimori and Minoru Kanno. On 22 March 1995, Toyo Ito's design, selected along with two others out of the 235 entries in the first phase, was declared the winner of the second phase. The proposal submitted to the competition underwent no substantial changes during the drawing up of the executive plans, although there were a number of interesting evolutions in this passage. The basic idea remained that of a large volume of glass, with a square plan of 50×50 metres and a height of around 37 metres. The conception of the building is founded on three main elements of composition: six linear planes, thirteen reticular columns and an external skin. The "planes" present the appearance of thin square sheets, suspended in the void at different heights to meet the needs of the client and to avoid a "classic" and constant rhythm on the façade. The thirteen "columns" (there were twelve of them in the competition project), formed out of tubular steel structures, support all the floors, running vertically through the building from the basements to the roof. The columns permit natural illumination of the central parts of the various floors and contain all the systems of vertical circulation and the ducts of the plant. The skin is made up of four façades and a reticular flat roof. Each front is characterized by an architectural solution that accentuates its two-dimensional graphic quality and differentiates it from the others.

Each of the three elements is separated from the others, forming an almost self-sufficient system. In fact the designer did not want to propose a large and solid volume in which columns, floor slabs and façades would be fused together. He has avoided any formal or plastic compromise between the elements. This type of decomposition makes it possible to lighten the image of the building and bring it into line with Ito's research into an ephemeral and insubstantial architecture. His buildings are not designed to last, they are not "palaces" of masonry based on models from the past, but light, almost immaterial structures, resembling temporary installations that reflect the fragile dynamism of the great Japanese cities. The functions are located on different floors, whose interiors have been entrusted to different designers. Each level is characterized by different colours, forms and materials, creating an effect of stratification as if various fragments of the city had been laid one on top of the other.

Visitors enter the building through the large entrance hall on the ground floor, which has the appearance of a covered plaza, completely open onto the urban surroundings. In the competition project, Ito had proposed an authentic concave plaza sunken into the ground and with no outside walls, so as to create an open filter between the building and the city. Unfortunately, the client later decided to enclose the ground floor so that it could be used as an entrance hall, information area and cafeteria. In order to maintain, at least in part, the interaction with the world outside, the four boundary walls are made entirely of glass, with no frames and shutters. In addition, a portion of the glass wall on the main front can be opened totally, transforming part of the interior space into exterior space.

The upper levels are open plan, traversed solely by the reticular columns that act as conductors of natural light and contain the vertical links and plant. The position of the columns has been changed from the design submitted to the competition: instead they are arranged in three parallel strips to rationalize the spaces of distribution, especially in relation to the exhibition galleries on the fourth floor and the structural logic of the floor slabs. The parts at the rear are generally used for service functions and reserved for the staff, while the south side, completely glazed and facing onto the main street, is open to the urban landscape and houses the spaces for the public.

Any constraint of a formal character applied to the project as a whole has been set aside in favour of a neutral system, in which the various solutions are defined floor by floor. Just as in the Yatsushiro Museum, built in 1991, it was the roof that defined the building's architectural image while the spaces inside remained neutral, so that they could be adapted to the museum's requirements, in the Mediathèque the tubular columns, the building's most distinctive feature, permit the creation of *plans libres* in the manner of Le Corbusier that are perfectly adaptable—precisely because they are free of formal constraints—to functional requirements.

On this neutral base, Ito and others have designed the interiors as installations. While on the ground floor Karim Rashid has proposed pieces of furniture-sculpture with organic forms and strong colours, on the first floor the spaces are bounded by retractable synthetic white drapes, lightweight divisions that do not interfere with the perception of a single open plan. On the second and third floor, Ito has laid out the library as a two-storey-high volume, with reading rooms on the south and north sides. The space is characterized by a regular grid of ceiling lamps and the furnishings are designed by KTA.

There are two types of exhibition space: on the fourth floor there is a gallery subdivided by partition walls of full height, some of which can be moved along tracks on the ceiling, allowing the

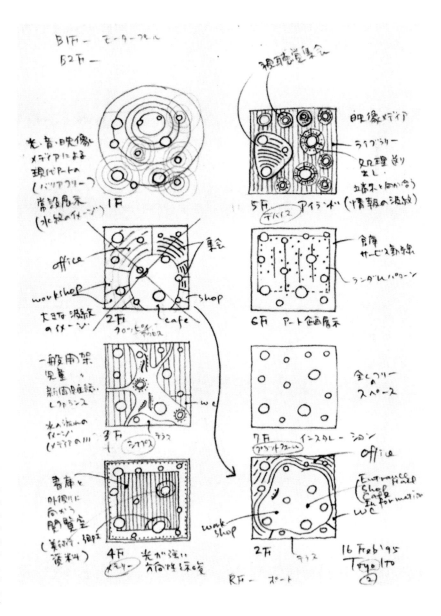

233

*Mutsuro Sasaki's
schemes of the
structural concept:
reticular
column-torsion-
deformation.*

*Scheme of the
assembly systems
of the prefabricated
modules.*

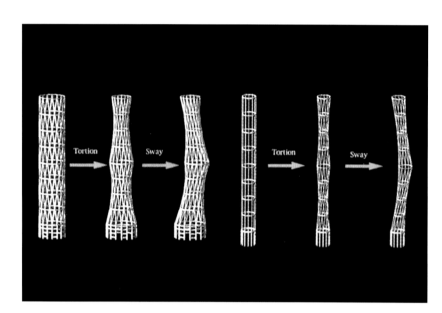

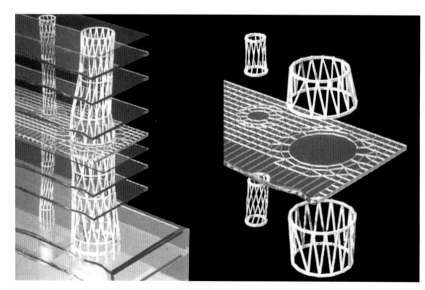

interior distribution to be varied according to need; on the fifth level an open plan can be adapted to any installation. The reticular columns can be left exposed to let in natural light, or covered up by drapes of synthetic black material.

The top floor houses the Mediathèque proper: a curved wall of translucent glass reaching all the way to the ceiling delimits a central volume containing an auditorium with seating for 180 people, meeting rooms, offices and a cafeteria. The outer walls of this floor are made entirely of glass. This creates a sort of belvedere with views onto the city in which the audiovisual spaces are concentrated, with video collectors and consulting tables designed by Ross Lovegrove.

The Sendai Mediathèque is a long way from the so-called high-tech style, in which technology determines the form of the building and is flaunted as the primary element of the architecture. Ito, by contrast, has been able to retain control of a technologically complex structure, placing the technical aspects at the service of his quest for a poetry of light and a dematerialization of the building. Special attention should be paid, in this connection, to the solutions adopted for the reticular columns. In the competition project, they had been faced with opaque glass which masked their internal structure. They had been conceived, in fact, as "columns resembling seaweeds". They were supposed to be solid, white and have the physical consistency of a homogeneous "material". Fascinated by the studies of Mutsuro Sasaki, who was responsible for the structural calculations and designs, Ito was drawn toward a progressive dematerialization of the originally solid form, eventually arriving at the final solution in which the tubular structure is left exposed, faced solely with transparent glass. Right from the start, it had been the intention to set skylights at the top of the columns in order to transform them into pillars of light. For this

*Graphic
elaboration
by 000Studio.*

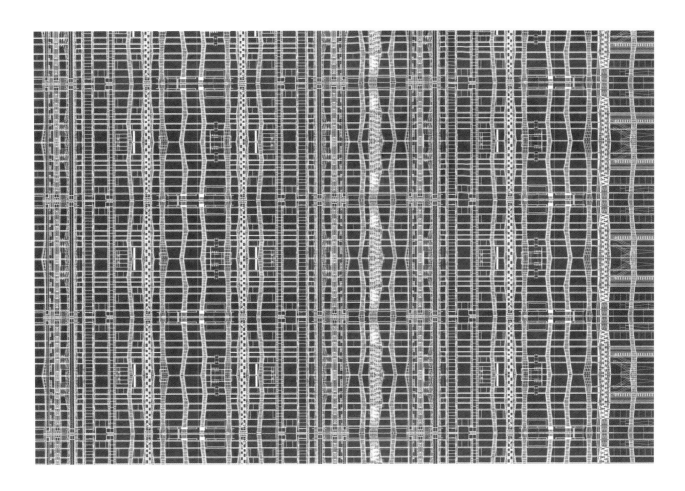

Bird's-eye view
of the completed
Mediathèque.

purpose, computerized systems of rotating mirrors have been installed in the upper part of the two central columns to reflect natural light down to the lower floors and permit automatic control of the internal illumination.

Mutsuro Sasaki designed the reticular columns in the form of hyperbolic paraboloids, with tubular steel elements reduced to the minimum possible thickness. The study of the form of the columns started out from the concept of a cylinder, subjected first to torsion and then deformed by oscillation. The torsion imparts greater stability to the structure. The diameter of the columns ranges from 2 to 9 metres, while the diameter of the tubes of which they are made up ranges from 140 to 240 millimetres and their thickness from 9 to 40 millimetres. The four reticular columns with the largest diameter have been designed as trusses with reinforced-concrete bases, to resist earthquakes. They are positioned at the four corners of the building so as to withstand any kind of eccentric torsion. The other nine, more slender columns make no contribution to the resistance to horizontal forces, but are located in positions where they are able to support only vertical forces. They are made out of bundles of tubes simply arranged in parallel to control the phenomenon of partial as well as total deformation, with the addition of a ring in the middle section to prevent compression.

The floors are designed as flat slabs of steel, as slender and light as possible, to improve the resistance to earthquakes. They have a sandwich structure, formed out of grids of beams covered with plates of steel above and below, using the same technique as in naval construction. The thickness of the floor slabs, with spans of up to 20 metres, has been reduced to just 40 centimetres, with frameworks of beams at a distance of 1 metre. The beams are welded together, with tubular components used for the most complex joints. The foundations have been designed to

absorb shocks from earthquakes in the basement levels and leave the structures of the upper floors free. This has been achieved by setting the reinforced-concrete slab of the ground floor on the outer walls of the foundations, allowing horizontal movements of up to 100 millimetres. The reticular columns are transformed into frame structures in the sunken storeys, with rounded heads that allow them to rotate. The transverse beams of the frame structures at the base of the columns have been designed to give way immediately in an earthquake, permitting the tubular structures to rotate and the ground floor to move. The shocks are concentrated and dampened in the basement, making the upper structure lighter and allowing greater freedom in its design.

The construction of such a complex structure has relied chiefly on prefabrication, as fabrication on site would have entailed much higher costs and less precision in the details. The steel sandwich slabs of the floors, along with the attachments and the base rings of the reticular columns, were prefabricated in modules of 3 × 10 metres and assembled on site. The structures of the columns were also broken down into modules the height of a single storey, and these in turn subdivided into prefabricated sub-modules. Before each module was brought to the construction site, it was pre-assembled in the factory so that the connections with adjoining modules and the floor slabs could be checked. Given the complexity of the design it would not have been possible to make corrections *in situ* and only prefabrication and checking in the factory could guarantee the security of the result.

Separate mention must be made of the elevations. Starting out from the idea of a building-aquarium, Ito wanted the main façade to be completely transparent. The façade was designed as a thin and independent sheet of glass, merely set against the structure behind. This effect was obtained by means of a dou-

ble, ventilated façade, with a slender and sophisticated internal structure of glass that accentuates its lightness. At the corners there is no connection with the adjacent façades but the panes of glass extend freely into empty space beyond the edges of the façade, underlining the two-dimensional effect. During the day, the façade reflects the sunlight and remains ambiguously transparent, creating a translucent filter between the inside and outside. At night, however, it almost seems to vanish so that the interior of the building is laid bare at every level. This produces an interesting effect of stratification, due to the different patterns adopted in the design of the internal lighting.

On the east and north sides, the internal floor slabs have been extended 50 centimetres outward solely for aesthetic reasons, so as to create the dark horizontal bands that characterize the lateral façades. The facing materials on each level are different—transparent glass, opaque glass, solid panels—to accentuate the effect of fragmentation that contributes to the abstraction of the building. In the competition design, the west front was the same as the other lateral elevations. While the executive plans were being drawn up, the need to add a series of fire escapes was exploited by the architect to create a façade that differed from the others, made up of a semitransparent structure in galvanized steel applied to the wall behind and faced with vertical slats running the full height of each floor: a sort of skin with a highly graphic effect. (A.M., from *Casabella*, nos. 684–85, 2000)

*Night-time view
of the stratification
of the interior with
different schemes
of illumination
for each floor.*

opposite
Main front.

239

West front with fire escapes faced with vertical slats of perforated aluminium.

East front with horizontal bands separating the different curtaining materials of the various floors to underline the effect of stratification.

Detail of the corner showing the two-dimensional, graphic effect created by the façades.

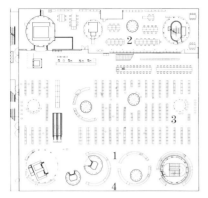

2nd floor

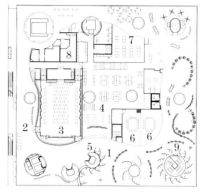

6th floor

1st floor

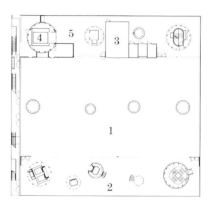

5th floor

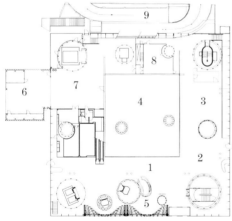

ground floor

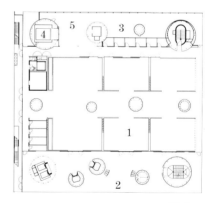

4th floor

242

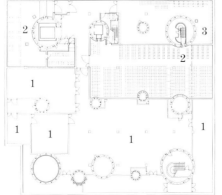

2nd basement

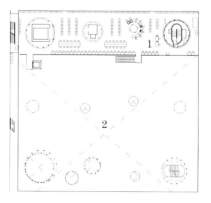

3rd floor

North, west and east elevations.

opposite
From top to bottom:
Plan of the second floor, legend:
1 library
2 staff service space
3 files
4 reading islands.

Plan of the first floor, legend:
1 children's library
2 meeting room
3 offices
4 voluntary workers' office
5 service space
6 deposit for children's library.

Plan of the ground floor, legend:
1 information
2 commercial space
3 cafeteria
4 internal plaza
5 sliding glass walls
6 loading-unloading area
7 unpacking area
8 storeroom
9 access ramps.

Plan of the second basement level, legend:

1 technical areas
2 book deposit for library
3 storerooms for exhibition space.

Plan of the sixth floor, legend:
1 mediathèque
2 cinema foyer
3 180-seat cinema
4 offices
5 information
6 meeting room
7 Internet point
8 service space
9 video room.

Plan of the fifth floor, legend:
1 exhibition spaces
2 foyer
3 display storehouse
4 freight elevator
5 unpacking area.

Plan of the fourth floor, legend:
1 exhibition gallery
2 foyer
3 service spaces
4 freight elevator
5 unpacking area.

Plan of the third floor, legend:
1 reading room
2 double-height space.

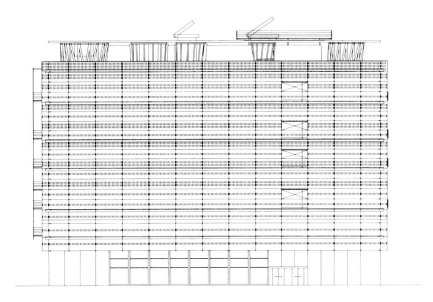

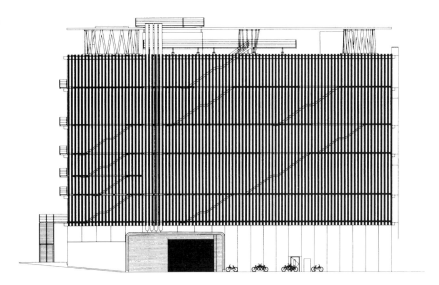

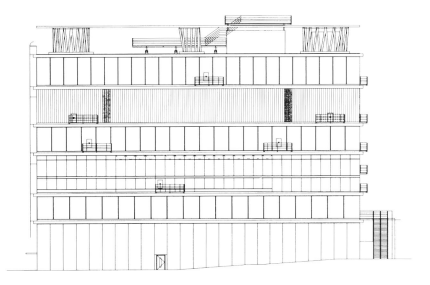

*Views of the
Mediathèque
at night.*

following pages
*Main entrance
hall.*

*Detail of the
furnishings of the
entrance hall and
air-conditioning
ducts.*

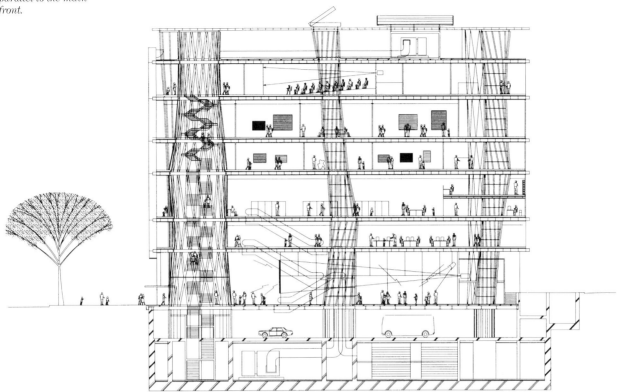

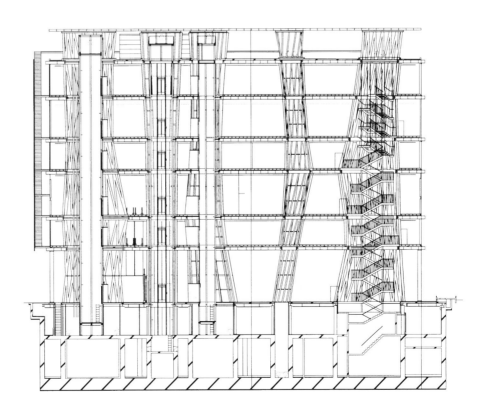

249

The children's
library on the first
floor.

Partitions
of semitransparent
white fabric and
furniture designed
by Kazuyo Sejima.

*Double-height
volume of the
library on
the second
and third floor
with interiors by
K. T. Architecture.*

Interiors of the exhibition gallery on the fourth floor with furniture designed by Karim Rashid.

The Mediathèque
on the top floor
with video and
multimedia
stations and
180-seat cinema.
Furniture designed
by Ross Lovegrove.

Project for the Trade Fair Centre
Hiroshima-shi, Hiroshima
1997–

A trade fair centre with a total area of 40,000 square metres, including an exhibition hall of 15,000 square metres and three conference rooms of varying sizes covering a total of 4000 square metres. The structure is roughly divided into three zones: the entrance area and the exhibition and conference spaces. The flat and simple plan allows the facility to be easily adapted to a wide range of uses. In spite of its enormous size, the building is easy to understand and convenient to use.

The structure consists of steel sandwich plates that serve as the roof and the floor of the upper storey, while the exterior is made of a mesh structure and tubes. This combination of sandwich plates, mesh and tubes was first employed experimentally in the Mediathèque at Sendai. Here the combination has been systematically developed and employed on a large scale.

The enormous flat plates of the roof are able to cover a maximum span of 72 metres with a thickness of only 1.35 metres by balancing the effect of continuous beams with the first floor suspended from the roof. The plates also serve as the infrastructure for plant, housing various pipes and ducts. The upper surface is fitted with large solar panels. The mesh structure supports the entire vertical load of the building and provides resistance to earthquakes. It is sandwiched between glass sashes so that it constitutes a double skin and a screen for control of the internal environment. Nine tubes covered in membranous material support the roof and provide natural lighting and ventilation. At night they light up to provide illumination.

The various elements have multiple functions. They do not work in isolation but relate to each other in different ways to create a single environment. The resulting space resembles an ocean or forest, in which great strength is produced by a soft system.

General plan of the site.

opposite
Plan of the ground floor, legend:
1 entrance hall
2 information
3 crater
4 cafeteria
5 shops
6 pools of water
7 trade-fair spaces
8 movable partitions
9 toilets
10 storerooms
11 outdoor exhibition spaces
12 restaurant
13 kitchens
14 restaurant car park
15 taxi stand
16 stop for public transport
17 footpath
18 bus park
19 entrance for bicycles
20 bicycle park
21 technical spaces.

View of the model.

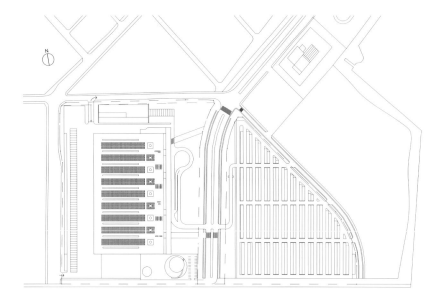

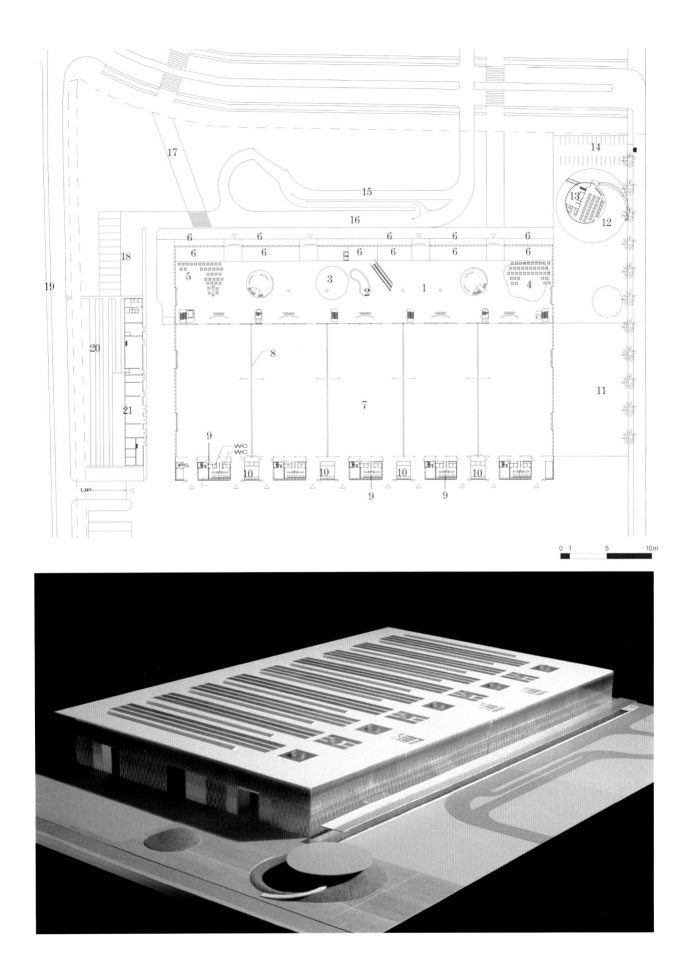

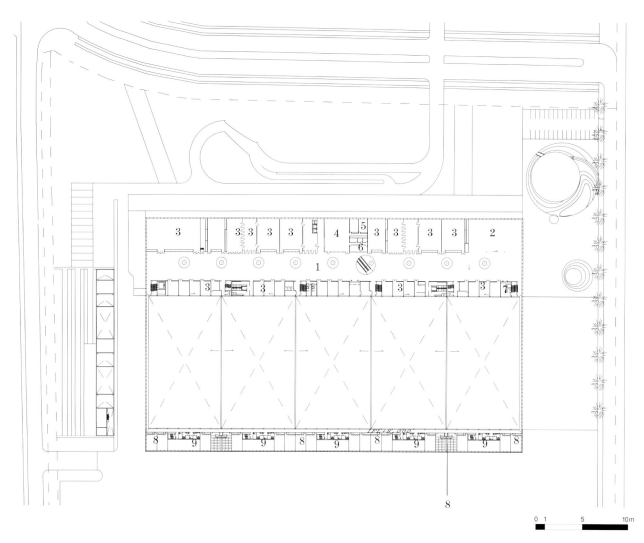

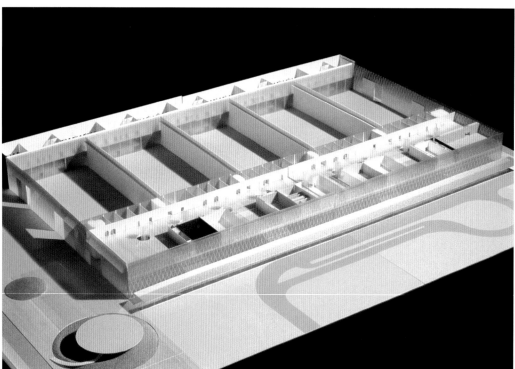

*Axonometric
exploded diagram
of the structural
scheme.*

*The model
uncovered at
ground-floor level.*

*Plan of first floor;
legend:*
1 foyer
2 reception
3 conference room
4 office
5 VIP room
6 storeroom
7 pantry
8 waiting room
*9 technical spaces
for air-
conditioning.*

*View of the
model uncovered
at first-floor level.*

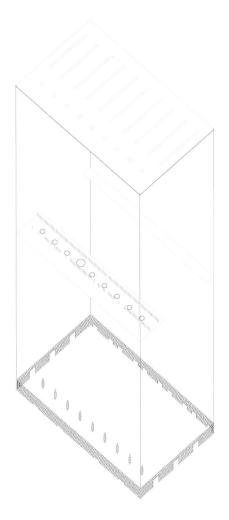

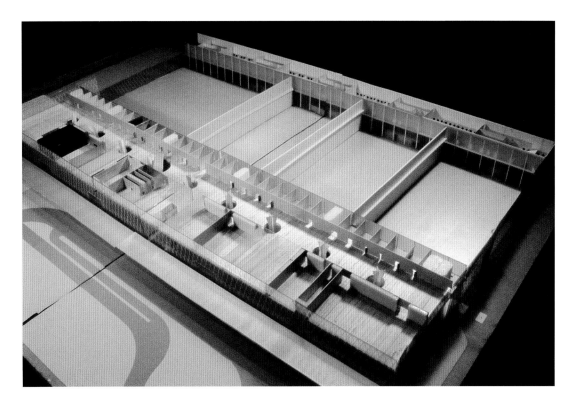

*Elevations
and longitudinal
section.*

opposite
*Partial view
of the main front.*

*Simulation
of the entrance hall
in the model.*

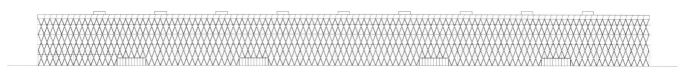

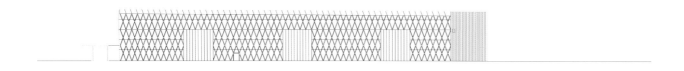

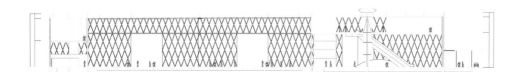

Project for the Extension of the Bank
of International Settlements
Basel, Switzerland
1998

The existing BIS building is a tubular tower with a lift core at its centre. It is divided into an upper section of offices and a base that broadens out in steps down to a platform at the bottom. The most important activities are located in the lower part, where they are clearly separated from each other horizontally. Our intention was to further refine and clarify the relations between the different functions of the building while creating open and flexible spaces that ensure a good working environment.

1. BIS base (lower office section/phase 1) Instead of creating a separate new building for the BIS in phase 1, the lower part of the existing building is extended. This emphasizes the horizontality of that part of the complex in contrast to the verticality of the tower section. At the same time, the functions and relationships of the more important departments are clarified spatially.
2. The breathing tubes
The wide, horizontal spaces are connected to each other functionally as well as

spatially by means of tubes that stretch from top to bottom of the building.
3. BIS east (phase 2)
A linear building containing additional office space is constructed on the Gartenstrasse. The building creates an impression of horizontal extension and is remarkably transparent, especially in contrast with the vertical tower building.

*General plan
showing the
location of the
project in the
urban fabric.*

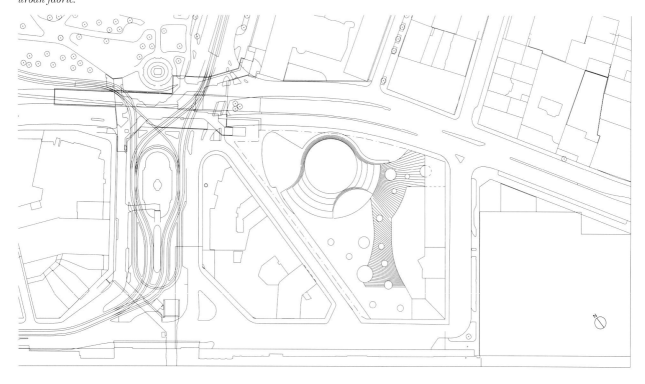

View of the model.

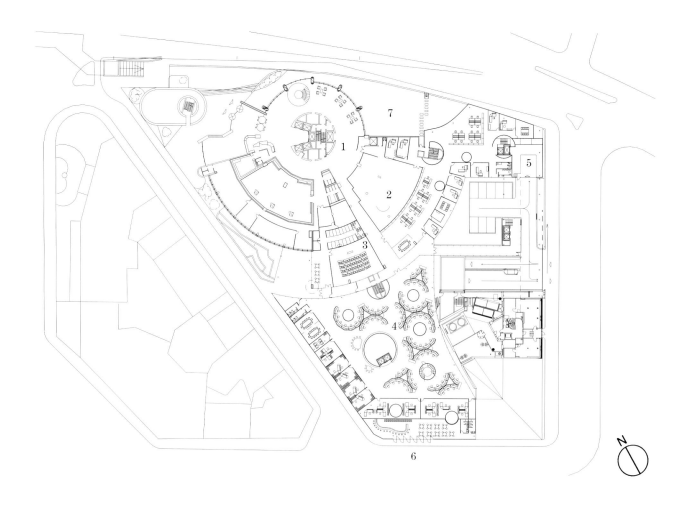

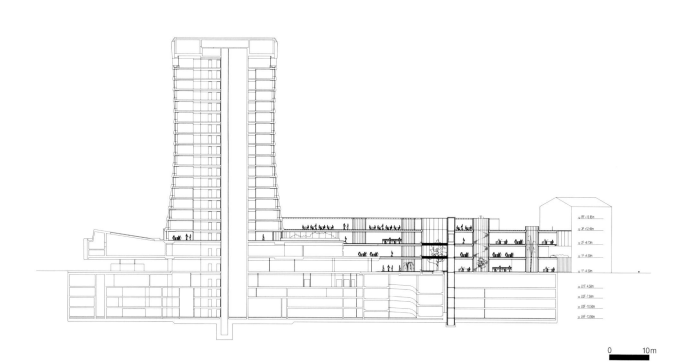

Ground-floor plan,
section, plans
of the second and
first floor, legend:
1 tower
2 offices of the
security service
3 press centre
4 offices
5 loading/unloading
6 main entrance
7 pool of water
8 terrace
9 meeting room
10 cafeteria
11 offices, second
phase
12 security check
13 bank offices.

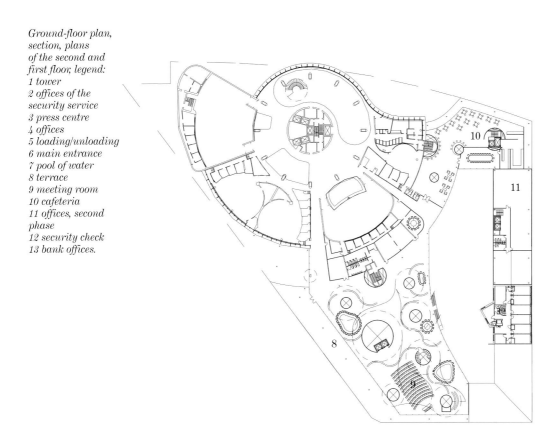

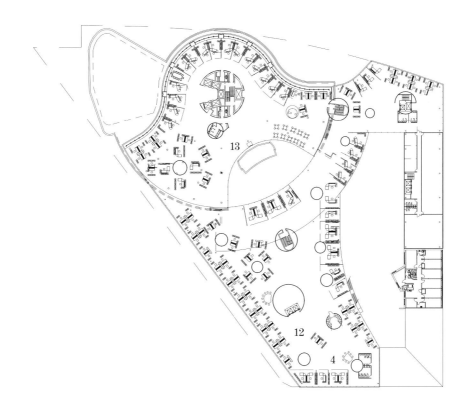

"Health Futures" Installation
at the Expo 2000, Hanover
Hanover, Germany
1998–2000

Plan, legend:
1 waiting room
with ticket office
and information
desk
2 theatre of water
with images
projected onto the
long wall covered
with mirrors
3 emergency exits
4 technical areas.

Internal view
of the installation.

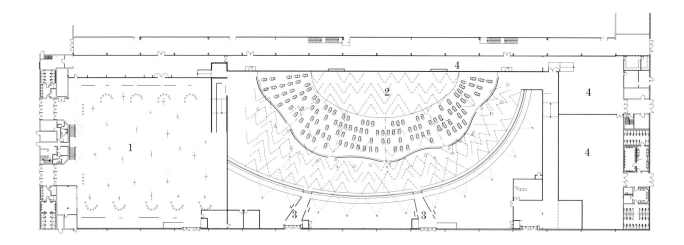

For the Expo Ito created a "Theatre of Water" in which visitors were offered the physical experience of spaces and parts of the human body through all of their senses. They could relax by lying down on the approximately 120–150 massage chairs, placed at random alongside the great expanse of water. They were gradually made aware of the importance of water, light and fresh air, as well as of the human body itself. As the space also functioned as a restaurant, visitors could enjoy the health food or futuristic space fare served on trolleys. At the same time, the space offered another experience, that of a different kind of water—"virtual water"—created by the flow of visual images and sounds. The images were created by 168 video projectors. The space filled up with these images and made visitors feel as if they were inside an amniotic fluid. The visual images did not provide comprehensible information, but an experience like that of being inside a human body, where they could sense the walls of the stomach, the uterus and even blood vessels, expanding their awareness of the function of genes. The space was not intended to educate visitors by showing them materials or supplying them with large quantities of information, but to convey to them a physical sensation of health and of "health futures" through their own bodies.

Cross-section;
longitudinal
sections.

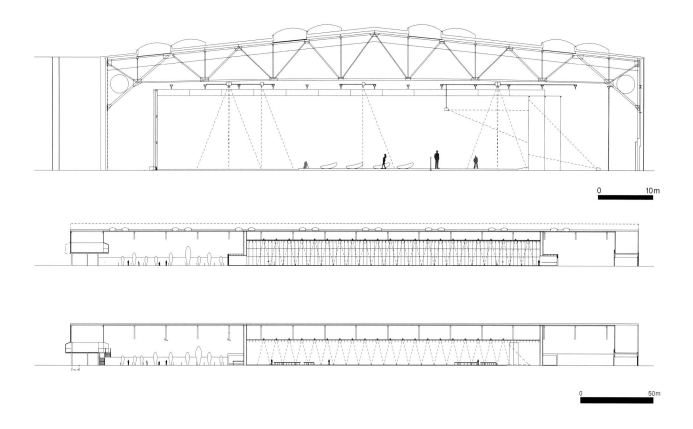

0   10m

0   50m

271

Variations
of three-dimensional
images projected
onto the floor
and walls.

Luminous
information screens
in the waiting room.

Groningen House, Project for a Residential
Complex in Aluminium
Groningen, Netherlands
1998–2001

At the request of the Dutch city of Groningen we took total charge of the planning of events to be held there in 2001. The plan included the construction of student housing on a site located in the old part of Groningen where its traditional architecture has been beautifully preserved. This will be a small, four-storey building with a café on the ground floor, rooms for students on the upper three floors and a rooftop garden for viewing the moon, in keeping with the project's name, "Blue Moon".

The nature of the events required the structure to be built in a very short space of time. We thought aluminium would be appropriate under these conditions. The project studies came up with two different solutions. The first was a "Dom-ino" model made up of stacked unidirectional slabs and the second a slender framework model made out of extruded aluminium.

Dom-ino Proposal: the building is supported by translucent mesh walls with bi-directional, bent aluminium plates set on the outer surface. The walls are assembled out of hollow, brick-shaped extrusions. Changes in load call for different thickness of wall so that the view from the side reveals a slight gradation. An abstract pattern of bricks is created in the middle of an old city built out of brick.

Light Framework Proposal: extruded aluminium panels are assembled to create a slender framework. The walls and floors are 100-millimetre-thick structures made of bent aluminium and all the interior fixtures, including insulation, are formed by attaching various materials to the surface of the walls and floor. The living space is created by attaching interior fixtures to the extremely thin aluminium structure. The astonishing precision of the extrusion and the texture of the aluminium serve to create a structure of unbelievable lightness and elegance.

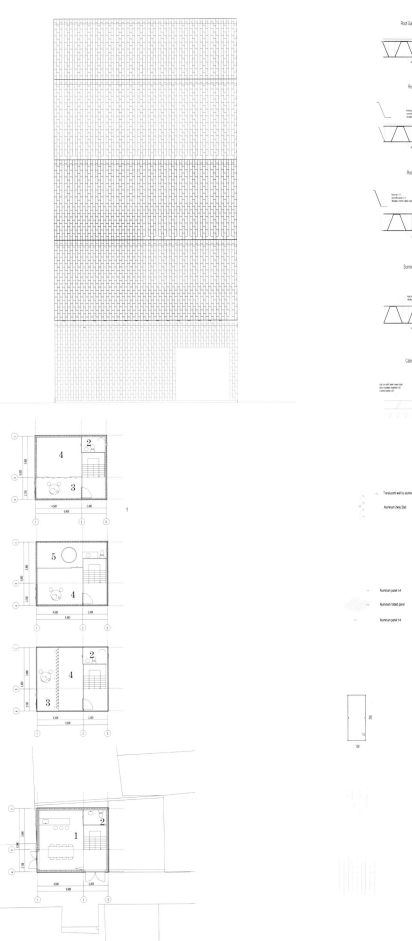
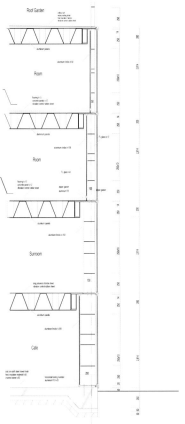

Printouts of the first proposal: the façade covered with sheets of aluminium.

Plans of the four levels, legend:
1 cafeteria
2 toilets
3 terrace
4 room
5 bathroom.

Detailed section of the aluminium supporting structures.

Structural schemes and detail of the 100 × 250 mm modules of the aluminium supporting structures.

275

opposite
*Scheme of the
aluminium
framework with
curtaining panels.*

*Detailed section
of the aluminium
supporting
structures.*

*Structural details
of the joints and
the prefabricated
aluminium
modules.*

*Plan and
disposition of
masses and plans
of three levels,
legend:
1 cafeteria
2 toilets
3 room
4 roof garden.*

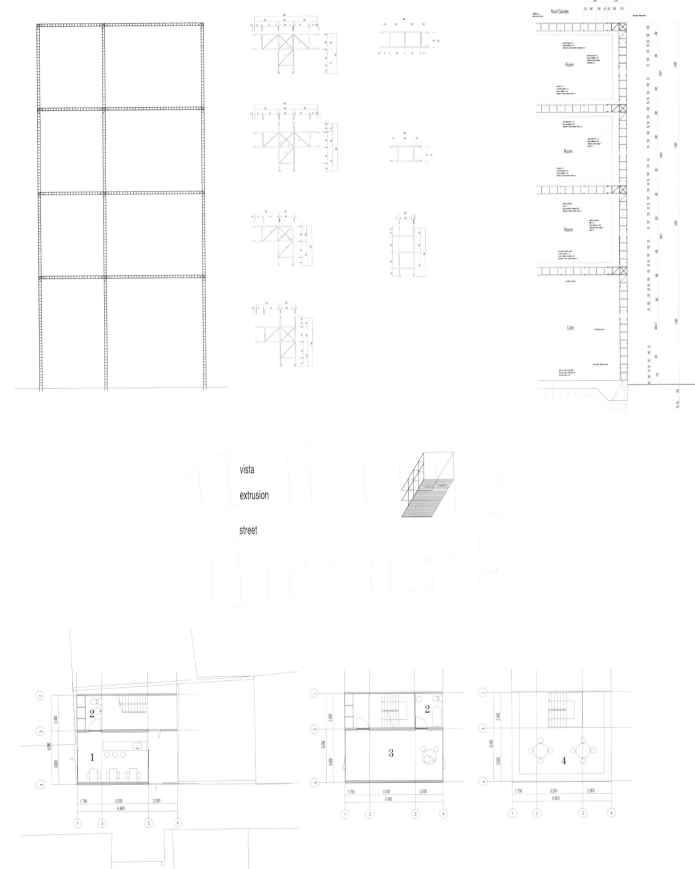

vista

extrusion

street

Roof Garden

Room

Room

Room

Cafe

2

1

2

3

4

277

Project for the Centre
for the Contemporary Arts
Rome, Italy
1999

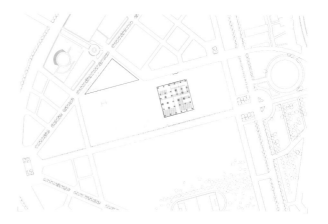

Unlike a conventional art gallery, our proposal for the new Centre for the Contemporary Arts is not a finished piece of architecture. Breaking away from the notion of a "mere space for exhibiting art works within an enclosure," we have proposed a "place" that potentially presents a great opportunity for generating a variety of artistic activities in which the process of creation is involved as well. In an attempt to realize such a conception, our proposal includes an environment in which the distinctive character of the site and its history and the new architectural synthesis can act as mutually enhancing cultural stimuli. The challenge is to create an integrated body of intelligence, a complex of different spaces that is in itself an urban space.

In other words, we propose to integrate the following:

1. The functional and spatial realization of an intelligent environment making use of advanced information and communication technologies.

2. The introduction of a place where creative activities (workshops) and networking are carried out interactively by curators and visitors.

3. The creation of an evolving space which constantly prompts innovative programmes of activity.

Vertical structural columns made of steel channel light from the skylights down to the ground floor and create an effect of "pillars of light" rather like that of the Mediathèque at Sendai. These columns regulate the light that reaches the exhibition spaces of the museum and house all the ducts for the system that regulates the natural ventilation of the rooms inside.

Plan showing the location of the project in the urban context.

Model of the competition project.

Plan at ground level and south elevation, legend:
1 internal plaza
2 main entrance
3 shop
4 gallery
5 information
6 ticket office
7 cloakroom
8 450-seat auditorium
9 workshop
10 multipurpose hall
11 restaurant
12 terrace
13 secondary entrance
14 storeroom
15 unloading area
16 technical areas
17 conservation
18 temporary exhibitions
19 security
20 spaces for independent exhibitions.

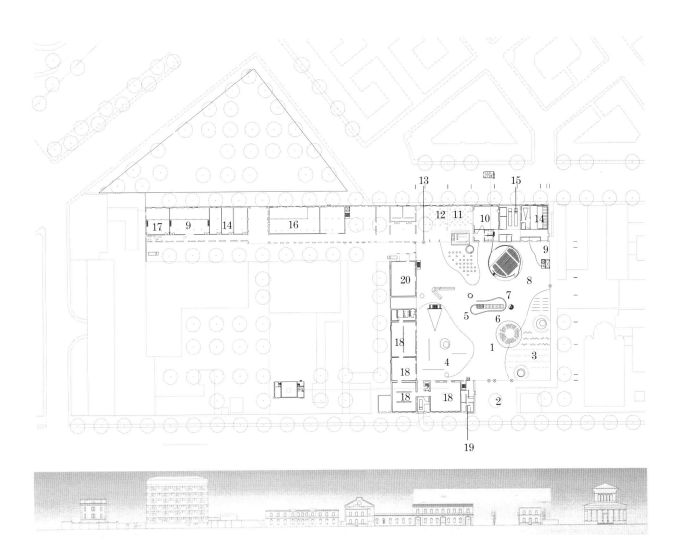

Section.

*Plans of ground
and first floors
and roof.*

*West, east and
north elevations.*

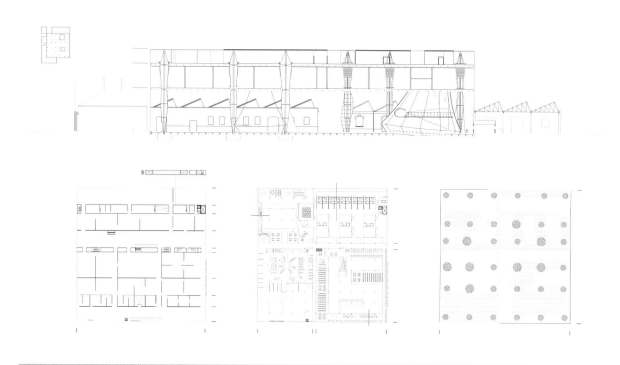

0   10   50 m

Computer graphics
simulating
the exhibition
galleries, entrance
hall and roof
terraces.

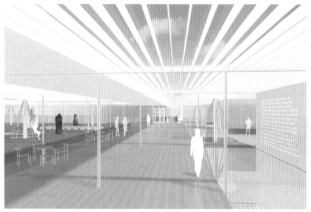

*Detailed section
of the structures,
columns of light
and lighting
control systems
in the galleries.*

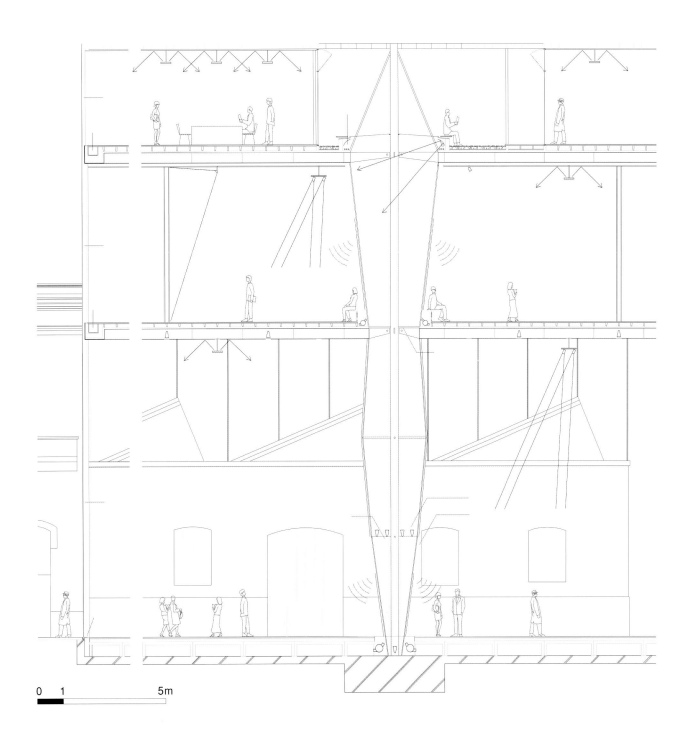

0 1   5m

Project for the Hôpital Cognacq-Jay
Paris, France
1999–(2004)

As it stands today, the Hôpital Cognacq-Jay is a fantastic, stimulating structure which virtually exudes a sense of history. Its tranquil garden, interior décor and appointments, along with the paintings and photographs hanging on the walls, convey an impression of harmony and the strange feeling that one is in a holiday resort rather than a hospital.

Our work has been about much more than simply providing the varied and complex functions required of a hospital. When the power of rationality is manifested in architecture as the fruit of our assembled intellects, people will find in that architecture the strength and the will to live.

We have tried to create human spaces where people feel relaxed and comfortable, and striven to integrate them in an organic manner. The hospital requires many different spaces adapted to each function. Their articulation lends a human scale to the hospital as a whole and creates an extremely powerful relationship, almost one of cohabitation, between nature and architecture. Here, in communion with nature, people can find health and healing. The richly varied spaces are organically connected through the garden, which serves as the focal point of the project. The interlocking arrangement of the structures results in a fusion of solid and liquid that makes the most of the front onto the garden.

It is our hope that the Cognacq-Jay Foundation will feel more like a home, a small museum, a private park or a lounge than a hospital. This is the concept that underpins our design: views of greenery from the patients' rooms, warm interiors and park-like gardens where people can take quiet walks and chat with their friends and family in the shade, alongside a stream or next to a work of art.

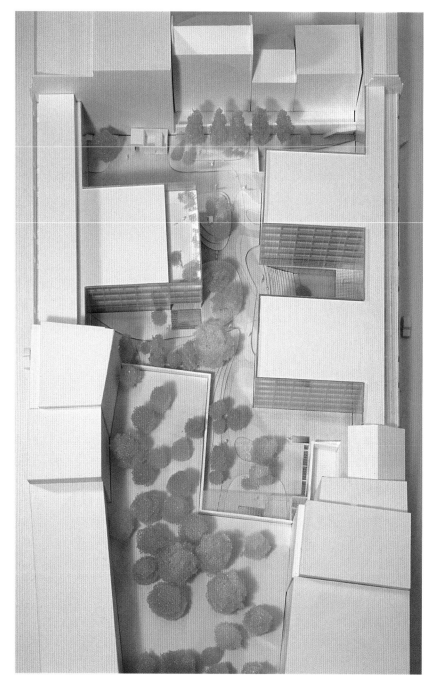

Model of the competition project.

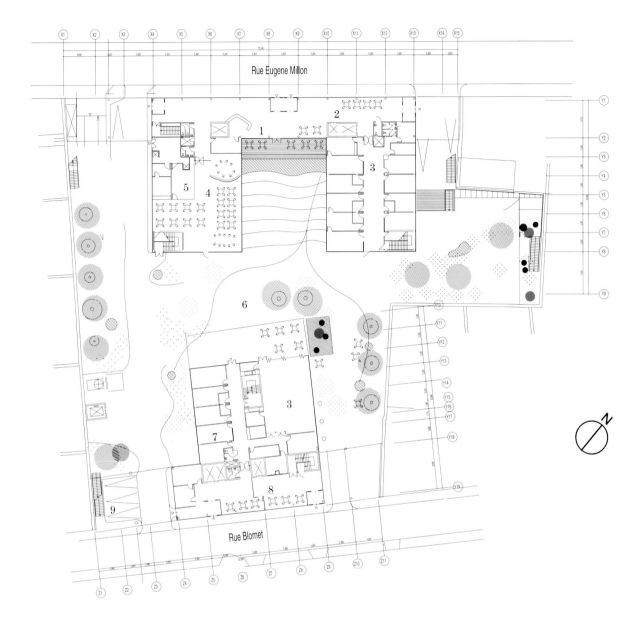

Rue Eugene Millon

Rue Blomet

General plan,
legend:
1 entrance
2 information
3 offices and
consulting rooms
4 cafeteria
5 kitchens
6 internal garden
7 staff areas
8 laundromat
9 loading/unloading.

View of the street
front from above.

following pages
Elevations and
views of the main
entrance from the
street.

285

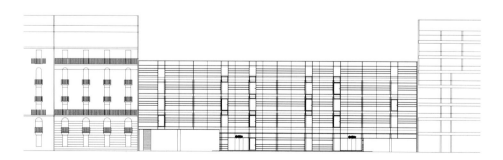

287

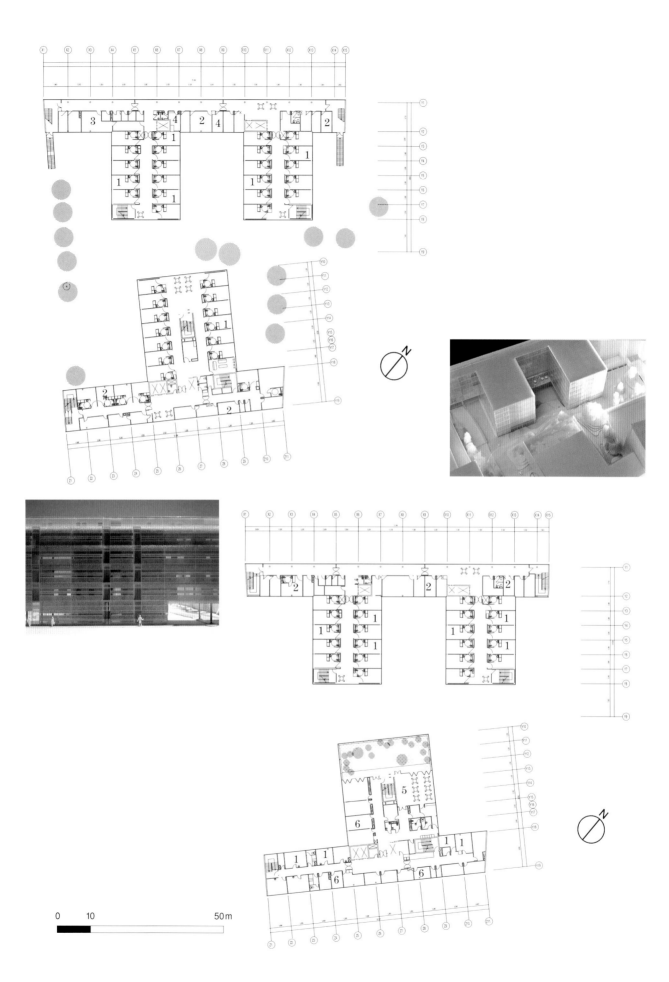

0   10   50 m

*Plans of the first,
third, fourth and
fifth floors, legend:
1 patient's room
2 consulting rooms
3 kitchens
4 toilets
5 restaurant
6 training areas
for doctors.*

*Details of the
model.*

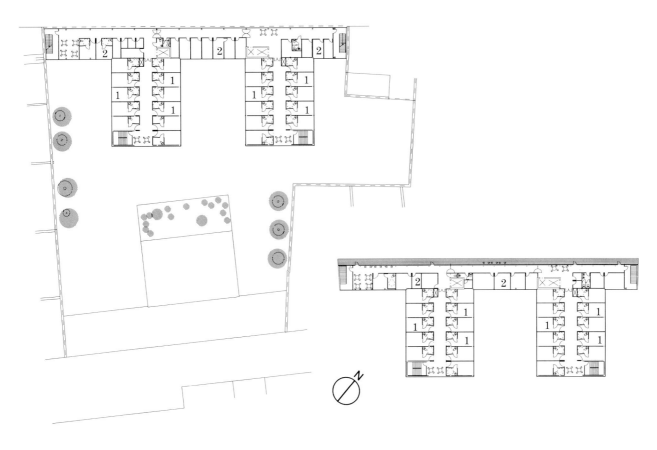

Oita Agricultural Park
Hayami-gun, Oita
2001

Oita Agricultural Park is a centre for the promotion of farming in the prefecture of Oita. Among other things, it introduces the general public to a variety of activities, carries out studies into the future of agriculture and holds training and exchange programmes aimed at fostering human resources. The site covers an area of approximately 120 hectares, with a lake and irrigation dam set amidst luxuriant vegetation. The main entrance is located on the western shore of the lake, where the park's principal facility (Rakuichi Rakuza), a spa and a parking lot for 700 cars are situated. Cottages with lots of farmland that can be rented out, orchards, a caravan site, a boat-hire agency and a zoo are also located on the lake's western shore. More than ten different facilities are dotted along a promenade that stretches for a distance of 5 to 6 kilometres. The building called Rakuichi Rakuza is an elongated greenhouse-like space measuring 300 metres in length and 24 in width. It comprises various functions, including a shop selling local products, a restaurant, an entomological museum and a botanical garden, and is open to the public, offering up-to-date information, training programs and activities related to the promotion of agriculture. The main entrance leads directly to Rakuichi Rakuza, with the lake to the east and the parking lot to the west. Various facilities located inside the building are arranged in a row parallel to the lakeshore and the parking lot. A plaza for a variety of events, a piece of terraced ground and flower gardens are intended to complement the indoor facilities, with spaces on the inside and outside penetrating one another. The natural environment, the terrain and the ecological system have been utilized to the fullest extent in the design.

Plan showing the location of the park in its surroundings.

Bird's-eye view of the whole complex.

*Elevations and
view from the lake.*

opposite
*Standard cross-
section and views
from the outside.*

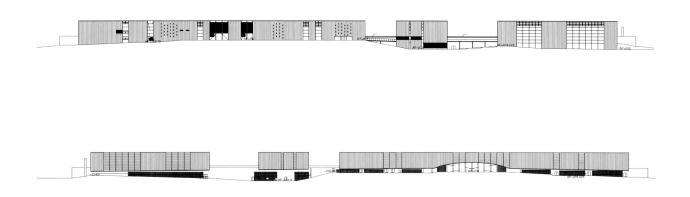

292

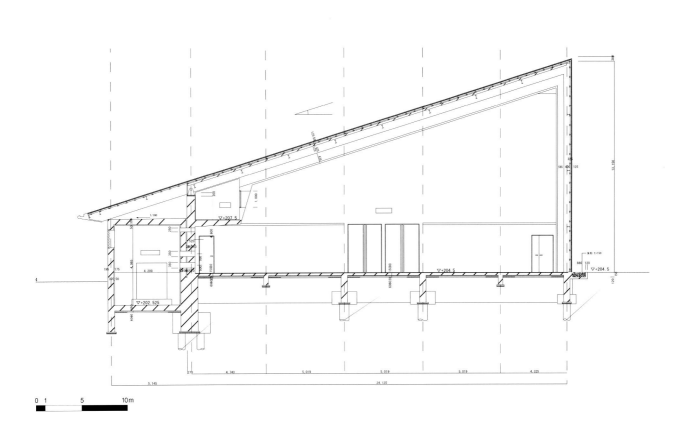

0 1 5 10m

View of an interior.

General and partial plans of the two levels.

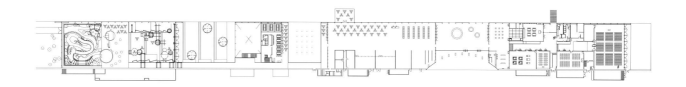

Project for Mahler 4 Office Block, Blok 5
Amsterdam, Netherlands
2000–01

In the South Axis zone of Amsterdam, between the city centre and Schiphol Airport, the Dutch studio Architekten Cie. has drawn up the detailed plan for a 200,000-square-metre block to be used for business, residential and commercial purposes. The planned block has an internal road cutting diagonally across the rectangular lot. The two passageways for pedestrians that also run through it demarcate six areas of intervention whose design has been entrusted to various architectural studios: Skidmore, Owings & Merrill, Foreign Office Architects, Michael Graves, Rafael Viñoly, the Office for Metropolitan Architecture and Toyo Ito. The disposition of masses laid down in the plan, in addition to defining the maximum heights and volumes of the buildings on the basis of their visual and functional relations with the urban context, imposes considerable restraints on the designers' freedom of composition. The solution adopted by Ito for his "Mahler 4" in block no. 5 sticks precisely to the form called for in the plan and its functional distribution on twenty-six superimposed levels. To overcome the heaviness of a compact disposition of masses and take it in the direction of an abstract form, he has applied a process of "corrosion" to the exterior as well as the interior.

The client had requested a reduction of the internal area from the maximum of 45,000 square metres available to 35,000. The architect attained this result by introducing rectangular empty spaces of varying sizes, used as hanging gardens, terraces and patios that create communal open areas amidst the offices. These geometric shapes cut out of the pre-established volume create points of reference and external characterization and define the appearance of the façades. More empty spaces are set inside the volume and snake vertically through the regular succession of floors to create relationships and introspections between the various levels and characterize the offices with elegant spaces. These solutions make it possible to exploit the core of the building, which would otherwise have been used exclusively for technical and service facilities, as indicated in the building regulations. The stratagem of having the terraces extend to the outer edge of the building allows the habitable spaces to extend further in. The ground floor is occupied in its entirety by commercial spaces surrounded by glass walls. Thus the base is eliminated and the construction appears to float in space. The floors are identified by horizontal bands of anodised aluminium panels. The strip windows, partially silk-screened, render the volume rarefied and vibrant. The façades of different colours resemble two-dimensional sheets set side by side.

(A. M., from *Casabella*, no. 689, 2001)

Model showing the location of the project in the urban context.

Models of the high-rise building showing the internal terraces cut into the volume and vibrant facing of aluminium panels.

Longitudinal section with the open spaces linking all the floors together shown in colour.

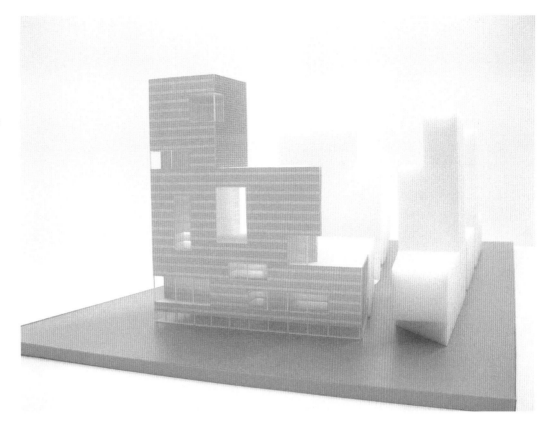

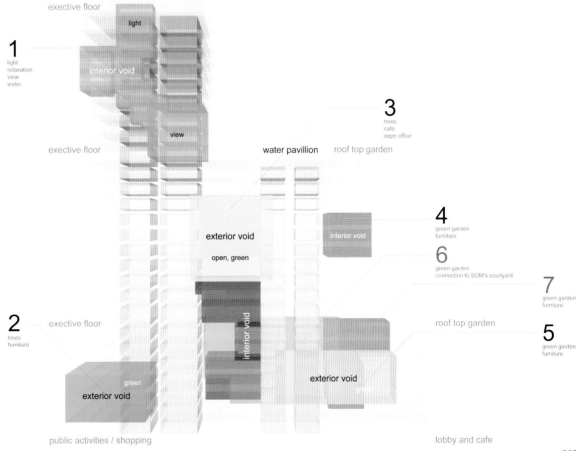

1

light
relaxation
view
water

exective floor

light

interior void

view

exective floor

3

trees
cafe
oepn office

water pavillion   roof top garden

exterior void

open, green

4

green garden
furniture

interior void

6

green garden
connection to SOM's courtyard

7

green garden
furniture

interior void

2

trees
furniture

exective floor

roof top garden

5

green garden
furniture

green

exterior void

exterior void

public activities / shopping

lobby and cafe

Study model.

opposite
*Study of the voids
and of the internal
relationships
between the various
floors of the
building.*

298

Computer graphics simulating the internal voids.

Plans of the various levels with shops on the ground floor and offices on the upper floors cut by the multi-storey voids and terraces leading to the outside.

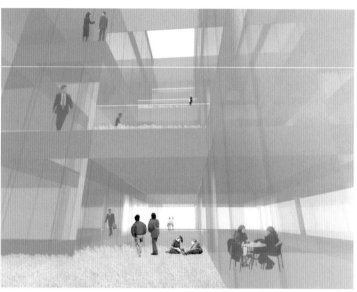

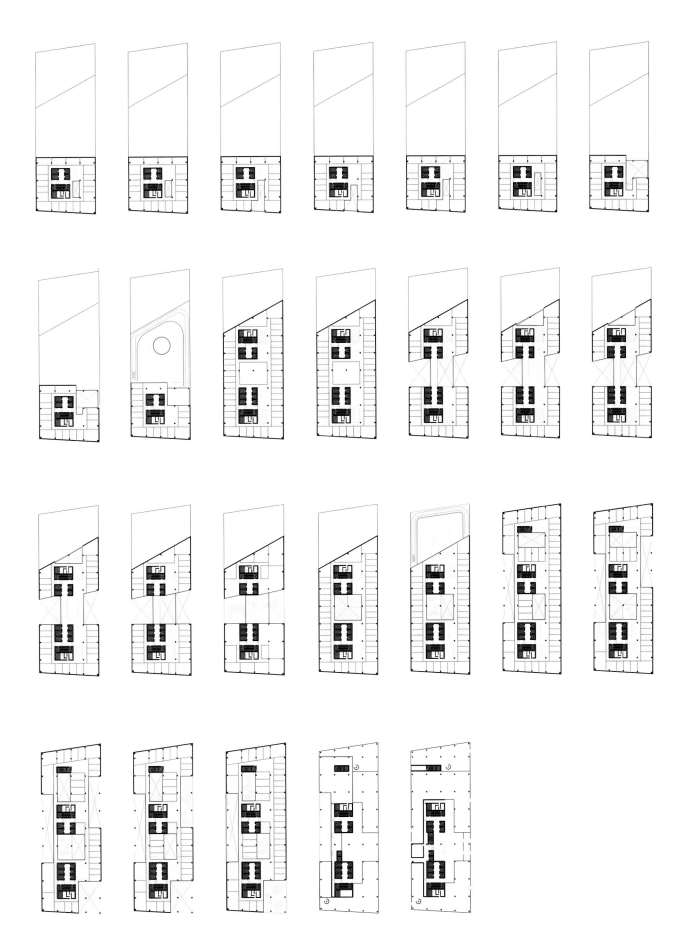

301

Chronology of Works

1970–71
Aluminium House
location: Fujisawa-shi, Kanagawa
site area: 379 m²
building area: 84 m²
total floor area: 110 m²
programme: house
number of storeys: 2

1973–74
Cottage in Sengataki
location: Nagano
site area: 996 m²
building area: 59 m²
total floor area: 63 m²
programme: house
number of storeys: 2

1974–75
Black Recurrence
location: Setagaya-ku, Tokyo
site area: 86 m²
building area: 43 m²
total floor area: 80 m²
programme: house
number of storeys: 2

1974–77
Hotel D
location: Sugadaira, Nagano
site area: 5242 m²
building area: 1152.48 m²
total floor area: 2437 m²
programme: hotel
number of storeys: 2

1975–76
White U
location: Nakano-ku, Tokyo
site area: 367 m²
building area: 151 m²
total floor area: 148 m²
programme: house
number of storeys: 1

1976
House in Kamiwada
location: Okazaki-shi, Aichi
site area: 198 m²
building area: 91 m²
total floor area: 91 m²
programme: house
number of storeys: 1

1976–78
PMT Building
location: Nagoya-shi, Aichi
site area: 7727 m²
building area: 428 m²
total floor area: 921 m²
programme: office
number of storeys: 4

1978–79
PMT Factory
location: Neyagawa-ku, Osaka
site area: 2120 m²
building area: 1098 m²
total floor area: 2236 m²
programme: factory
number of storeys: 2

1979
PMT Building
location: Fukuoka-shi, Fukuoka
site area: 897 m²
building area: 457 m²
total floor area: 895 m²
programme: office
number of storeys: 2

1979
House in Koganei
location: Koganei-shi, Tokyo
site area: 147 m²
building area: 50 m²
total floor area: 94 m²
programme: house
number of storeys: 2

1979
House in Chuorinkan
location: Yamato-shi, Kanagawa
site area: 128 m²
building area: 74 m²
total floor area: 122 m²
programme: house
number of storeys: 2

1980
JAL Ticketing Counter
programme: lobby

1980–81
House in Kasama
location: Kasama-shi, Ibaragi
site area: 865 m²
building area: 155 m²
total floor area: 290 m²
programme: house
number of storeys: 2

1981–82
House in Umegaoka
location: Setagaya-ku, Tokyo
site area: 138 m²
building area: 60 m²
total floor area: 118 m²
programme: house
number of storeys: 2

1982–83
House in Hanakoganei
location: Kodaira-shi, Tokyo
site area: 242 m²
building area: 77 m²
total floor area: 152 m²
programme: house
number of storeys: 2

1982–83
House in Denenchofu
location: Ota-ku, Tokyo
site area: 161 m²
building area: 69 m²
total floor area: 135 m²
programme: house
number of storeys: 2

1982–84
Silver Hut
location: Nakano-ku, Tokyo
site area: 403 m²
building area: 120 m²
total floor area: 139 m²
programme: house
number of storeys: 2

1985
**Pao I, Installation for "Pao:
A Dwelling for Tokyo Nomad
Women"**
location: Seibu Department Store,
Tokyo
programme: furniture

1985
**Competition Project for the Sports
Complex in Owani**
location: Minami-Tsugaru-gun, Aomori
programme: sports complex
number of storeys: 1

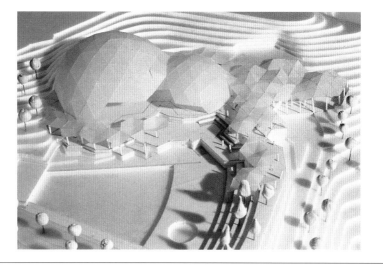

1985–86
House in Magomezawa
location: Funabashi-shi, Chiba
site area: 100 m^2
building area: 50 m^2
total floor area: 81 m^2
programme: house
number of storeys: 2

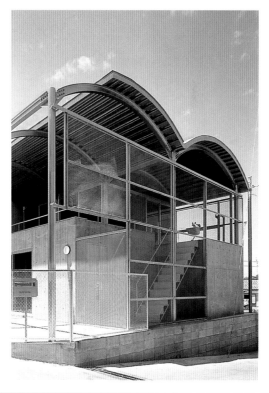

1985–86
Honda Automobile Showroom
location: Setagaya-ku, Tokyo
site area: 333 m^2
building area: 181 m^2
total floor area: 393 m^2
programme: showroom
number of storeys: 3

1985–86
Competition Project for the
Fujisawa Municipal Cultural
Complex
location: Fujisawa-shi, Kanagawa
site area: 7970 m²
building area: 4015 m²
total floor area: 12,280 m²
programme: cultural complex
number of storeys: 3

1985–87
M Building in Kanda
location: Chiyoda-ku, Tokyo
site area: 142 m²
building area: 128 m²
total floor area: 671 m²
programme: office
number of storeys: 6

1986
Project for the Exhibition:
"Furniture for Tokyo Nomad
Women"
programme: furniture

1986
Nomad Restaurant
location: Minato-ku, Tokyo
site area: 333 m²
building area: 272 m²
total floor area: 429 m²
programme: restaurant
number of storeys: 3

1986
Tower of Winds
location: Yokohama-shi, Kanagawa
site area: 43 m²
programme: reconstruction
of an obsolete tower
height: 21 m

1986
Project for House in Saijo
location: Saijo, Hiroshima
site area: 1848 m²
building area: 200 m²
total floor area: 242 m²
programme: house
number of storeys: 2

1986–88
House in Takagicho
location: Minato-ku, Tokyo
site area: 203 m²
building area: 121 m²
total floor area: 324 m²
programme: house
number of storeys: 3

1987
Project for Noh Theatre
programme: theatre

1987
MAC Project
location: Machida-shi, Tokyo
site area: 5800 m²
building area: 4700 m²
total floor area: 43,700 m²
programme: commercial complex
number of storeys: 9

1988
Roof-garden Project
location: Tokyo

1988
**Katai Kyoro: series of designs
for furniture produced in Italy**

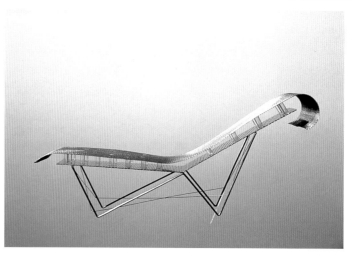

1988–89
I Building in Asakusabashi
location: Taito-ku, Tokyo
site area: 127 m^2
building area: 97 m^2
total floor area: 676 m^2
programme: office
number of storeys: 9

1988–91
Yatsushiro Municipal Museum
location: Yatsushiro-shi, Kumamoto
site area: 8223 m²
building area: 1433 m²
total floor area: 3418 m²
programme: museum
number of storeys: 4
structures: Toshihiko Kimura
Structural Engineers
plant: Uichi Inoue Laboratory,
Otaki E&M Consultant

1988–92
Amusement Complex H
location: Tama-shi, Tokyo
site area: 6400 m²
building area: 4570 m²
total floor area: 23,830 m²
programme: commercial complex
number of storeys: 7

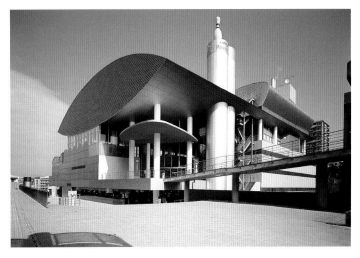

1989
Guest House for Sapporo Brewery
location: Eniwa-shi, Hokkaido
site area: 318,369 m²
building area: 1196 m²
total floor area: 1139 m²
programme: guest house
number of storeys: 1

1989
Pastina Restaurant
location: Setagaya-ku, Tokyo
site area: 181 m²
building area: 123 m²
total floor area: 341 m²
programme: restaurant
number of storeys: 2

1989
**Pao II, Exhibition Project
for "Pao: A Dwelling for Tokyo
Nomad Women"**
location: Brussels, Belgium

1989–90
T Building in Nakameguro
location: Meguro-ku, Tokyo
site area: 584 m²
building area: 402 m²
total floor area: 1444 m²
programme: office
number of storeys: 6

1989–91
Gallery U in Yugawara
location: Yugawara-cho, Kanagawa
site area: 1276 m²
building area: 267 m²
total floor area: 256 m²
programme: gallery
number of storeys: 2

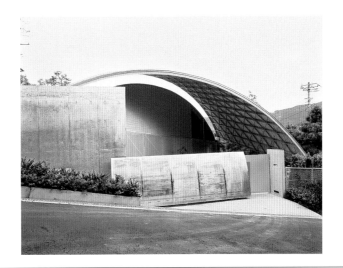

1989–91
F Building in Minami-Aoyama
location: Tokyo
building area: 114 m²
total floor area: 337 m²
programme: office
number of storeys: 3

1990
**Competition Project for the Maison
de la Culture du Japon**
location: Paris, France
site area: 1670 m²
building: 1260 m²
total floor area: 6865 m²
programme: municipal complex
number of storeys: 6
prize: honourable mention

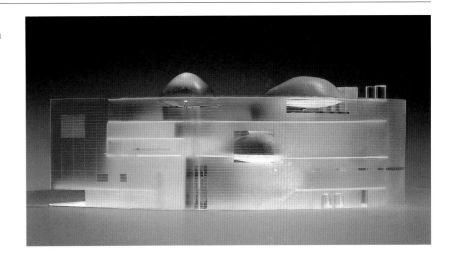

1990–91
**Gate of Okawabata River City 21
("Egg of Winds")**
location: Chuo-ku, Tokyo
building area: 119 m²
total floor area: 115 m²
programme: main gate

1990–93
Shimosuwa Municipal Museum
location: Shimosuwa-cho, Nagano
site area: 5276 m²
building area: 1370 m²
total floor area: 1983 m²
programme: museum
number of storeys: 2
structures: Toshihiko Kimura,
Matsumoto Structural Design
plant: Tetens Engineering, Setsubi
Keikaku

1991
"Visions of Japan" Exhibition
location: Victoria and Albert Museum,
London
programme: exhibition

1991
Gallery W in Yatsushiro
location: Yatsushiro-shi, Kumamoto
site area: 637 m²
building area: 94 m²
total floor area: 94 m²
programme: gallery
number of storeys: 2

1991
Lighting for the Opera House
location: Frankfurt, Germany
programme: ceiling of the main
auditorium

1991–92
Hotel P
location: Shari-gun, Hokkaido
site area: 6604 m²
building area: 983 m²
total floor area: 1418 m²
programme: hotel
number of storeys: 2

1991–93
ITM Building
location: Matsuyama-shi, Ehime
site area: 832 m²
building area: 486 m²
total floor area: 1256 m²
programme: office
number of storeys: 3

1991–94
Tsukuba South Multi-storey Car Park
location: Tsukuba-gun, Ibaragi
site area: 6477 m²
building area: 4904 m²
total floor area: 20,433 m²
programme: parking facility
number of storeys: 6

1992
**Competition Project
for the Olympiad 2000 Sports Hall**
location: Berlin, Germany
total floor area: 40,000 m²
programme: sports hall
number of storeys: 3
prize: honourable mention
(gymnasium)

1992
**Planning and Urban Design
for Luijazui Central Area**
location: Shanghai, China
site area: 170 ha
total floor area: 4,000,000 m²
programme: planning and urban
design
height: 240 m

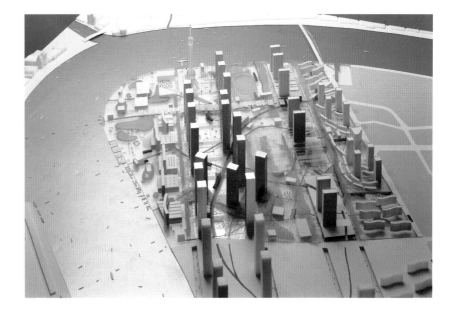

1992
**Competition Project for the
University of Paris Library**
location: Paris, France
site area: 126,433 m²
building area: 14,755 m²
total floor area: 19,710 m²
programme: library
number of storeys: 3

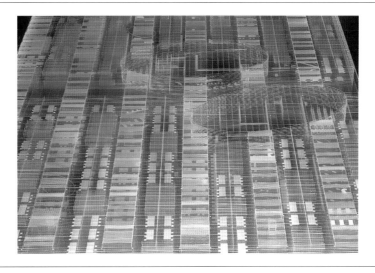

1992
**Competition Project
of Rejuvenation for Antwerp**
location: Antwerp, Belgium
site area: 59 ha
building area: 238,390 m²
programme: park, residences, cultural
and commercial institutions
prize: 1st prize

1992–94
Old People's Home in Yatsushiro
location: Yatsushiro-shi, Kumamoto
site area: 7425 m²
building area: 2183 m²
total floor area: 2467 m²
programme: old people's home
number of storeys: 2
structures: KSP-Matsumoto Structural
Design
plant: Otaki E&M Consultant/N.E.
Planners

1992–95
Yatsushiro Fire Station
location: Yatsushiro-shi, Kumamoto
site area: 8390 m²
building area: 3329 m²
total floor area: 5392 m²
programme: fire station
number of storeys: 3
structures: Toshihiko Kimura
Structural Engineers
plant: Uichi Inoue Laboratory,
Otaki E&M Consultant/N.E. Planners

1993
Eckenheim Municipal Kindergarten
location: Frankfurt, Germany
site area: 2900 m²
building area: 653 m²
total floor area: 703 m²
programme: kindergarten
number of storeys: 1

1993
**Competition Project for O Hall
and Museum**
location: Okegawa, Saitama
site area: 9390 m²
building area: 7430 m²
total floor area: 10,945 m²
programme: museum of modern
literature, public theatre
number of storeys: 4

1993–96
Nagaoka Lyric Hall
location: Nagaoka-shi, Niigata
site area: 39,700 m²
building area: 9708 m²
total floor area: 6682 m²
programme: concert hall, theatre
number of storeys: 4
prize: 1st prize
structures: KSP-Hanawa Structural
Engineers
plant: Uichi Inoue Laboratory

1993–97
Dome in Odate, Competition
location: Odate-shi, Akita
site area: 110,251 m²
building area: 23,218 m²
total floor area: 21,914 m²
programme: multipurpose dome
prize: 1st prize
number of storeys: 2
structures and plant: Takenaka
Corporation

1994–95
S House in Tateshina
location: Tateshina, Nagano
site area: 1689 m²
building area: 232 m²
total floor area: 126 m²
programme: house
number of storeys: 1 below ground,
1 above

1994–97
**Community Activities & Senior
Citizen's Day Care Centre
in Yokohama**
location: Yokohama-shi, Kanagawa
site area: 3026 m²
building area: 1755 m²
total floor area: 2802 m²
programme: day-care centre
number of storeys: 2
structures: KSP-Sasaki Structural
Consultants, Hanawa Structural
Engineers
plant: Kawaguchi Mechanical
Engineering, Yamazaki Electric
Engineering

1995
Tokyo Frontier Project
location: Koto-ku, Tokyo
site area: 66,000 m2
building are: 21,600 m2
total floor area: 21,500 m2
programme: produce area

1995–96
S House in Oguni
location: Oguni-cho, Kumamoto
site area: 1822 m²
building area: 179 m²
total floor area: 115 m²
programme: house, studio
number of storeys: 2

1995–98
Ota-ku Resort Complex in Nagano
location: Chiisagata-gun, Nagano
site area: 18 ha
building area: 9419 m²
total floor area: 5404 m²
programme: resort complex
number of storeys: 1 below ground,
3 above
prize: 1st prize
structures: Sasaki Structural
Consultants, Hanawa Structural
Engineers
plant: Tetens Engineering

1996
**Project for an Information Centre
in Urayasu**
location: Urayasu-shi, Chiba
site area: 33,537 m²
building area: 998 m²
total floor area: 767 m²
programme: information centre
number of storeys: 2

1996–98
Notsuharu Town Hall
location: Notsuharu-machi, Oita
site area: 12,324 m²
building area: 2325 m²
total floor area: 3399 m²
programme: offices; meeting rooms
number of storeys: 2
prize: 1st prize
structures: Sasaki Structural
Consultants
plant: Kankyo-Engineering

1996–99
T Hall in Taisha, Competition
location: Taisha-cho, Shimane
site area: 20,400 m²
building area: 5565 m²
total floor area: 5903 m²
programme: hall, library
number of storeys: 4
prize: 1st prize
structures: Sasaki Structural
Consultants
plant: Sogo Consultants Mechanical,
Electrical Engineers Associates

1997
**MoMA 21, Competition Project
Extension of the Museum
of Modern Art**
location: New York
total floor area: 6,120,000 m²
programme: gallery, theatre, office,
food service, art storage
number of storeys: 3 below ground,
7 above

1997
**Crystal Ballpark, Competition
Project for the Seoul Dome**
location: Seoul, Korea
site area: 109,770 m²
building area: dome 44,470 m²
future commercial facilities 14,760 m²
total floor area: dome 198,700 m²
future comercial facilities 165,000 m²
programme: multipurpose dome
and shopping complex
number of storeys: 2 below ground,
3 above

1997
**Redesigning the Waterfront
of Thessaloniki, Project**
location: Thessaloniki, Greece
site area: 2,120,000 m²
programme: redesigning
the waterfront
prize: 1st prize

1997–99
T House in Yutenji
location: Setagaya-ku, Tokyo
site area: 182 m²
building area: 80 m²
total floor area: 148 m²
programme: house, studio
number of storeys: 2
structures: Masato Araya Structure
Design Office Oak. Inc
plant: Kawaguchi Engineering
Consultant, Yamazaki Engineering
Consultant

1997–2000
Aluminium House in Sakurajosui
location: Setagaya-ku, Tokyo
site area: 184 m²
building area: 86 m²
total floor area: 109 m²
programme: house
number of storeys: 2

1997–2000
Sendai Mediathèque, Competition
location: Sendai-shi, Miyagi
site area: 3949 m²
building area: 2933 m²
total floor area: 21,682 m²
programme: library, gallery, theatre
number of storeys: 2 below ground,
8 above
prize: 1st prize
structures: Sasaki Structural
Consultants
plant: Urtec, Taihei Electricity, Tozan
Electricity

1997–
Project for the Trade Fair Centre
location: Hiroshima-shi, Hiroshima
site area: 81,400 m²
building area: 29,928 m²
total floor area: 41,266 m²
programme: exhibition hall, convention
hall
number of storeys: 1 below ground,
2 above

1998
**Competition Project for
the Extension of the Bank
of International Settlements, Basel**
location: Basel, Switzerland
building area: 34,274 m² (including
existing area)
total floor area: 13,123 m² (phase 1),
5052 m² (phase 2)
programme: office
number of storeys: 4 below ground,
4 above
prize: 1st prize

1998–2000
**"Health Futures" Installation
at the Expo 2000, Hanover**
location: Hanover, Germany
building area: 9000 m²
total floor area: 5400 m²
programme: installation

1998–2001
**Groningen House, Project
for a Residential Complex in
Aluminium**
location: Groningen, Netherlands
site area: 47 m²
building area: 41 m²
total floor area: 166 m²
programme: house and café
number of storeys: 4

1999
Hanover Acrylic Tower Project
location: Hanover, Germany
area: 785 m²
height: 18 m

1999
**Project for the Centre
for the Contemporary Arts, Rome**
location: Rome, Italy
site area: 2.2 ha
building area: 8491 m²
total floor area: 28,567 m²
programme: museum, auditorium,
library, office
number of storeys: 3
steel structure

1999–(2003)
**Project for Apartment House
in Shinonome (B Block)**
location: Koutou-ku, Tokyo
site area: 7070 m²
building area: 4930 m²
total floor area: 35,232 m²
programme: housing, shop, parking
number of storeys: 1 below ground,
14 above

1999–(2004)
Competition Project for the Hôpital Cognacq-Jay
location: Paris, France
site area: 4976 m²
building area: 3207 m²
total area: 14,754 m² + 3214 m² parking
programme: hospice (total terminal-care facility)
number of storeys: 2 below ground, 7 above
prize: 1st prize

1999–
Blue Moon Project
location: Groningen, Netherlands
programme: master-plan, housing, landscape, demonstration

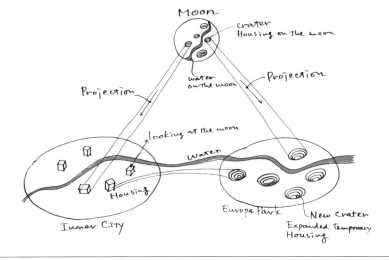

2000
Intercommunication Competition in Morioka
location: Morioka, Iwate
site area: 9860 m²
building area: about 6500 m²
total floor area: about 43,000 m²
programme: library, convention centre, information centre
number of storeys: 8

2000–01
**Project for Mahler 4 Office Block,
Blok 5**
location: Amsterdam, Netherlands
site area: 2700 m²
building area: 2700 m²
total floor area: 35,000 m²
programme: offices, shops
number of storeys: 26

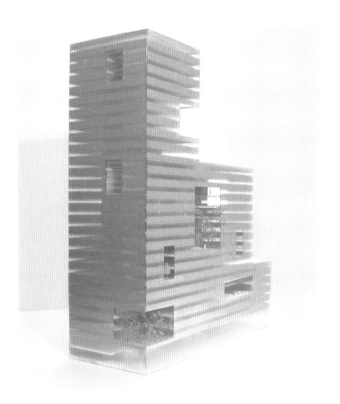

2000–(2002)
**Project for an Aluminium Pavilion
for Bruges 2002**
location: Bruges, Belgium
building area: 144 m²
total floor area: 40 m²
programme: pavilion
number of storeys: 1

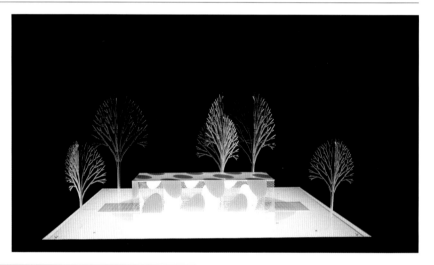

2001
Oita Agricultural Park, Competition
location: Hayami-gun, Oita
site area: 800,000 m²
building area: 7352 m²
total floor area: 7911 m²
programme: meeting room, study
room, store, restaurant, exhibition
space
number of storeys: 2
prize: 1st prize

Selected Writings by Toyo Ito

Architecture in a Simulated City

Video images of Tokyo projected onto the floor, aerial photographs that seem to form a map and scroll past, one after the other. A photograph, taken automatically from a height of 300 metres and graphically processed on a computer, corresponds to a flat and uniform landscape. Another shows a row of kids from the back, playing a videogame. Suddenly the screen changes and a landscape with an expressway appears: it looks as if it has come from the videogame. The landscape vanishes with the sort of speed that Akira reaches on his motorbike. In this case too, as a consequence of the graphic processing of the scene that appears on the screen, the sense of depth has been eliminated completely and the whole thing transformed into a sort of cartoon landscape.

An undulating floor, 10 metres wide and 28 long, covered with translucent acrylic panels. A screen of the same material, 5 metres high and folded longitudinally, incorporating in turn a liquid-crystal screen that can be controlled by an electrical system and that oscillates between transparency and translucence. On another side wall are set a few aluminium panels, with a sheet of translucent material hanging in front of them. All the panels are screens reflecting images from forty-four projectors: eighteen slung from the ceiling project onto the acrylic floor, while the other twenty-six are located under the floor, so that that the different images are superimposed.

Numerous recordings on twelve laser disks display scenes of daily life in Tokyo: groups of people making their way over pedestrian crossings, businessmen chatting on the platform as they wait for their train, a boy talking on a public telephone, etcetera. The video images form a collage and change continually on the forty-four screens where they are projected in a random sequence; every now and then the same image appears on all the screens. The space is filled with environmental sounds processed by a synthesizer, emitted by sixteen-channel speakers which help to make the place seem more three-dimensional.

I have just described the third room, entitled "Dreams", of the "Visions of Japan" exhibition held in London. Visitors were immersed in the pictures that flowed past and remained submerged in this space made up of sound and images. They floated on the surface of the river formed by the acrylic floor and staggered as if they were suffering from sea sickness. When Crown Prince Hironomia of Japan, present at the exhibition's inauguration, visited this space he remarked that he would have been able to grasp its reality more fully if he had drunk some sake first. Charles, Prince of Wales, on the other hand, asked me what there was beyond the images. When I told him there was nothing, he asked me if I was an optimist. I certainly am.

Originally Arata Isozaki, curator of the exhibition, had chosen to call that room "Simulation". When the organizers in London objected that such a name would have been difficult for the public that usually visited the museum to understand, it was decided to change it and call the room "Dreams" instead. Yet this space was an exact simulation of the reality of Tokyo. Perhaps it would be more correct to say that Tokyo itself is a simulated city. It can be claimed, for example, that the experience of walking through Kabuki-cho at night and that of immersing yourself in these images are very similar. In both places our bodies float in a sea of images and noise. Looking at the screen of the videogame we are submerged in it. Like Prince Hironomia we experience a sort of seasickness as a result of the illusion of light and sound, and like Prince Charles we are immersed in a space with no future. Does that mean we have no future?

Certainly there is one marked difference between the "simulation" of the exhibition hall and the Kabuki-cho district. While the real district brims over with noise and confusion, the collage of the city projected on the screen ends by filling up with white noise, or dissolves into the "info-graphic" flow. Briefly, the landscape of the city loses its outlines and vanishes, as if wrapped in morning mist. The landscape of reality continues to dissolve into a state of tranquil and serene "nothingness" that could be described as nirvana. What else can we expect from the future if not this dimension of absolute technological control?

In this space were set five objects submerged by video images. Created by the young designer Anthony Dunne, they could be described as "unpacked television sets" or "comical androids that breathe the air of information". In any case they were objects that modified the images by reacting to the noises around them and emitting mysterious sounds. While the mass-produced television sets sold to the public, all as identical as the grey and monotonous suits worn by businessmen, continually transmit newscasts without bringing about any change as a result, Anthony Dunne's objects were personal and poetic and allowed us to perceive how our environment is filled with sounds. Could it not be that an apparatus for breathing sounds has developed in some part of our body? Are we not becoming like these objects? Although we are unable to see it, our body is in continual contact with the air of technology—and this we do perceive—and this type of air also governs its rhythm. The fact is that, without us realizing it, our bodies are turning into androids with the passing of time.

The entrance to Okawabata River City 21, called the Egg of Winds, is based on the same concept. An egg 16 metres long and 8 wide, clad in aluminium panels, floats in front of two tall residential buildings. By day it is a simple object that reflects the sunlight. At sunset the five liquid-crystal projectors installed inside enter into action. Images from videocassettes or televisions are projected onto the partially perforated surface of the aluminium panels, as well as onto the screen located inside. The aluminium-clad egg that gleams during the day loses its conventional identity as night falls and is transformed into a vague three-dimensional entity composed solely of images. People passing by look at it, stopping for a moment in amazement to wonder what on earth it could be, and then go on their way. It is not a television set installed in the street and looks different from the enormous coloured panels that adorn the façade of the building in front of the station. It is an object made of images that can be seen through the air, filled with information coming from the surroundings that appears and disappears with the wind.

During the construction of the Egg of Winds, a model of similar form was suspended in a gallery in Brussels. To be precise, it was the original model of the River City 21 Gate, which had the shape of a ship or a polyhedron with triangular facets. The Egg of Winds in Brussels was covered with sheets of translucent material and perforated aluminium panels. Even the floor was made of transparent acrylic. Visitors could not go inside it but, through the translucent sheets illuminated by natural light from above, were able to see the chairs and tables, also made out of translucent material, that it contained. People looked at the urban life packaged inside the egg as if it were an illusion. All those objects had lost their materiality and sense of existence, as if they were nothing but a hazy mirage. They had no structure, and yet appeared to be a transient natural phenomenon, similar to the rainbow that appears in the sky and vanishes soon after.

If the two "Eggs of Winds" were to be superimposed, then they could almost be defined as "design of the air". Air that is not visible, even though it is saturated with information. If any kind of spray is released in it, objects appear that are only just visible, transformed into images. Might not the architectural development of today be the discovery of this spray, that is to say of a filter that makes this visualization possible?

In this sense, the Tower of Winds built some years ago in front of Yokohama Station could also be said to perfectly embody the concept of "design of the air". The tower is distinctive because it is not a work of art located in a museum, but a lighting system intentionally situated in the middle of an environment filled with neon lights. From the purely aesthetic viewpoint, its lights can in no way compete with those of the neon signs. Reportedly, however, even though almost the same rate of intermittence as that of the lights in the surroundings was used, people had the impression that the air was purified only around the tower. It is clear that in this case a substance could not have been expected to emit light into the air. Instead, the air itself became light.

Originally, the Egg of Winds at River City 21 was intended to represent the model image of a new kind of dwelling; it was from here that the house of the future was to be born. However, the project was never realized owing to the high cost of building the external structure. Originally what I attempted to show through the air was the new style of life in a simulated city.

On the other hand, the Egg of Winds in Brussels has been called Pao after the nomadic woman of Tokyo, and for me it has become the model of a city house. I wanted to trace the image of urban life that day after day grows less real, in parallel with the transformation of urban space into images. Consequently, what the two eggs have in common is the fact that they are both containers alluding to a new way of life. In other words, I intended to demonstrate that the loss of the reality of urban life and architecture understood as image are two sides of the same coin.

In every era, the desire for a new life has given rise to a new space. The so-called "modern living" of which people dreamed in the fifties was a space that embodied the image of a simple and carefree life surrounded by electric household appliances. Brightly-lit houses covered by flat roofs with large openings or by very gently sloping lightweight roofs, a kitchen with a shiny built-in refrigerator, the chairs of the dining-room made out of galvanized metal tubing and thin backs of flexible wood: this style of "modern living", decorated and with a cheerful appearance, guaranteed a modern way of life to the nuclear family on which it was based. The idyllic scene took place when the breadwinner came home after spending the whole day at the office, this too decorated in a clean and lively fashion and furnished in steel and glass, and was welcomed by his smiling wife and children in the kitchen-cum-dining-room equipped with all the latest electric household appliances. And if there was a Volkswagen "Beetle" or a Citroën 2CV parked in the garage, then the image of the new way of life was absolutely perfect.

If the ideal life in the age of electricity found concrete expression in "modern living", what will be the image of the ideal life in the era of the computer? Up to now we have not discovered a suitable space. Rather than in the difference between the homes people live in, the situation is symbolically represented by the difference between the Volkswagens and Citroëns of the past and the Toyotas and Nissans of today. Just as the design of the former alluded to their function, in which form took the place of mechanism, the design of modern Japanese cars equipped with a series of electronic brains is skin-deep and extremely harmonious and does not allude in any way to the technology they contain. The image of today's cars has almost nothing to do with their mechanics. The same could be said of the design concept of the various electric appliances. If industrial and automobile design adapts to the needs of the consumer, i.e. to the modern style most in vogue, where the house is concerned this coincidence is very superficial. Instead, the project in the proper sense of the word is decidedly biased toward conservatism. In the world of architecture, where there has been no close relationship between function and form since the very beginning, the style tends to express a nostalgic form of life linked to economic prosperity.

If that is how things are, what is the new life of today? We do not have time to reflect on this, distracted as we are by the gleaming objects that surround us and that increase in number every day. The many products, foodstuffs, clothes and articles that fill the department stores and supermarkets have a shiny appearance and look as if they are capable of satisfying our desire for a new life. Consuming them, however, wearing those clothes, or keeping them at home, their splendour fades. And immediately we want more.

Behind these apparently highly personal articles—from those of everyday use to the house itself—is concealed an ever greater homogenization. In other words, as we see in the design of the latest cars, the homogeneity of content means that small superficial differences provide an apparent individuality. The same fate is shared not just by houses but by architecture itself. The development of air conditioning, for instance, has allowed architecture to ignore climatic factors, so that the same architectural style can be used in any part of the world. Not just the same architectural style but any style. Is it not true that even the numerous designs which seem to have a rich personality and to attract the public's attention mostly have the same content and are merely decorated on the surface? The same happens with the perishable foodstuffs wrapped in transparent plastic that adorn the aisles of supermarkets. The different foods, rich and varied, are able to do this as long as they remain frozen, wrapped in transparent film and kept in conditions that do not vary.

Since the emergence of steel and glass, we have been constantly searching for homogeneous space, so-called universal space. Like the coordinates of Euclidean geometry, universal space is homogeneous only in theory. Indeed, it could be said that the purely neutral process of homogenization has been curbed by the preference for the local or by the propensity for monumentality. In any case, the total standardization of architecture has been automatically checked by the devotion that architects themselves display, in an almost unconscious manner, for "architecture" in itself.

So it can be said that the phenomenon of the homogenization of modern architectural space is somewhat different from the aesthetic quest for universal space of the past. Today it is society itself that is homogeneous and architects have embarked on a struggle to combat this situation, but to no avail: the more individual they try to be, the more they fall into the simple homogeneity of Euclidean geometry, limiting themselves to joining up two points on the axis of coordinates. Today, society is wrapping itself in a great sheet of transparent plastic.

In other periods, architects yearned for a homogeneous pattern because the society of the time was considered opaque. What they were trying to do was introduce a neutral and transparent element into a society as heterogeneous and opaque as lava. As a consequence, even if the space of an office could create the homogeneity they were seeking, it was only an attempt confined within a closed space. Just one step outside the office lay a real and opaque space.

The environment in which we live today is covered completely by an empty clarity. Our cities are totally arid, just like the products that fill the supermarket shelves. In the last ten years the dampness of the city has been eliminated as if a gigantic hairdryer had been turned on it. Even if we are surrounded by every kind of article and product, we are immersed in a total homogeneity. All this wealth is supported by nothing more than a sheet of transparent plastic.

Simulated life is based on this transparent film in which society is wrapped. At sunset, for example, businessmen and office workers on their way home get off the train a few stops early: in the centre they eat, drink, sing, dance and comment on the events of the day. Sometimes they go to the cinema, the theatre or play the slot-machines. Otherwise they go shopping, head for the gym or swimming-pool or go jogging. For them the time and space between the office and the house are totally fictitious. They eat and drink trustingly, as if they were consuming delicacies cooked by their own mothers.

335

They sing and dance as if they had turned into movie stars. They talk and argue drunkenly, as if they had been friends all their lives. They buy everything, as this makes them feel rich. They do exercises in an artificial space, as if they were swimming in the open sea or running through the grass. The space, gestures and even the objects they have managed to get hold of are simulated. Moreover, this simulated life and space are not confined exclusively to the intermediate zone of the city centre, but have invaded their offices and houses as well. Our whole life, including family and work, has become a simulation. It could even be said that the sense of the distinction between real and unreal has been lost.

We have lost the sensation that not just our vision but also our taste, hearing and smell are real. We can no longer be sure of what is really tasty, of what we are hearing or touching in reality. All this because, independently of our consciousness, our bodies are changing. In similar fashion, our way of communicating with objects and with each other has changed. We now have bodies that with a single function of image, whatever it may be, can easily turn the relationship between real and unreal on its head.

Advances in the media have meant that the word has been separated from things and that its own reality has been blurred. We have reached an extreme in which we can develop impressions only with words and images, and not with things. In this way, simulated life has independently extended its sphere of action. It follows that communication through the media, i.e. communication devoid of substance, has become so commonplace that it is now impossible to establish communication except through the network of the media. Communication limited to a particular area or place has lost its meaning. It can be claimed that what has made the city in which we live grow out of all proportion is the formation of this indefinite, as well as provisional and fleeting network in which physical distance has been cancelled out.

As a consequence, when you set out to create a work of architecture in the simulated city you are faced with two problems that are hard to solve. In the first place, how to create a work of architecture that has substance, at the very moment when the significance of the things as such is being lost? In the second place, how to create a work of architecture that will last in a context in which the concept of local community is vanishing and the networks of communication established by the media are continually appearing and disappearing?

These two problems are really difficult to solve as they are contradictory conditions. On the one hand there is no alternative to building something real, even though the object in question has almost no reality. On the other, it is necessary to create a permanent space in the midst of a relative and transitory set of relations that change incessantly. Given these contradictory conditions, what sort of architecture can exist?

Of course it is not possible to come up with a definitive answer to the dilemma. Personally, I believe that it makes no sense to fall back on a position that does not accept the contradiction as such, i.e. to place yourself outside these conditions without acknowledging them. Will not whatever solution is left, then, be linked to the need to reduce the gap between these contradictions? As far the first problem is concerned, it is a question of being able to create a work of architecture that is fictitious or resembles a video image; the second problem can be solved by creating a short-lived and provisional work of architecture. By this I do not mean to claim that video images can replace architecture, nor that I consider it possible to use temporary elements in architecture. What is necessary is to create a work of architecture that has a lasting and permanent substance on which a fictitious and temporary appearance is bestowed.

We have to exploit the provocative capacities of space, based on the images created in this city. What I'm trying to say is that we must make the most of effects of simulation, given that real urban space offers us a vast quantity of suggestions. In the Tower of Winds and Egg of Winds, for example, fictitious and ephemeral images were evoked by means of real fire and real images, while in works like the project entered for the competition for the Maison de la culture du Japon in Paris, the T Building in Nakameguro and the S Building in Aoyama, the images look like natural phenomena, an effect produced by screens of glass that contain a film of liquid crystals (in reality in the last two projects we limited ourselves to applying a transparency made out of silk). In projects like the Guest Quarters of the Sapporo Brewery on Hokkaido and the Municipal Museum of Yatsushiro I also set out to produce natural images, creating an artificial landscape on a originally level site.

All these manipulations are already simulations in themselves. I believe that in a simulated city there can be no architecture without a simulated manipulation. The small hill constructed at the entrance of the Municipal Museum of Yatsushiro, for example, is totally fake but, once created, looked as if it had been there for over a hundred years. It seems to me that at this point reality is something that is formed beyond fiction. In architecture the same thing happens with materials: by now the frontiers between real and unreal have totally vanished. Today the whole of society is wrapped in an enormous transparent film. Should we not be trying to make the wrapping more visible, rather than attempting to make the content look real? I believe that from now on the destiny of architecture will depend on its capacity to reveal the structure of fiction.

Kenchiku Bunka, December 1991

A Garden of Microchips

*The Visual Image in the Era
of Microelectronics*
I believe that the 1990 exhibition entitled "Information Art – The Diagramming of Microchips", held at the Museum of Modern Art (MoMA) in New York, was an event of great importance for the world of architecture and design. I did not see the exhibition but, judging by the catalogue, it consisted of numerous photographs of microchips blown up hundreds of times, in other words diagrammatic images of the integrated circuits used in computers.

The microchips look like delicately woven textiles, made up of patterns of bright colours applied to the silicon in such a way as to form grids. Each image, however, is different from the others. In some striped patterns are repeated, while in others they are subdivided into blocks, each with a different colour and pattern as in a patchwork. Many chips have borders and are composed of cell-like squares, arranged like the representation of buildings in a plan. One shows a complex diagram with a pattern that is reminiscent of an organic form, looking like the nervous system of the human body superimposed on a checkerboard.

In any case, the patterns of microchips are electronic textiles that suggest the image of the plan of a contemporary city. A chip, so small that it has to be enlarged hundreds of times before it is visible to the naked eye, can contain millions and, more recently, tens of millions of transistors. Currently, a chip containing billions of them is under development. In addition, the patterns that look like flat surfaces are in reality three-dimensional structures made up of anything from ten to twenty-five layers.

The exhibition at MoMA seemed truly innovative to me because the photographs of microchips were used to make the aesthetics of the era of microelectronics visible in images. It succeeded in giving form, for the first time in a decisive manner, to the image of the existence of a new aesthetics that is replacing that of the machine age which dominated the twentieth century.

Almost fifty years have passed since the invention of the transistor and as far back as the sixties the computer had already made surprising progress. You will probably be asking why it is only now that I am referring to the microelectronic era, given that the

transition from mechanics to electronics occurred a long time ago. It is true that even at the time of the Tokyo Olympic Games, the booking system for the Shinkansen high-speed train showed us that computer technology was going to modify society in an irreversible way.

And yet, despite the fact that microelectronics had made amazing progress, we had not yet succeeded in moulding it into clear visible images, as had been done for the machine age. In the field of architecture and design, however much effort we made to imagine the society of the future, we continued to be dependent on visual forms of expression. This difficulty was evident in the images of the city and the works of architecture produced in rapid succession by the Archigram group, which so fascinated young architects and students in the sixties. Projects like Peter Cook's Plug-in City (1964) and Instant City (1969) and Ron Herron's Walking City (1964) represented visualizations of a technological utopia arising out of a system made up of the machine and the human being playing with the computer.

Although extraordinary imagination went into their design, these cities of the future remained within the aesthetic realm of the machine. They were collages of mechanical objects like huge cranes, three-dimensional structures, launch ramps for missiles and space shuttles on their way to the Moon. Looking back at these projects, only the one called Computer City (1964) by Dennis Crompton traced the image of a network, a grid, resembling the nervous system. Nevertheless, even this project seems to be a substitute for an integrated circuit, enlarged and configured as the layout of a city plan. In other words, the structure of the city is once again determined by a simple visual analogy. It is precisely at this point that we discover the reason why it is almost impossible to outline the aesthetics of the era of microelectronics. Whereas in the era of machines aircraft, ships, cars and their mechanical components such as motors, screws and hubs in and of themselves constituted an image of the age, in the electronic era we have not yet found a visual form that can produce a representative iconography.

The form of mechanical objects expresses some sort of causal relationship, however ambiguous, with their function. In the case

of vehicles, a dynamic form that opposes less resistance to the air or water results in greater speed. The myth that the best form is the one that most closely matches function dominated the world of design throughout the twentieth century. In the case of electronic objects, on the other hand, there is no causal relationship between function and form. Even in objects that generate images or sounds, such as audiovisual devices, form does not follow function. The enormous memory and calculation capacities of the computer conjure up no formal image. All that appears before our eyes are the data to be entered and the results obtained. We cannot even imagine the electric current, its speed and its huge volume. It is for this reason that, in order to "see" the image of the electronic age, we have started to use the image of mechanical objects as a surrogate.

Yet microchips set out in this way clearly suggest images totally different from those of mechanical objects. Such images are not so much forms as spaces in which invisible things flow. It could be said that what we are dealing with here is a transparent space in which, as soon as the flow is produced, different phenomenological forms emerge. It seems, in this case, that the visualization of the image of a space that generates expressions is more important than the forms expressed.

It has often been claimed that the design of new cars in our country is a product of the electronic era and that it does not express an immediately recognizable, solid form as in the case of such celebrated European cars as the Porsche or Mercedes-Benz. Japanese cars are delicate and present an image as subtle and elusive as mist. Their speed is not necessarily translated into an aerodynamic form; on the contrary, one has the impression that they have been designed to circulate silently in a world with no air. At the base of such vehicles must lie the electronic and transparent space symbolized by the microchip. Does not that mean that forms as subtle and elusive as mist are fragments of phenomenological design, images that are born and vanish in the middle of that space?

The City Is a Garden of Microchips
The blown-up diagram of a microchip looks like an aerial photograph of a city, processed on the computer. If transformed by means of

an effector, the photograph of an urban area can become an abstract diagram that shows only the empty outline of the buildings and the works of civil engineering, filled with luminous and coloured points. The real appearance of urban space is cancelled out and the image starts to resemble a photograph of a microchip.

So the fact that as soon as the substance of urban space is eliminated another city emerges, the city as microchip, acquires a symbolic value. In that moment the city is not just diagrammatically analogous to the microchip, but even begins to display similar characteristics to it. These common characteristics can be summed up by three terms: 1. Fluidity, 2. Multiplicity of layers, 3. Phenomenality.

I have already pointed out on several occasions that urban space is made up of immovable objects like buildings and works of civil engineering, and is at the same time an accumulation of various elements that flow. These flows are generated by a range of different forces such as water and wind or people and cars, as well as by different types of energy and information.

Originally Japanese cities developed by exploiting the variety of the natural terrain, due to the topography of the ground and the action of rivers and other currents of water, which was then overlaid with the networks of roads and canals constructed by human beings. At Edo [the old name of the city of Tokyo] in particular, an interesting urban space was created, where natural variations of relief, roads and canals were fused in a harmonious way. Looking at the *Bushu Toyoshima-gun Edo Shozu*, considered the oldest surviving map of Edo and representing the city as it was around the middle of the seventeenth century, what we see is a network of rivers, roads and canals that extend outwards in spirals from Edo Castle as if in a dynamic configuration. Here we see clearly how the pattern, which in theory should have been traced by the roads, is twisted and bent under the influence of the spiral configuration of the different undulating lines and transformed into a profoundly organic and fluid space. The space formed is totally different from the Western one, in which geometric patterns are imposed in a rigorous fashion on the natural relief, even though based on it. In the *Edo ikkenzu byobu* [a screen with a panoramic view of Edo], which is thought to have been painted at the beginning of the nineteenth century by Esaitsuguzane Kuwagata, the spiral configuration of the space is even clearer. The picture is a view from above, looking in the direction of Edo Castle and Mount Fuji, painted from the highest point of the Fukagawa district. In it we see groups of houses, corresponding to the residences of feudal lords and the homes of ordinary people, which form undulating lines along the watercourses and the areas of greenery. And it is clear that at that time there was a living urban space which flowed in a dynamic manner, something totally unimaginable in modern Tokyo.

Referring to the construction of this city, beautiful as a "garden", in which the groups of houses, the vegetation and the water were combined in an extraordinary fashion, Hidenobu Jinnani asserts that it "can be interpreted as a balance between the 'desire for planning', common to all cities that grow up around a castle, and the 'flexible adaptation to the uneven terrain' of the Musashino highlands. ... A clear and strong urban structure that would dominate the surrounding space was not created. Rather the area was carefully studied, taking the terrain with its delicate changes of level as a reference, and a pattern traced that was similar to a harmonious mosaic embedded in the ground, with the aforementioned individual urban elements distributed in an appropriate manner" (Hidenobu Jinnani, *Tokyo no kukan jinruigaku* ["Spatial Anthropology of Tokyo"], published by Chikuma).

So it appears that the garden-city called Edo consisted of an area in which the artificial elements, such as buildings, roads and canals, blended in with nature at all levels, forming a single space. In other words, it seems to me that technology and nature were fused into a single system, from the urbanistic macro-scale that formed the general plan of the city to the micro-scale that coordinated the relationship between the individual houses and the gardens.

From the Meiji period onwards, new and artificial elements, such as means of transport, were introduced into this extraordinary space that destroyed the balance in a one-sided way. In particular, the increase in the size of the buildings and the introduction of the network of expressways, together with the rapid economic development of the post-war period, contributed in a decisive fashion to the elimination of the natural system.

In the Tokyo of today the confusion created by the tyranny of technology and the accumulation of heterogeneous systems is evident. In my view, however, it makes more sense to try to discover the fascination of what is concealed in the urban space of our own day than to complain about the disastrous conditions of modern Tokyo and to look back with nostalgia to Edo, the garden-city of the past.

In comparison with the urban space of Edo, it is clear that Tokyo has lost the dynamic fluidity of plants and water. As I have already pointed out, what has increased instead is the flow of artificial elements. In the centre of the metropolis, in particular, vast systems of transport have been superimposed on one another at different levels, from a depth of tens of metres under the ground up toward the sky. At each level there is a highly complex horizontal transport network, linked to the other horizontal networks by a vertical system. In different zones of the metropolis these networks form different layers, something that could certainly not have been imagined in ancient Edo.

In addition, it is significant that it is not just people and vehicles that flow through the city. The flows of energy and information have increased explosively, to the point where it can be said that these invisible currents are dominating the urban space to an ever greater extent. We cannot mould this space of information into visible images inasmuch as it does not constitute a physical network and can only be observed through terminals. Given the increase in electronic flows and consequently in data, urban space can only be phenomenological. In other words, the real urban space made up of works of architecture is overlaid with another that stems from phenomena such as light, sounds, images, et cetera. This phenomenological city also comprises different areas, from the space created by light and images in a totally spontaneous manner to the abstract one formed by the web of signs of the so-called media. As a phenomenon the city is, after all, a space with a transient function (effect), generated by the invisible flow of electrons, and does not assume a morphological expression. The city as phenomenon transforms the real city into an illusory one, coated with light, sounds, images and signs. If we were to eliminate the concrete part, an enormous quantity of energy would be revealed, along with the network of electronic flows that manipulates this illusion.

As a consequence, the spatial characteristics of the contemporary city are fluidity, a multiplicity of layers and phenomenality, exactly the same as those of the microchip.

Nevertheless, I believe that describing this city as a "garden of microchips" would be an excessive idealization, since the presence of the artificial objects introduced during the process of modernization, of the networks of different means of transport that ignore the natural relief, of filled-in canals and above all of groups of huge buildings that completely ignore the natural flow is overwhelming. So we have to bring to light the delicate network of flows covered up by these other presences, as if we were carrying out an archaeological dig.

Could we not uncover the structure and the natural flow historically present within the constructions of the machine age, superimpose on them the networks of the electronic era and allow the whole thing to be re-created as phenomenological space? Only then would it be possible to describe this city as a "garden of microchips", only when the superimposed layers of the networks of new technologies and the flow of nature itself begin to give rise to reciprocal effects.

Architecture as a Device for Storing and Transmitting Information

If urban space today has already been transformed into a garden of microchips, is it possible to give this phenomenological space a concrete expression in the form of architecture?

I have always conceived my architecture by superimposing it on a garden, which means that I saw my works as gardens and not that my aim was necessarily to create an architecture that blended into the landscape. Nonetheless, in several of the projects I have produced in recent years I have tried to integrate the architecture into the landscape. So I have attempted to conceal the volume of the buildings or to establish a positive relationship between the individual buildings and the space outside by removing or adding earth. These intentions were very stimulating in themselves. In addition, the insertion of a natural environment of artificial form between buildings in the urban areas of Japan, where it is difficult to find a context between the constructions, seemed an effective stratagem.

Yet when I talk about architecture as a garden, I am thinking of an architecture as fluid and phenomenological as urban space. It does not reveal itself as a whole straightaway. Rather, it is people who link up the phenomenological spaces that succeed one another in each scene, in such a way that the overall image emerges in the end as a continuous series of all the scenes.

The scenes should not remain detached like the rooms of a building. What I want to create is a space in which some of them leave room for the following ones, leaving behind a sort of echo, just as happens in a film in which the images progressively appear and disappear.

It can be argued that architecture in which the temporal sequence takes on a fundamental importance is closer to the space of sound than to that of vision. It is a space in which innumerable sounds float. Of course these are not sounds emitted at random like those of urban space, but selected in such a way as to insert them in a relationship based on choice. Not even the whole is organized into a form, like a classical music score or a Japanese *kaiyu* garden. As far as the choice of sounds to be combined is concerned, everyone can pick the ones that he or she prefers. As a consequence, even though there is a musical space that generates the score, the chronological order in which the notes are placed varies from person to person. For me, architecture understood as a garden has the image of a soundscape.

Yet my first attempt to produce a work like a garden, the House at Nakano or the White U, resulted in a space that resembled a *kaiyu* garden. A "garden of light" was created between two concrete walls that curved to form a U. A luminous space rich in effects of light and shade, produced by the natural illumination from above and the sides, was formed within this tubular ring of spotless white. The phenomenon of light was used to create a space filled with currents and vortices. People entering the space could linger for a moment but could not change their route. They were only allowed to circulate around the empty space in the middle of the courtyard. The space was vigorous because the simplicity and clarity of the closed ring made it so, alluding precisely to a complete universe, i.e. to the force of cosmology, just like in a *kaiyu*.

The recently completed ITM Building in Matsuyama could also be described as a "garden of light". Rather than the White U's interior enclosed by concrete, what has been created here is a space filled with delicate light wrapped in translucent glass; the intensity of the light is controlled by a transparent membrane. The various architectural elements situated inside this volume of light reveal their dimensions in a horizontal as well as vertical direction, maintaining a gradual relationship between them as if they were sounds wafting through the air.

Although the horizontal and vertical relations are maintained, the terms "above" and "below" have little significance here. Hence those architectural elements whose significance derives from their relationship with the force of gravity, such as floors, walls and roofs, have been lost and even if we were to imagine the space rotated through 90 or 180 degrees, their significance would not change at all. The floors, stairs, partition walls, etc. are made of translucent panels that let light through. Inside this new "garden of light" the public, no longer confined by gravity, can walk around freely choosing sounds (the architectural elements) and singing their own musical notes.

If the House at Nakano and the ITM Building in Matsuyama are "gardens of light", the Silver Hut and the Municipal Museum of Yatsushiro are "gardens of wind". What the two projects have in common are their continuous, light and thin vaulted roofs, constructed out of a framework of steel slats, and the free space between the independent columns that support them. Should not such a space be regarded as a garden that induces currents of air, like the wind blowing through a wood? In the case of Yatsushiro in particular, the different scenes staged vary in sequence: the curved bridge built on the top of a small hill covered with vegetation, followed by the space under the vaults that offers a view from an elevated position and then the exhibition hall with its supports resembling a natural clump of trees, the room open to the sky that offers a totally different space next to the entrance of the museum, etc. This building has been assigned the function of a museum, but a garden divided up into internal and external areas has been created in the zone that serves as the exhibition space proper. Visitors perceive the currents and vortices of air, and by walking and stopping weave the "garden of the wind".

My interest in electronic phenomena commenced with the Tower of Winds in 1986. The project cannot exactly be defined as a work of architecture, but it was the precursor of a series of works in which both light and images have been utilized. At the base of the Tower of Winds lay the intention of selecting the air (wind) and sound (noise) from the various currents flowing through the surroundings and turning them into luminous signs, i.e. into visual information. To put it briefly, it was a question of introducing information into the environment.

The project that I presented at the Yokohama "Urbana Ring Exhibition" in 1992 had a similar aim. In this case, data on the conditions in Yokohama Bay had to be transformed into a visual and aural space by means of instruments like light, sound and images. The space of light and sound that resulted from this—and that was to have been called a "media park"—was in reality another space of phenomenological water superimposed on that of the real water. Thus the project set out to turn information into environment and at the same time to introduce information into the environment itself.

So it might be asked how it is possible to transform data into environment in order to formalize architecture as a "garden of

microchips". By its very nature the architectural act represents the creation of a new environment that is at one and the same time physical and phenomenological through the addition of information to the existing environment. In this case architecture becomes a device for emitting information and storing it. The architecture has no need of a physical form of its own but is transformed into a means of interpreting form as phenomenon (environment).

In the competition project for the University of Paris Library, drawn up last year, I also tried to create a work of architecture that could be used as a means of controlling the environment. In the first place, this consisted of a large oval room (centre) on a vacant site between three buildings of the university campus. That room is the information centre which, by linking the three constructions, transforms the free space from negative into positive. In concrete terms, it is a functional space laid out around the reading room of the library, i.e. an instrument for the storage and emission of information, since it is also a communication centre for students and teachers. The oval space is traversed by two levels of walkways arranged in parallel lines, architectural elements that make up the floor and ceiling and at the same time serve as a device for controlling the environment, for controlling light, sound and heat. They constitute a large horizontal slit for ventilation, making the oval room a pleasant place, suitable for reading. Just as these openings are devices for regulating the passage of light and wind, the two layers of walkways do not separate the interior from the exterior but create an environment that is similar to the outside only more comfortable. So the concept of façade is absent from this architecture. However much the space is subdivided by panels of glass, you have the impression that it is continuous. On the one hand, what we have here is a device for the storage and emission of information, a place in which the electronic flows form vortices; on the other we are in the presence of a mechanism for filtering light, heat (air) and sound, a place in which the flow of nature is modified. The oval and the line, respectively symbolizing the two aspects, are superimposed, forming a layered space. So could not this project be considered the architectural realization of the garden of microchips, inasmuch as it is characterized by fluidity, a multiplicity of layers and phenomenality, especially since such characteristics take the material form of architectural elements like walkways and screens?

The same concept of layered space has been adopted in the two projects still under construction in the municipality of Yatsushiro, the fire station and an old people's home. In both cases, what I wanted to create was a place that would not only be able to fulfil the functions specific to the two constructions but also resemble an open garden. In my view, in the first case it was not just a question of solving the problem of the physical construction of the layered space, but also of overlaying the specific functions of this firefighting park with the more ambiguous one of the garden and ensuring that these functions interact

Simple Lines for Le Corbusier

with one another, creating a particular garden within the park as a consequence of their mutual permeability. The latter consists in the transparent relations between the two social functions, and is what we have to compose as materialized architecture. The situation is absolutely the same in the case of the old people's home.

Projects like the Redevelopment Plan for the city of Amberes and the Redevelopment Plan for the Luijazui Central Area of Shanghai also set out to create a "garden of microchips". Here it is easier to take real urban spaces as a reference in so far as they are projects on an urban scale. By organising the multitude of networks present in the real urban space, and establishing a transparent relationship between the networks that form layers, new gardens appear.

In any case I am convinced that the task of visualizing the images of the microelectronic era coincides with the aim of designing the dream of the "garden of microchips". That is to say, it is a question of producing an electronic vortex in the space of the electronic current, of creating a place of information that will take the place of the *genius loci* of the past.

JA Library, 2, July 1993

I don't know exactly why, but over the course of my career I have kept stumbling across Le Corbusier, even though I have never consciously followed in his footsteps. I don't think about him when I'm drawing up my projects. I only become aware of his influence when people point it out to me, after looking at my models or my plans.

Le Corbusier has played an important role in the works that I have designed so far. Although I am not aware of the end result that I am going to attain right from the outset, the fact is that the architecture of the Swiss master is always somewhere along the line of the route to be followed in order to get there. It is strange, but every time I deviate from the course I have laid down for myself and am then forced to change direction, I run into Le Corbusier again.

This is exactly what happened in the early eighties, when I designed a series of houses that I myself called Dom-ino. The small and cubic constructions of this series—steel structures with outer walls made of concrete panels—such as the House at Koganei (1980) and the House at Umegaoka (1982) alternated with others of a different type like the House at Chuorinkan (1980) and the House at Kasama (1982), characterized by a saddle roof, a treatment of the surfaces that can be regarded as decorative and a formal manipulation of the set of volumes. In other words, Dom-ino was a response to the search for refinement, expressed in the attention paid to surfaces and manipulations of form, characteristic of my works from the seventies onward.

That project provided me with the cue for a new examination of the city and its rapid changes, and a point from which to start to reconsider architecture from the viewpoint of urban life. There too Le Corbusier's Dom-ino system represented an opportunity to find out what the homes of a new era were supposed to look like, after the destruction of the First World War. It was an innovative design that demolished the style which had held sway up until then, and one which contained the essential energy that was to be released in the following works, Villa Stein at Garches and Villa Savoye. It also embodied the bases of the "five principles of the new architecture" that were to become famous all over the world.

In the early eighties I was looking for just

this type of active energy in architecture. In the vision of modern urban life I hoped to discover something definite and vital that concerned the living essence and was not merely a conceptual manipulation of forms. Just as Le Corbusier never stopped trying to express the simple emotion that the sun and plants instil in human beings, even when surrounded by geometric and abstract forms, I too wanted to have a secure base that, even if the world were falling to pieces, would impinge on the most hidden corners of the body.

The Silver Hut (1984) was my response to that desire. Like Le Corbusier's, the work was the outcome of a quest for an architecture that would be able to enter into contact with the sun, with plants and above all with the wind. Perhaps the very form of the roof with its depressed and continuous vaults might have hinted at the existence of a connection with works like the Henfel Weekend Home at La-Celle-Saint-Cloud or the Roq and Rob Apartments. Probably what those projects had in common was an inclination toward the vernacular house.

However, there is an important distinction between the life that Le Corbusier envisaged for the inhabitants of his houses and the one that I had in mind. I think that the Silver Hut was in a way more open to nature than the series of dwellings designed by Le Corbusier. The separation between inside and outside was more marked in his houses: I wanted to create an architecture in which these boundaries were eliminated. This difference of intention may stem from the diversity of our architectural traditions. Both Le Corbusier's houses and my own seek to establish a positive relationship with nature. Yet the mode of existence of human beings and architecture in a computerized society and one in which the computer is yet to put in its appearance are profoundly different.

Every time that I have been given the opportunity, I have stressed my conviction that in a society like ours, in which informatics has invaded every area, human beings have two bodies. The "real body", made up of our physical essence, and the "virtual body", linked to the world of information. Of course in daily life the two entities are not clearly divided but constitute a single, interactive body. The virtual body exercises an ever greater influence and is radically modifying the dynamics that bind together the units of which society is composed, from individual relationships to those between families, neighbours and communities.

In reality it can be said that nowadays the relationship between groups, and with it the concept of community based on the real body, has been completely replaced by group relations established through the virtual body. Even the existence of the last surviving unit, the family, is threatened by the virtual body. In contrast to the period in which Le Corbusier lived, we are now obliged to take this reality of society into account in architecture. And it was in the Silver Hut that I wanted to represent the difference between my work and Le Corbusier's.

The decision to use the term *pao* to describe a house covered with a translucent sheet, and to call its inhabitants "nomads", is a direct consequence of the image of those who live in the city and have a virtual body and a house. So I wanted the Silver Hut to stand at the meeting point between the house of residents with real bodies and the *pao* in which nomads live.

In Le Corbusier's time no one could have imagined inhabitants who on the one hand yearn for a strong and united family and a home for it to live in, and on the other are constantly trying to set themselves free of that family and that home. Yet the inhabitants of the city of our time live in a society steeped in information, are equipped with virtual bodies and cannot help but adopt this ambiguous attitude.

At the time my ideas about "nomads", the *pao* and the Silver Hut as their materialization drew considerable criticism: in particular, that my peculiar vision did not at all lend itself to generalization. In spite of this, the only image of city-dwellers I could summon up was that of beings with two bodies. And this conviction has grown stronger and stronger as time goes by.

It would be easy to go back to the image of the home and community based on a single cosmology as Le Corbusier understood it and design our architecture on this basis. It is clear that it would win the favour of society. However, when we try to give material form to those images, we find that they are founded solely in nostalgia, that they are superficial expressions totally divorced from the reality of the city. In the eighties we saw many examples of this kind. If we are to think of the future even just for a moment, we cannot ignore the image of the house and the community based on the virtual body.

For this reason, after the Silver Hut, Le Corbusier vanished from my mind for a long time. Occupied as I was with the question of the virtual body, I thought that the Swiss master would have no further bearing on my work.

And yet with the two projects located in the city of Yatsushiro, the Old People's Home (*Hozyuryo*) and the Fire Station in the firemen's park, Le Corbusier reappeared without me realising it. Does not the Old People's Home have aspects in common with the architectural image of Chandigarh, such as the Law Courts? My work has the appearance of a three-dimensional rectangle with a large flat roof, a single element made up not of concrete slabs but of layers of metal plates supported by steel girders. The roof rests on a concrete wall and on slender steel tubes and has a series of different oval apertures. Some are closed by sheets of glass to form skylights, while others are simple openings that let in light. Perhaps it is this flat roof with openings, designed to cope with the strong sunlight in the south of Japan, that reminds people of Le Corbusier's works in Chandigarh.

The free space formed under the flat roof is subdivided by screens made of different materials into rooms in which the old people live their daily lives. The residence is a long way from Tokyo and, although the site cannot be compared with the Mediterranean for beauty, here too the sun is very hot, the vegetation luxuriant and it is possible to watch evocative sunsets over the Shiranui Sea.

The elderly will live a new life in contact with nature, under this vast and flat roof that covers them and protects them from the intensity of the sun's rays, while letting light through for illumination. Yet this does not mean that their existences are not bound by a highly spiritual constraint, as a result of which, although they are in community with one another in the physical sense, they also need to have a set of human relations on the outside. From this point of view they are old people with real bodies suited to living together, but are they not at the same time nomads with virtual bodies in their consciousness?

As a consequence, the Old People's Home is not simply a container for community life, but also a house in which every resident in his or her capacity as a nomad would want to live. In other words, it was necessary to design a house that could be inhabited by a community of spirits not closely bound to the place. I created various connections between this container and nature, but I did not want the space to represent a single cosmology. What I wanted was to create a not very defined space that would have no centre other than the dreams of the residents (collective illusion). And so there is nothing of the cosmology or materiality that Le Corbusier tried to express in Chandigarh in my project. Although different materials may have been utilized, they have been treated in an abstract manner so as to establish a relationship with the virtual bodies. The work could be called "Le Corbusier along simple lines", in the sense that the real depth and breadth of existence have been eliminated.

The Fire Station in the firemen's park, another project in the municipality of Yatsushiro, has also been realized on the basis of these principles. If the Old People's Home can be compared to Chandigarh, the front of this building is reminiscent of the Villa Savoye. The prism set on pilotis, the proportion of the whole with its accentuated horizontality and the horizontal strip windows all point in this direction. Yet I was not aware of it during the design phase. The pilotis, for example, were adopted to trigger a reciprocal reaction between the raised volumes and the landscape at ground level, just as I had done in the Redevelopment Project for the city of Amberes (1992).

The most important space in this project is in fact set at ground level. Areas planted with grass are located under the pilotis. It could be argued that it is a sort of park in which citizens can stroll freely, except for the space reserved for the vehicles, ambulances and training activities of the fire service. A park in which red vehicles are lined up in the midst of the vegetation, while other, silver-coloured ones shoot off with sirens blaring. As people walk by with their dogs, the firemen carry out aerial exercises as if they were trapeze artists. A common and at the same time decidedly unusual scene. In this way people are immediately transported from their everyday lives into a futuristic space that seems to have come out of a science-fiction film.

In recent times we have all had the experience of being bored in parks, places that certainly do not facilitate communication between the inhabitants of a city. You can't expect to create a natural space worthy of the name with a bit of grass, a bit of water and a bit of space for children to play. Ought not our parks also to be fabulous and fanciful spaces that act on the virtual body and not just on the real one?

Just as Le Corbusier had proposed, in this project the pilotis delimit a space for the public. Today adding vegetation is no longer sufficient to turn an area into a place for the community. The unexpected combination of greenery and an extremely unusual function, like that of the firemen's park, produces new stimuli in people's virtual bodies. As in the Old People's Home, people dream another community.

"Le Corbusier along simple lines" is my current interpretation of the Le Corbusier who is still transmitting energy to us today. Previously I have written about my ideas concerning the process of evolution from the machine age to the electronic one (*A Garden of Microchips – The Visual Image in the Era of Microelectronics*). This essay was an attempt to assess the extent to which today's architecture and cities produce messages aimed at the virtual body. Le Corbusier had an important message for the body of the machine age. My job is to translate that message for the electronic age, i.e. to propose a version along simple lines of Le Corbusier's architecture in all its force.

April 1994

The Image of Architecture in the Electronic Age

Architecture in the Electronic Age is the Figuration of a Vortex of Information

Since primitive times, the human body has been linked with nature as a member through which water and air circulate. People today are equipped with an electronic body in which information circulates, and thus are linked to the world through a network of information by means of this other body.

The virtual body made up of a flow of electrons is drastically changing the model of communication in the family and community, while the primitive body in which water and air flow still craves for the beauty of light and wind.

The biggest challenge we face is how to integrate these two types of body. Today the same applies to architecture as well. Our architecture has traditionally been linked with nature through the figuration of the vortices that occur in water and air. In contemporary architecture, we must link ourselves with the electronic environment through the figuration of vortices of information. The question is how can we integrate the primitive space linked with nature and the virtual space linked with the world through the electronic network. Space which is able to integrate these two types of body will probably be envisaged as electronic and biomorphic. Just as the figure of a living body represents the locus of movements of air and water, virtual space will most likely be represented as the locus of human activities in the flow of electrons.

Architecture in the Electronic Age is an Extended Form of Media Suit

In the 1960s Marshall McLuhan said that our clothing and our shelters are forms of our skin. Since ancient times architecture has served as a means of adapting ourselves to the natural environment. Contemporary architecture needs to function, in addition, as a means of adapting ourselves to the information environment. It has to function as an extension of our skin in relation to both nature and information. Architecture today must be a media suit.

Clad in mechanical suits called automobiles, people today have had their physical bodies expanded. Clad in media suits, people have their brains expanded. Architecture as media suit is the externalized brain. In the whirlpool of information that surrounds us, people browse freely, controlling the outside world and appearing in it themselves. Instead of dealing with the outside world by armouring themselves in a hard, shell-like suit, people can now do so by wearing a light and pliant media suit which is a figuration of the information vortex.

People clad in such suits are Tarzans in the forest.

Architecture in the Electronic Age Is a Convenience Store of the Media

The curtain has fallen on an age in which museums, libraries and theatres proudly flaunted their archetypal presence. Paintings on walls and books on paper no longer have an absolute existence. They have been turned into something relative by the electronic media.

Media with established styles, such as paintings, books and films, will in future be ranked at the same level, with no hierarchical distinctions, as electronic media such as CDs, CD-ROMs and videotapes. People will use both types of medium in mixtures and in a complementary manner.

Enjoying paintings and books through electronic media will surely demolish the once established, archetypal form of the museum and the library. They will all be fused into one and there will be no boundaries between a museum, an art gallery, a library and a theatre. They must be reconstructed as a *mediathèque*. This will be a convenience store of the media where a variety of media are laid out in arrays, and a convenience store of culture which performs different cultural functions.

This new form of public building resembling a convenience store should not be a symbolic presence standing on a public square. Rather, it should be located near a railway station and stay open until midnight to serve members of the public as they go about their daily lives.

Architecture in the Electronic Age Changes the Concept of Barrier

Various types of barrier in today's society define the form of architecture. These are not just the barriers to be found between healthy people and the elderly or handicapped. There are also great barriers between the administrator of a building and its users, between private and public spaces, between archetypes of different genres such as libraries and museums, between one's mother tongue and a foreign language and between different media such as visual images and printed matter.

The development of electronic media may break down these barriers one after another. The introduction of personal computers is radically changing our mode of communication. The educational and social systems, which have been rigidly restricted by traditional media such as printed matter and painting, will also have to confront the need for drastic reform. In the future, the distinction between the different physical senses, vision, hearing, smell, taste and touch, may become meaningless if the development of electronic media enables signals to be fed directly into the brain or the nervous system without having to rely on organs like the eyes, ears or nose.

The advent of navigation systems for cars has altered the concept of the map. Drivers are constantly informed of their location and guided to their destination by communication satellite. They do not look at the map but are immersed in a virtual space called a map. Such a navigation system can also be employed to guide people around urban or architectural spaces.

Architecture in the electronic age will probably radically change our concepts of the contrast between healthy people and people with handicaps, between administrators and users or between public and private spaces.

Architecture in the Electronic Age Is What Designs Time

The process of design will be changed by the introduction of computers. This does not simply mean that plans drawn in pencil on tracing paper will be replaced by images displayed on the computer screen. We can now erect a virtual building and experience it during the design process. Later we experience another building as a physical entity. The process of shifting from virtual architecture to physical architecture is continuous. These two types of architecture overlap and proceed simultaneously.

Eventually, the physical building will emerge. By that time, however, yet another virtual space will have been created by the introduction of electronic media. Even after

Tarzans in the Media Forest

the physical building is completed, its architectural programmes may continue to undergo modification as new media evolve. Thus there will be no end to our spatial experiences as the real and virtual spaces overlap in our experience. Design in architecture will refer not only to traditional hardware design but also to a more flexible software design that includes programmes. We will be designing time in the same way as we design space.

Kenchiku Zasshi, Tokyo 1995

Mies's Barcelona Pavilion stands out as the most remarkable of all twentieth-century works of architecture. This is overwhelmingly true even in comparison with all of the same architect's subsequent works. Nowhere else do we find a space filled with such "fluidity".

Although the structure is a combination of steel, glass and stone, it does not imply the hardness of these materials. The glass and stone are merely the flat and simple, planar components of the space. Spaces created by the combination of abstract, horizontal planes have an infinite extension, described by Giedion as a mutual intrusion of interior and exterior spaces. Similar results can be found in works by architects of that time belonging to the De Stijl school and by Frank Lloyd Wright, but none of them produces as strong a sense of fluidity as Mies's. This is not simply because of its spatial composition but owes a great deal to the brilliance of the materials. Everything, from the glass to the stone and metal, appears to fuse and flow out into the space. All the elements interact and create an atmosphere of eroticism within the space by their reverberation with the nearby surface of the water. The sensation created by the space is not the lightness of flowing air but the thickness of molten liquid. In the early 1920s, Mies made several drawings of skyscrapers. His later works, such as the Seagram Building and the Lake Shore Drive apartment houses, are generally considered to represent his image and idea of a highrise. Personally, I think it is the pavilion in Barcelona that best embodies the image presented in those drawings. The space composed of glass is given no distinct structure but stands like a pillar made of ice, beginning to melt in the air. It is an architecture born out of images alone and does not yet have a definite form. Of course the pavilion in Barcelona has a structure and a form as it stands on the ground, but the original image of the glass architecture contemplated by Mies in his earliest days is brought vividly to life. This is a work of architecture in which the architectural style is not yet manifest.

Mies is said to be a proponent of the "universal space" which swept through twentieth-century cities: a space created by a homogeneous continuum of grids extending both vertically and horizontally. True, Mies was one of the very first architects to come up with a skyscraper supported by a glass-and-steel curtain wall. And yet the image of a skyscraper that looks like a pillar of ice or the space embodied by the Barcelona Pavilion appear to differ considerably from the transparent office buildings that fill contemporary cities. The transparency of Mies's space seems to be entirely different from that of other modern architecture.

In the essay entitled "Chicago Frame" (in *The Mathematics of the Ideal Villa and Other Essays*, MIT Press, 1976), Colin Rowe discusses this difference. Rowe points out how the space defined by steel frames that already existed in late nineteenth-century Chicago differs from the universal space studied by Mies van der Rohe. It is the difference between a space created as the result of a rational pursuit of pragmatic economic advantage and an ideological manifestation, symbolic of a future world based on technology. This difference, or antagonism, is still seen today between large corporate firms of architects and so-called avant-garde architects. Since there are no other architects who have been as faithful to the use of steel and glass as Mies, his buildings are unquestionably transparent. But the transparency of the Barcelona Pavilion is not that of clear air. Rather, it makes us feel as if we are looking at things deep underwater, and would better be described as translucent. The infinite fluidity we sense in the pavilion must arise from this translucent, liquid-like space. What we experience here is not the flow of air but the sense of wandering and drifting gently underwater. It is this sensation that makes the space distinct and unique.

The simultaneous fluidity and density of the Barcelona Pavilion gradually disappeared even from Mies's own architecture. Its place was soon taken by architectural formalism instead. The once fluid space was lost, as if a liquid had been turned into a solid. And as we await the arrival of the twenty-first century, we are once again in search of an erotic architecture that fuses with the environment.

One night I was given the opportunity to speak at the side of the pool next to Mies's now restored pavilion, using visual images reflected in the water. Several days later, I landed on Lanzarote in the Canaries. The island was a staggering place. It was quite unlike anywhere else I have ever been and far exceeded our expectations. It felt like sitting on the sea bottom. The island must once have been submerged by the sea. There was little fertile soil for plants to grow and most of the surface was covered by rocks, gravel and sand. Strong winds must blow constantly, as there were no plants that grew higher than the waist of a human being. In spite of the fact that it was mid-summer, the plants looked withered and had hardly any green leaves. The bare bushes resembled a coral reef—a coral reef on dry land, the terrain of the sea bottom exposed on the surface.

Underwater, organisms have far greater flexibility than on dry land. On dry land, gravity makes it necessary for fauna and flora alike to be armoured with a rigid and self-supporting framework. Animals can never overcome the rigidity of motion imposed by this framework. But in water, the bodies of animals are subjected to pressure as well as the effects of buoyancy. Pliant and flexible structures stand up better to the flow or pressure of the water. It is better to be receptive and surrender to the forces than to resist them. Thus aquatic flora and fauna tend to sway and dance gracefully. These motions define the forms of living beings. The forms of aquatic creatures represent motions more explicitly than those living on the land. The forms of living beings are the loci of their motions. Indeed, they are "fluid bodies".

What characterizes the Sendai Mediathèque project is the tubular columns that support the floors in six tiers. The slabs, measuring about 50 metres on a side, are supported by thirteen tubes that act as the structure. Each tube is made up of a combination of thin steel pipes and looks like a bamboo basket. The tube houses the means of vertical distribution, such as lifts and stairways, ducts for the air-conditioning system and conduits for the power supply, but it is essentially hollow. Natural light enters from the top of the tube. The tubes have different sizes and shapes depending on the functions they house. The design can be modified to adapt to the plan of the corresponding floor. In other words, these tubes are organic in nature, resembling plants in their forms and actions. They can be said to be biomorphic structures.

On the drawings that I made at the very first stage of the project I scribbled the words "seaweed-like columns" next to the tubes. The columns were conceived as structures that sway and dance like seaweed in the water. Thus the volume, measuring 50 metres on a side and about 30 metres in height, is the embodiment of a tank of water. What we had pictured in our minds was thirteen tubes softly swaying in the virtual water that fills the tank.

The Sendai Mediathèque is a new type of public facility that features a library and art galleries. Naturally, it should be a model library and a model museum of the next generation, equipped with an advanced computer network. What is the true image of an architectural space where new media are used in abundance? Why must we picture the space intended for electronic media as "water" or as "fluid bodies in water"? A graphic designer skilled in the use of the computer says he has the odd sensation that part of his body starts to flow into the screen whenever he sits at a computer. "The inside of a computer is of course not inside myself, but it is not outside either." The boundary is vague and he cannot tell how far the self extends. In the electronic media time and space are different from those we experience in daily life. As we step into their world, as the designer says, "a strangely comfortable sensation surges up inside me". And he goes on, "when I am sitting at a computer, I feel like I'm wading in the water's edge, that I am being linked with another world" (*Asahi Shimbun*, 19 July 1994).

Fluids such as blood and lymph make up some 50 to 60% of the human body and more than 80% in the case of a newborn child. We may compare the human body to a stream in so far as fluids flow and circulate inside it. It connects with the world by means of water. Notwithstanding that fact that people, even today, cannot live without water, the system by which it is supplied to us is completely hidden from our eyes in contemporary cities. And we tend to forget that our bodies are part of nature. But we are reminded of this fact very clearly if we pay a visit to Bangkok. The city of Bangkok has a very well-developed network of canals and a large number of people live by and on the water. Looking at the way they live, we realize that our own lives must once have been very closely related to water. Water jugs stand in line on terraces. People dip and bathe in the turbid water and wash their clothes and dishes in the canal. They live like amphibians. Watching them, we can understand why Buckminster Fuller assumed that humankind originated at the waterfront in Southeast Asia.

The fact that the Thais worship Naga, the god of water, supports this. The gently rippling sea-snake Naga frequently adorns buildings and ships in Thailand. The elegant movements of Thai dancers also remind us of Naga. It is hard to believe they have the same rigid skeleton as other terrestrial organisms. Rather, they seem to lead a supple existence like plants and animals that sway and dance in the water.

The graphic designer poses a serious question when he says, "just as water makes us realize that a human being is part of a greater nature, electronic media may modify or change the meaning or boundary of a human being, especially of the individual". By entering into the computer screen, he became aware of the possibility of orienting the self toward the outside, a self that used to be excessively introverted. In other words, recognizing the flow of electronic media inside him made him realize once again that the human body is part of nature.

The new technology is not antagonistic to nature. Rather, it is creating a new kind of nature. If nature as we have always known it is to be considered real, then this artificial nature should probably be called virtual. And we people of the modern age are provided with two types of body to match these two types of nature: the real body which is linked with the real world by the fluids flowing inside it, and the virtual body linked with the world by the flow of electrons.

In the East, "nature" has always meant the basic principle of the cosmos. In 4 BC, for example, the Chinese philosopher Lao-tzu taught that nature continues along its own path in accordance with cosmic rules regardless of any human act. According to this philosophy, the human body is not independent of the world but an integral part of a continuum that links it with the world.

Banzan Kumazama, a Japanese philosopher of the early Edo period (seventeenth century), discussed the integrity and continuity found in humankind and nature in terms of the Neo-Confucian concept of *ki* or "spirit": "As our body is born from nature and nurtured by it, we human beings exist in nature as its children, no matter how small we may be physically. The *ki* of yin and yang and the five elements that fill the heaven and the earth make up our body. Turbid and thick *ki* takes a physical form and becomes the body, while clear and light *ki* fills the inside of the body to make it act" (Toshio Kuwako, *Philosophy of Ki*, Sin'yosha).

"Circulating in the cosmos like air, the spirit or *ki*, becomes condensed and solidified to form the bodies of organisms. Bodies are made up of liquid and solid, but basically they are gas. The gas condenses and solidifies to form the body, and the air is taken inside and fills the body. Once inhaled, the air is quickly exhaled again, and there is no distinction between the self and others."

According to this way of thinking, each creature in the cosmos is given a certain form, but creatures are all fluid and constantly changing. They continually undergo phase shifts from gas to liquid to solid while remaining linked with the world. "All things are in flux" indeed.

In the modern era, however, this cosmic view was forgotten, and people began to attach importance to the individual, physical body. People are now obsessed with a way of thinking that places the individual at the centre of the world, and then dissects the world into pieces. We have lost sight of human relations rooted in the community and are now beginning to lose sight of blood ties as well. Today, even the family unit is no longer secure. People end up as isolated beings and start to feel alienated and empty.

Just as we reached this point, electronic technology began to emerge and reminded us of the world we had almost forgotten. The "flow of electrons" overlapped with the flow of "*ki*" and "water".

Electronic devices such as personal computers, fax machines, mobile telephones and car navigation systems alter our physical senses from day to day. Mobile telephones are an essential tool for today's high-school students. They carry them wherever they go and are constantly communicating with their peers. For them, talking with their friends over the mobile telephone is like chewing gum. It is not their mouths but their eardrums that demand stimulation. By hearing the voices of their friends at all times, they seek to avoid being left alone. Their bodies crave for the flow of electrons just as they need water and air.

A car navigation system also alters our physical senses. It allows us to confirm the position of our cars by radio waves transmitted from a satellite. The location of a car and the instructions needed for it to reach its destination are displayed on the screen at all times by means of a map on CD-ROM. With a conventional map printed on a sheet of paper, our physical bodies existed on a different plan, outside the map. The space on the map was abstract and we had to translate it into a three-dimensional space in our minds in order to learn the actual location by comparing it with reality. With the new system, the location of a car on the display overlaps with reality. We no longer have to dislocate our physical bodies to a different plane from that of the real world.

As the aforementioned graphic designer said, our isolated self is linked with the outside world by means of electronic media whether we like it or not. The concept of inside and outside is deeply rooted in the autonomy of the self. The emergence of new media obscures the boundary between the inside and the outside without our realizing it.

When viewed from that angle, we have to admit that the real, physical body and the virtual one no longer contradict one another but overlap completely. To an analytical mind, there may appear to be a division into two bodies, but in fact they are integrated and unified. If we are determined to make a distinction, we could say that the former is an analogue kind of body which is not transparent, while the latter is a digital body and transparent.

What I have said so far about the physical body also applies to architecture and urban space. We have long defined architectural and urban space as something independent of nature. In Asia, however, they were extensions of nature and therefore fused with it. They maintained a relative position in nature and were alive, breathing in and out in response to the natural flux. The boundary between inside and outside was vague both in architecture and in urban spaces.

The houses that line Bangkok's canals clearly show us that the people who live there are totally free from the architectural concept of inside/outside. Broad terraces overhang the water, stairs run down into it and rooms are usually left open onto the terrace. Bougainvillea in full bloom almost invades the houses. Even though the canals provide their essential means of transport, their homes are left exposed to them, defenceless. There is no vanity or concealment. Here the concept of inside/outside refers to the relationship between architecture and environment and not to that of interior/exterior in the symbolic sense it has in society. An ideally comfortable relationship is formed between a human being and nature as there is no boundary between inside and outside, no matter how poor he or she may be. Not very long ago, we used to live like this in our traditional houses. People in contemporary cities, however, can no longer return to such a life even if they see it as a kind of utopia. It would be inconceivable for them to give up their mobile telephones or fax machines.

So what kind of environment should people be looking for when they are surrounded by electronic devices?

Marshall McLuhan once said that clothing is an extension of our skin and that shelter is the communal skin or clothing. As early as the 1960s, he predicted that the development of electronic media would cause our then heavily vision-oriented culture to shift toward a dependence on cutaneous sensations. If we are to define hearing as one of the cutaneous senses, people fitted with electronic devices like a cyborg will no doubt grow obsessed with cutaneous sensations. Young people who cannot live without a mobile telephone need to stimulate their skin continually through their organs of hearing.

If clothing and architecture are both extensions of our skin functioning as mechanisms for controlling energy and protecting us from the world outside as McLuhan said, then their function as membranes would certainly be very important. In other words, clothing, architecture and cities must train and polish their epidermises (outer layers) to make them extremely sensitive and delicate. This epidermis can no longer be the conventional thick and heavy layer of cloth or wall that used to protect us from the outside world. It must operate as a highly efficient sensor capable of detecting the flow of electrons.

Moreover, the membrane needs to be soft and flexible. Rather than being rigid and dense like a wall, architecture as epidermis must be pliant and supple like our skin and be able to exchange information with the world outside.

It would be more appropriate to call architecture clad in such a membrane a media suit. Architecture is an extension of clothing and therefore a media suit. It is a transparent suit meant for a digitalized and transparent body. And people clad in transparent media suits will live in virtual nature, in the forest of media. They are Tarzans in the media forest.

2G, 2, 5 January 1997

345

Three Transparencies

1. *Fluid Transparency*

Standing in front of a gigantic tank at the aquarium means experiencing the curious sensation of being in two different places at the same time. With just a transparent wall in between, "here", on this side, lies the dry land surrounded by air, while "there", on the other side, stretches a world of water. Not long ago, tanks in aquaria were relatively small structures, with openings in their walls like windows which you could look through. The aquaria of today, by contrast, are equipped with incredibly large tanks containing huge volumes of water that exert a terrific pressure, held back by layers of acrylic just a few tens of centimetres thick. Looking through walls of this type constitutes a considerable paradigm shift, comparable to the difference between an architectural elevation and a cross-section. When you look through a window, the view of what is on the other side remains intact and self-contained. This is not true of a transparent wall: an environment that ought to be penetrable everywhere is suddenly limited by an invisible boundary, leaving the sectioned front exposed. In the past, visiting an aquarium was like going to the circus; now it is an experience of total immersion.

Thanks to these new aquaria, we now have a clearer vision of aquatic life, of how underwater plants and animals move in ways that would be unimaginable on dry land. Especially in deeper parts of the ocean, inaccessible in the past, where the greater pressure of the water renders divers lethargic and weighs down the waving fronds. Like the serene dramatic art of the Japanese Noh Theatre, everything is in continual movement but time is slowed down, with each cell and body part held in suspension by a halving of its speed. Moreover, in the reduced transparency of water everything looks as if viewed through a silk curtain. A soft scattering of light that, at a certain distance, brings out the reality of things. The vital physicality is lost and what you see looks like candied fruit floating in a gelatinous universe.

The image I started out with for a project that is currently under construction was an aquatic scene. A transparent cube, situated right in the middle of the city, faces onto an avenue lined with tall and beautiful cedars and rises seven storeys from a square plan with sides of 50 metres. Seven slender floors are supported by thirteen tubular structures. Each element is an irregular and non-geometric tube and resembles the root of a tree that grows thicker towards the top, diverging and bending slightly as it approaches the surface of the ground. These tubular elements are clad with steel cables woven like basketwork and mostly covered with frosted glass so that they look like hollow and translucent candles.

In the margin of my first sketches of the tubular elements I had written: "Columns like seaweeds". I had imagined soft tubes that waved slowly under water, rubber tubes filled with fluid. Without resorting to the typical wall with windows—neither a glass façade separating the building from the street, nor a sheet of transparent acrylic borrowed from an immense fish tank—I wanted the front to be a section opening onto a different world.

But why an aquatic image for a building on dry land? In the first place, water is the primary moulding element, the source of all the forms of life. When trees, for example, fork repeatedly from the trunk to the branch to the leaf tip, they resemble rivers which collect water from their tributaries and carry it to the sea. The opaque density of the trunk that splits into more and more slender branches gradually forms an intricate membrane and finally attains the virtual transparency of the leaves—the very image of fluidity.

If this is true for a tree on land, how much more fluid must be the plants and animals that live under water? Their very forms incorporate this movement. As we see in the fins of fish, the parts involved in movement grow ever more diaphanous towards the extremities. Movement and form come together in fluidity, and the fluidity is always translucent tending to transparency.

2. *Erotic Transparency*

Translucent objects seem always to be in transition from the opaque to the transparent. I am reminded of the metamorphosis of insects: immediately after emerging from their hard chrysalides the transparent creatures are covered with a milky liquid; and then, in a moment, contact with the air turns them into adult insects with hard and crystalline wings. An incomplete, translucent, gelatinous state evokes images of transformation; as soon as it becomes transparent, solid and fixed, it loses its ambiguous fascination.

Some architecture, like the early works of Mies van der Rohe, almost achieves this gelatinous and semi-fluid translucence. Famous as the man who invented the transparent glass-and-steel architecture of the twentieth century, at the beginning of his career Mies used opaque building materials—brick and stone. And then, in the twenties, his architecture underwent an abrupt metamorphosis. In the sketches for his "glass skyscrapers" and in the pavilion in Barcelona, truly translucent and fluid spaces were created.

The German Pavilion for the Barcelona Exhibition of 1929 had a steel structure, but its flamboyant dynamism came from the stone and glass. The mosaic of stone that faces the flat and abstract composition of the walls traces an undulating motif that is audaciously fluid. Suspended between these stone-clad walls, the screens of greenish frosted glass create the impression of tanks filled with water. The various floors are reflected in an orthogonal pattern without ever really meeting up. Instead, they are superimposed on the lower surfaces of the external pool to create a fluid space, producing the image of a solid form that is slowly dissolving into the liquid state. A highly erotic space.

In the same way, the Japanese designer Shiro Kuramata was very much in tune with this transparency in contemporary society and pursued it actively in his creative work. This too he tackled in an extremely creative manner, sometimes taking on the part of the "villain" who proposes things in bad taste. From the start of his career in the sixties, he frequently made use of transparent acrylic in his furniture designs. In one of his acrylic chairs, the piece of furniture disappears completely as an object, leaving nothing visible but the "primitive" act of sitting. His transparent cupboards and chests of drawers were even more effective in this sense for the simple reason that the act of storing things, of putting things away, consists essentially in concealing objects in opaque containers where they are invisible. Here, on the contrary, the clothing on hangers and the folded garments are openly displayed, as if suspended in empty space. The material forms of the containers vanish and only the act of storing remains—in a space that is also steeped in eroticism. The effect of this transparent touch is not very different from that of going into a forbidden room and glimpsing something that you are not supposed to see.

Three years before his death, Kuramata made a direct reference to the eroticism of transparency in one particular object. The transparent acrylic chair "Miss Blanche" (1988) attained a high degree of transparency thanks to the artificial roses that were scattered in its "empty" interior. The red petals floated all over the place as if they were being carried by a stream; floral designs set free of the heavy upholstery fabrics of the past and transformed into real flowers suspended in a crystal-clear and liquid space.

Just where making things transparent ought to have been the most abstract of gestures, the liberation of form in a pure space, it unexpectedly has a presence that is almost too real and seductive. This polarity, these surprising inversions, this ambiguity between the real and unreal, are choices clearly dictated by the taste for the transparent.

3. Opaque Transparency

Yet transparency is not always so light and clear. We Japanese have readily renounced all our opacity in order to fit in with today's society. We live transparent lives that cannot be distinguished from those of other people within an extremely efficient system of regulation. Urban Japan has become a drugstore crammed with convenience foods wrapped in plastic and put out on display on its shelves. We are just signs, totally transparent and lacking any scale of values. Moreover, this mediocre and transparent existence is very comfortable. And yet, as the individual grows increasingly transparent in contemporary society, architecture and the city are on the contrary becoming more and more opaque.

One of the characteristics of the contemporary city is that each space is completely isolated from the next. Inside houses each room is separated from the others; there are walls everywhere. Perhaps this is the destiny of social control: that a vast and standardized urban landscape is fragmented into places almost totally devoid of mutual relationships. And this is particularly true of commercial outlets, where the split between the spaces inside and outside dramatically facilitates the "outfitting" of the rooms. Seen from a certain distance, these appear to be clearly organized on the basis of similarities and peculiarities: apparently idiosyncratic spaces that are in reality nothing but the accumulation of introspectively inflated fragments of homogeneity—this is the city of today.

Walking through the stations of Shinjuku or Shibuya, two of the most complex spatial configurations in Tokyo, is a really strange experience. The levels of communication that intersect, the interchanges of railway and underground lines, the three-dimensional nodes of interposed walkways and the commercial spaces that surround, penetrate and rise above this labyrinth are all designed to make us lose our way in a world without views and almost completely isolated from the outside. The only clues we are given are provided by signs and verbal directions. When we find ourselves inside this complicated spatial experience, the only thing we can do is create an equally abstract and semiotic mental space for ourselves.

What is asked of an architect today is to discover the "relationships" between these fragmented and hermetically sealed spaces; to find the opaque-but-transparent connections between the stratified spaces. I attempted to create an "opaque transparency" in a project commissioned by a Japanese city, a fire station that was completed two years ago. Almost all the functional aspects of the building have been raised on rows of pillars and located on the upper floor. This so-called "pilotis" structure made it possible to maintain a continuity with the street on the ground floor in the form of open spaces planted with vegetation that resemble a park and are freely accessible to the public. The only proviso to be respected in the layout of this space was that it had to include around a dozen fire engines and ambulances, as well as equipment for the training of the firemen. At the centre of a grass-covered area are set two tower structures, one large and one small, fitted with ropes and a long rope bridge linking the two towers for the daily exercises of the firemen. The station is also equipped with a swimming-pool for practicing rescues in water and a small gymnasium. Ordinary citizens can visit the complex and watch the firemen doing their exercises. At the same time, they can see the activities that are being carried out on the floor beneath from the corridors that link the individual rooms on the upper floor. There are also skylights set in the floor of the upper story that permit communication between the different levels. The basic concept of the project was that the fire station should be a "presence" in the daily life of the small city and not just in emergencies.

The building in itself is not glazed or transparent but several openings set at random in the floor create a certain dynamic relationship between the levels above and below—creating what I call an "opaque transparency". Building with glass it is not the only way to obtain transparency. On the contrary, the work that needs to be done today is the establishment of relationships between spaces otherwise separated by walls.

In *The Mathematics of the Ideal Villa and Other Essays* (1976), Colin Rowe defined these relationships as "phenomenal transparencies" rather than "literal transparencies". In the introductory essay he cited as examples of "phenomenal transparency" the early works of Le Corbusier or the painting of Fernand Léger, and as "literal" examples, the Bauhaus architecture of Walter Gropius and the works of art of László Moholy-Nagy. In other words, while the latter examples are simply made up of transparent elements, the former stratify "blind", non-transparent elements to create transparent interrelationships. Let us take the example of a famous work by the young Le Corbusier, the Villa Stein at Garches (1926–28) with its abstract stratification of overlapping vertical and horizontal floors. The effect is such that, notwithstanding the real volume of the material building, the composition becomes a Cubist painting with floors without visual depth that advance and recede in a non-Euclidean space.

Now, more than ever, architecture has to produce spatial relationships of this kind because, in spite of our apparent transparency, we go on, like faded products lined up on the drugstore shelves, building ever more solid barriers between us. I'm not saying that we should go back to the collective life of the world-without-walls in the past—even if we could. The key lies in introducing new openings into the walls that we have already built.

Suké Suké, Nuno Nuno Books, Tokyo 1997

A Body Image Beyond the Modern: Is There Residential Architecture Without Criticism?

1. *Fissures in Contemporary Society*

The first house I designed was completed twenty-eight years ago. This was also the first time I used the medium of architecture to send out a message to the world.

"There is no doubt that the position of architecture in the city is fast losing its social meaning. But if, as a lone and frail individual, one insists on continuing with the work of design after the inexpressible and futile collapse of logic in the world of architecture, the only way to do so is to expose the absurdity of one's surroundings ... For me, designing a home is a question of tracing the deep rift between myself as the designer and the future occupant of the house. Perhaps one should use the term "bridging" rather than "tracing" when speaking of this gap, but the fact is that we lack the common terms that would be required to bridge it. So this effort can only begin in contradiction: by building insurmountable walls with an awareness of that unbridgeable gap" (from "The Act of Design is the Tracing of One's Thought Processes as They Become Distorted", in *Shinkenchiku sekai*, October 1970).

As this passage suggests, I began the work of design out of a sense of unbearable frustration over the state of society and the city. This feeling was given blatant expression in aluminium-clad exteriors that flaunted their dents and irregularities in the sunlight, and in cylinders of light thrusting upwards without meaning. At the time, this was the best and only critical tool I had.

Over the last ten years my design work has focused almost exclusively on public architecture. The feelings I have about this work are almost the same as those expressed in the message I sent by way of that small house twenty-eight years ago. It is impossible to conceive of a common language capable of bridging the gap with the systems of actual cities and societies. We are left dumbfounded by our awareness of the vast size of that gap. Not a few times, during discussions with local authorities, I have been tempted to smash the models and storm out of the room.

Recently, however, I have begun to worry that staring into that gap has closed me off from the world around me. Sometimes I wonder if I am not taking refuge in the comfort of the "critique" as a selfish justification for my own condemnation of society.

Architecture and other creative practices often draw their inspiration from a sense of frustration and anger about the world outside. Sometimes they also stem from irritation and insecurity arising out of an inability to express one's emotions directly. Whether hot or cool, these emotions are linked to the desire to express oneself.

Yet even if their origins lie in individual impulses, the resulting expressions ultimately leave the hands of their creators and take on a life of their own. Paintings and novels remain in the museum or the bookstore, but architecture makes its appearance in our surroundings. Buildings are there for anyone to see in unmediated form. They are intended for use in people's lives and for specific purposes. Architects have no choice but to face up to the social or public nature of their work. Can antisocial, negative expressions arising out of personal frustration and anger ever be redeemed socially as individual expressions of rejection or questioning? This has been the most difficult issue I have confronted designing public architecture over the last ten years. Is it possible to turn negative expressions into positive ones that inspire trust without sacrificing their energy?

But even private residences take on an independent existence in their environment once they are completed. Their status as private property does not stop them from having social significance. In this sense the same problem exists in theoretical terms for both public and private architecture, but there is a difference when it comes to the actual process of designing public architecture.

2. *The Misunderstanding of Criticism*

By complete coincidence I had no opportunities to design private residences for some time after I began designing public facilities. It was not until two years ago that I finally got the chance to design two homes for the first time in many years. I was lucky enough to have two excellent clients and it was wonderful to rediscover how enjoyable it can be to design a private house. More than that, though, I was just happy to be dealing with people's homes again.

Both of the projects were low-budget, but the sites were unexpectedly large, which meant we had to cut back on finishing materials. The exteriors ended up looking like simple factory sheds, but the projects were eventually completed after tense but friendly disagreements with the clients. For the first time in years I felt certain that the clients and I were occupying the same space. This sense of commonality made the spaces modest ones, but also kept them from straying into too radical an expression.

It is impossible to experience this sort of commonality with public architecture. There are moments in certain projects when one feels that one has shared a space with specific individuals. But the communication as a whole is interrupted by a succession of gaps, so that it is nothing but an assemblage of irreparable fissures.

I have used the term "criticism" to refer to the absence or presence of this kind of rupture. At a round-table discussion I once claimed that there is no criticism in the design of private residences. For me, this was a natural expression of how I felt just after completing the two residential projects mentioned above. I felt there were no fissures and no need to directly vent any anger or frustration. I felt at once disoriented and happy to have been able to design something that lay outside my usual obsession with the language of criticism. And yet I was not sure if this particular solution was mine alone, so I added the caveat that this depends of course on how one defines criticism.

So I was quite astonished to read a response to this comment of mine which took it to mean that I had set my sights exclusively on public architecture and had no interest in looking for themes in the design of private residences. And even that established architects in general were no longer concerned with the design of homes. I felt sorry for myself at having been so completely misunderstood. But I prefer not to bring the discussion down to such a personal level here.

I think it would be more interesting to expand on the theme of the critical character of residential architecture as it has moved from the level of my personal feelings to a more general one. This has to do with the fact that when I designed my first home in the seventies I thought that a critical attitude towards society was part of the architect's ethic. Yet this is an idea that has been with us since the dawn of modernity. Architects have maintained a negative attitude towards society ever since modernist architecture set out to change it. And they have worn their rejection by mainstream society like a badge of honour. But as long as architects fail to find more positive terms in which to speak to their society, they will go on creating an architecture of exclusion. And residential buildings offer us the easiest way out from this narrow path.

This is why the subtitle of this essay is not "Is there criticism in residential architecture?" but "Is there residential architecture without criticism?".

3. A Flock of Reclusive Aesthetes

When I sat down to write this article I looked through the designs of young architects discussed in this journal over the last two years and found that many of them had a symptom in common. They were large and cubic and strived for transparency. Hasegawa Isamu has aptly caught the essence of the "transparency syndrome" that affects these designs in the passage from his article for the April 1998 issue of this journal that I quote below.

"The structures are made of reinforced steel or wooden frames and the entrances extremely large, with a peculiar insistence on transparency. The slightly built walls are flat, utterly neutral and make not the least pretence of structural strength … Pleasantly light and somehow makeshift, these houses nonetheless contain inconspicuous citations of the avant-garde architecture of the twenties, with whose forms they are gracefully enlivened. These are all houses designed by young architects born in or around 1960. As I look at them my sense of taste goes numb and I feel a kind of aphasia coming on."

The prevalence of this kind of design in the pages of this journal may simply be the result of selection by the editors, but it has become quite common in the real world as well. Of course my own work has many of the same characteristics. And I am certainly conscious of the fact that as someone who has made lightness, impermanence and transparency his own themes, I must bear some responsibility for this syndrome affecting those born twenty years after me. And yet I cannot help but sympathize with Hasegawa when he says that these works have numbed his sense of taste and left him speechless. Many of these houses built by young architects seem to be characterized by a kind of feeble introversion. Of course this does not hold for all of them, but for the most part they begin and end with the sophistication of a light and transparent aesthetic. They are beautiful and delicate, but they avoid conflict with the outside and remain disdainfully closed to reality. In other words, the vast majority of homes designed today fail to come up with any clear critique even while they the continue to insist on the critical character of modernism. Only a precious few manage to confront reality in a proactive fashion.

But if we were to trace the roots of the negative criticism seen in these residences we would end up right back in the twenties. They do in fact subscribe to the language of modernism and are characterized by the strong critique of reality that was the goal of early modernist architecture. I myself, as I mentioned earlier, have also insisted that my own work be critical. But I cannot help feeling that a negative attitude towards today's society tends to separate you from the land you live in and cause you to turn your back on it.

4. A Home of the Purest Modernism, or the Tragedy of O'Gorman

This spring I was the curator of an exhibition at a gallery in Tokyo devoted to a single home built in the early 1930s, the Diego Rivera and Frida Kahlo House located in Mexico City and recently restored. I was lucky enough to see this house on a recent visit to Mexico, though I knew nothing about it beforehand. I did not even know the architect's name.

From the moment I got out of the car in front of the grounds, this house made a powerful impression on me. First of all, its pure and stoic form was more than enough to overturn all the images I had associated with Mexico. The house was designed by Juan O'Gorman for the two highly original painters famous for their tumultuous relationship and completed in 1932, just one year after Le Corbusier finished his Villa Savoye. The two painters were married but worked independently of each other, so O'Gorman designed the house with two living spaces and studios in separate wings. The two wings, connected only by a bridge stretching from roof to roof, are each simple cubes that seem to float in mid-air. Painted Indian red and marine blue respectively to evoke the Mexican landscape, the two wings are surrounded by a cacti fence and raised on pilotis, so that they are completely cut off from the ground. Composed in the language of pure modernism, this work of architecture was not just separated from the earth but seemed utterly independent of the land of Mexico, where a sense of place still hangs thick in the air.

Contemporary Mexican architecture is perhaps most strongly associated with the work of Luis Barragán, but this house by O'Gorman is profoundly different in character. Barragán's homes blend much more gently into the Mexican landscape. Unlike O'Gorman, he often used festive colours to create harmony with the surroundings. The rough textures that denote his surfaces and the liberal use of trees in his substantial entryways only serve to heighten the sense of an intimate relationship with the earth. The volume as a whole may be based on the language of modernism, but there is always a tendency to downplay it, to dull its edges and cover it in vegetation in order to avoid as far as possible any clash with the environment. Barragán's architecture is an accommodation of modernism to the land, a revisionist truce with the local. As such, it offers not just a new lifestyle, but one that is tranquil, rich and established.

In O'Gorman's house, the Diego wing in particular, with its sawtooth roof and external spiral staircase built out of concrete, was clearly inspired by the Ozenfant House and Studio (1923), but it goes even further than the early houses of Le Corbusier in its pursuit of functionality. The quest for rationality and economy evident in the columns, floors, walls and staircases, all of which O'Gorman is said to have designed right down to the structural calculations, is taken to the extreme. The same is true for the precision of the horizontal and vertical surfaces and each element (from the doors to the window sashes, the dust ?chute?, the gutters and even the furniture) was thought out down to its last detail with a view to pure functionality and economy. A comparison with the Villa Stein at Garches (1927) and Villa Savoye (1931), regarded as two of Le Corbusier's early masterpieces, will make clear the extent to which O'Gorman's work was shaped by the search for pure functionality. Like the Rivera and Kahlo House, both these buildings have clean-cut edges based on simple geometrical volumes, but the architectural meanings embedded in them are quite different. Le Corbusier's works are concerned with functionality and proposing new ways of living, but at the same time they are skilfully infused with tendencies derived from both classicism and abstract painting. As Colin Rowe points out (in *The Mathematics of the Ideal Villa*), the proportions and phrasing of the exteriors are reminiscent of Palladio's villas, while inside curved lines like the ones used in Purist painting form layers (creating an impression of transparency). Even while Le Corbusier was making proposals for a new kind of city, he went on incorporating both the order of historical architecture and the experiments of avant-garde art.

Seen in this light, Le Corbusier's *Five Principles of Modern Architecture* (1926), which were supposed to make possible a new lifestyle, come to look like little more than a means of justifying his own architecture through the logic of modernism. More than Le Corbusier, it was the twenty-six-year-old O'Gorman who was dreaming up the new life that could be made possible through the five elements of pilotis, roof gardens, horizontal rectangular windows and free vertical and horizontal surfaces. All five of these elements were offered to society in the purest form in the Rivera and Kahlo House. Could we not say that it was only in this moment of single-minded pursuit of functionality that the language of modernism was able to burst out of its closed context and sublimate its identity as critical language? The best evidence we have of this surely lies in the fact that Rivera and Kahlo, in spite of all their fanatical championing of the culture of ancient Mexico and their support of the Communist movement, were so proud of this purely modernist space.

But O'Gorman's quest was not sustainable. In the early thirties he worked on many social programmes, including schools and communal housing, but gave up architecture by the end of the decade in order to take up painting. Later he threw himself into the mural painting movement, partly under Rivera's influence. His commitment to social reform remained constant, but the form it took shifted to the opposite pole from the pure, abstract space of Western modernism.

But O'Gorman's transformation did not stop there. In 1953 he moved into a cave-like home he had designed and filled with Amerindian furnishings. Finally, in 1982, he moved into a modernist house he had designed as a young man and took his own life. O'Gorman's pure and thoroughgoing pursuit of modernist space most likely forced upon him an all too clear vision of the gulf separating the language of modernism from the Mexican culture. This was indeed an unbridgeable gap.

5. *A Body Image beyond the Modern*

The two worlds that Juan O'Gorman expressed symbolically in his life are linked with two contrasting images of his body, one conceptual and one visceral. The former was an unnatural body aiming for an abstract, utopian world conceived on a conscious level, while the latter was a natural one which related to the traditions of ancient Mexico. People of every age have tried to preserve in their domestic space memories of the land that are inscribed in their bodies. This transformation of memory into space happens not just with personal memories but also with those of families and whole local communities. Houses built in this way pass through generations of desperate struggle with nature until they become almost like extensions of the human skin.

At the same time, however, people have always striven to build another kind of home to house their memories of the future. In this century in particular, with the startling advances made by technology, many have dreamt of that other house. Examples of this are provided by the attempts to bring the exhilarating sensations we experience in such mechanical spaces as cars and airplanes into our homes. When people try to slip into skins made of steel, glass, aluminium or plastic, they experience a liberation of their bodies as if they were moving into another dimension. And they try to expand that feeling of liberation into another skin and another body. It is a liberation from the ties of their land and from the customary life of earthbound families and communities.

I referred to the body that seeks a home which will be a memory of the future as an unnatural one, but now it is changing into one which experiences the universe. By now it should be possible to think of it as one that is seeking a new and different kind of nature. The body in search of the machine has gone through further expansions until it has begun to seek nature as a memory of the future. This is what we call the virtual body.

O'Gorman's Rivera and Kahlo House was shaped by the search for a body on the part of a consciousness bewitched by the machine age. But the attempt failed when it was rejected by another body of strong communal memories bound to the earth. Brought back to himself, O'Gorman tried to give himself back to the memories of the earth, only to fail again. He could not bear having two bodies at once.

But these two bodies are still with us as we live our lives today and the chaos of our urban environment can be seen as the consequence of our striving towards them. Many architects continue in the modernist tradition and use its language to speak of their work, lingering ambivalently and never finding a place to touch down. And yet the power of the land that was supposed to engage our fire has lost its strength to modernization and finds its body exposed in the shrunken world of the local. The situation may not be comparable to that of revolutionary Mexico at the beginning of the twentieth century, but it seems to me that the flock of young architects mentioned earlier symbolizes a Japan that has passed the peak of its modernization and lost sight of its goals. Hasegawa's taste and words succumbed to their ambiguity, to the sight of these architects without the confidence to be the heirs of modernism and without the power to create something of meaning to society. To lose one's social language and shut oneself up in a sophisticated aesthetic is merely to justify a stifling frustration in the name of a negative critique. We can only hope that these frustrated architects can go beyond their bodies as the inheritors of modernism, since no future memories are going to arise from the impasse of two bodies locked in a stalemate. And we must think of a new body image that will help us out of this deadlock. It would not be an unnatural body, but one accustomed to a new nature, and one which would still be able to accept the old. It is only when these two natures come together that houses seeking new bodies will start to speak a positive language.

Shinkenchiku, 1998

Blurring Architecture

Sendai Mediathèque Report
"Under Construction"

Two operations are proceeding simultaneously at opposite extremes, one on the construction site and the other on the computer screen.

The site is filled with steel. Countless steel sheets and pipes are suddenly plumped down in the middle of urban space. Gradually they are being fastened together and assembled to make one massive sculpture in steel. The sound of dozens of welders hammering on their sheets of metal echoes from morning to night, while sparks fly from their torches. And the steel dust dyes the air as black as smoke belched from a chimney. It is work that somehow seems too primitive for a construction site in the computer age, work that draws our attention to "things" through what looks like a violent act in this world of mass consumption.

Meanwhile, innumerable drawings scroll across an enormous screen. Ground plans, elevations, cross-sections, exploded views, facility plans, detailed plans... Plans abandoned when the designs changed, plans still under study. A panoply of two-dimensional architectural signs rendered on the screen and printed out on paper. Superimposed on one another, they appear and disappear by turns, flowing ceaselessly across the surface of the screen. They almost seem to follow in the trail of the design process in the office. This space has nothing to do with "things" and entails nothing more than the manipulation of symbols, signs folding over and into each other without end.

"Blurring architecture" is architecture that unsettles.

By pursuing two kinds of architecture at once, I am attempting to "blur" the field of architecture. In one instance by making "things" as visible as possible, and in the other simply by transforming the flow of "signs" into space.

1999

1. Under Construction
Construction of the Sendai Mediathèque is now complete, almost six years since the City of Sendai first sent out open competition guidelines in December 1994. Furnishings and fixtures are now being installed toward the January 2001 opening date.

This project has been totally unlike any other design work in my experience. Altogether unusual because, to put it bluntly, it was "out of my control". Up until now, with every building I've ever been involved in designing, I always thought I could see how it would come together.

Granted, I encountered problems in planning and on site, and in virtually every case the realized projects came to differ from the initial image, changes I'd like to think I myself kept in sensitive focus. Yet I always had a sense of heading toward something. This time, however, there was no telling where this was going until the very end.

The decisive difference here was that this mediathèque was of no set building typology such as a "museum" or a "library", and the architectural spaces and construction technologies we proposed differed radically from the norm in architecture. And so our confusion began from the very day after our competition proposal was accepted, if for no other reason than we were aware of just how great the gap was between the high ideals sought through the competition and the customary practices to be utilized toward realizing them. The gap went far beyond anything we'd previously experienced following public facility competitions—it was, in a sense, the very embodiment of the essential contradictions and difficulties intrinsic to contemporary architecture. So that in the course of trying to fill in this gap little by little, repeatedly going over mistaken thinking, we were given a rather unprecedented opportunity in the whole of Japanese public facility planning processes.

Most public buildings in Japan come together via unquestioned execution of unquestioned customary programs. Never tread on unfamiliar territory is the general rule. Thus disputes are singularly avoided, and everything gets decided in-house and completed at incredible speed. With the Sendai Mediathèque, however, starting so far afield from the "rules", both the local government and we ourselves initially fell into such confusion that there was no avoiding arguments at various levels.

In fact, during the one-year of construction, the sessions were many where words flew and disputes dragged on irredeemably. Yet after such fruitless arguments, gradually these sessions were replaced by regular round-table discussions between persons specifically concerned with shaping what the mediathèque was to be. These round-table discussions no longer took the form of City-sponsored committees, but were held as volunteer efforts in which our planning team participated together with young researchers and journalists from Tokyo and the Sendai region. But what gave these round-tables meaning was the presence of persons from City Supervision (Sendai City Lifelong Learning Department). That is to say, it was all very ambiguous in character: while the City did not necessarily regard the motions as binding in any way, neither were they seen as entirely inconsequential. It was this very ambiguity that allowed the discussions to move into unknown, thus all the more substantial, territory.

Or to put it the other way around, the building was "already in use" even during construction. And not just in the sense that the homepage was up and running on the Internet. No, here at these sessions to discuss the various unknown quanta of the mediathèque another building took shape, and in it workshops were already in progress.

For instance, one result was the 1988 pamphlet *Sendai Mediathèque Now Under Construction* put out by the Mediathèque Planning Room, which comprised a guide to the project up until the scheduled January 2001 opening. A simple A3 [double-fold] affair, but beginning from the introductory "What is the Sendai Mediathèque?" it presented concise descriptions of the Founding Principles, General Operations, Floor Plans and Special Features of the building, and Pre-opening Activities.

For a city to issue such a limited-period guide to a public facility still under construction is rare enough, but this was not a *fait accompli* pronouncement to the citizens of Sendai. Rather it was an expression of intent to elicit ideas at large about the ways and means of this new public facility mediathèque.

Under "Founding Principles", for example,

we find the following three clauses:
1. To provide the very latest thinking ("spirit") in service
  * flexibly responding to user needs
2. Not an end-point ("terminal") but an interconnection ("node")
  * actively utilizing the advantages of networks to the fullest
3. Free from all handicaps ("barriers")
  * overcoming obstacles to both the healthy and handicapped, users and administrators, whatever the language or culture.

We came to call these Principles the "Mediathèque Charter". These were based on working concepts established in 1995 by the mediathèque project review committee, then further formulated through round-table discussions and exchanging e-mails. Here in particular Eishi Katsura (Assistant Professor, Library Data Science, Tokyo University of Art) and Akira Suzuki (Head, Workshop for Architecture and Urbanism, Tokyo) made major contributions.

And not just the ideals, but the actual business of the mediathèque and all its pre-opening activities, the various proposals worked out by round-table and e-mail between the specialist group centered on these two and project liaisons for the City were all summarized in this pamphlet. By which I mean to say that alongside the construction of the building, the very kind of creative activities inside the mediathèque were already taking place.

Then there were the occasional Mediathèque Planning Room News issued in the form of A4 mini-newsletters. These consisted of interviews with persons involved in various aspects of hardware or software and other work-in-progress reports. Such outreach efforts did more than just let people know about the facility; they actually served as a forum for this new mediathèque direction in thinking, virtually building on paper what might be called the "other mediathèque" apart from the physical structure that was now taking shape.

Then in November 1999, a symposium entitled "Aims for the Mediathèque" was held at the Tokyo Design Center. Panelists included media art curators and designers, educators and journalists; many lively presentations were heard, Katsura and the Lifelong Learning Department Head joining in long hours of talks. One after the next, extremely concrete proposals came forward for things the mediathèque should undertake, functions by which a public facility in the new century might promote media literacy and media consciousness. Such an "open seminar" directed at general participation where, moreover, the specifics of the building are open to deliberation is highly unusual, to say the least.

Usually, by a year before opening, the programmatic dimensions of most public buildings are fixed and immutable. By this point it would be rare for a local administration to offer comment on their project even in a committee of its own convening, let alone open up to outside discussion by those on the receiving end. What made this possible at a symposium jointly sponsored by the City Board of Education was that these

strange relationships had already been going on for several years since construction began.

Of course, arrangements like this do not make for stability. Particularly as they depend upon the voluntary efforts of so many people. Yet if the tension from so many ambiguities and uncertainties could somehow hold through until after the opening, it might well prove a first step toward an ideal "unfinished" public institution that remains open-to-change. A brief review of the actual developments over the last six years should give an indication of the possibilities for such extended free-form circumstances.

2. The Mediathèque Concept
Looking back on the 1995 Sendai Mediathèque competition, it still stands as an altogether unusual event in the history of open competitions in Japan.

One unique aspect, more than distinctive expression as a building per se, was that what was sought was a whole new building "type" (typology). Another peculiarity was the uncompromising transparency and openness of the competition itself.

The Sendai Mediathèque was, in the very first planning stages, conceived as an amalgam of four different programs: a new building for the Sendai Civic Gallery whose lease was coming term (it was housed in a space rented within a department store), a replacement structure for the delapidated Aoba-ku Branch of the Sendai Public Library, improvements in the Sendai Audiovisual Learning Center, and the necessity for an information services center for the audiovisually impaired.

In order to firm up the design competition criteria by which to select an architect for the mediathèque, as well as to sort out the various programmatic complexities from a specialist perspective, the City of Sendai entrusted a research team headed by Professor Sugano at the Architectural Faculty, Tohoku University, Sendai with the task of drawing up competition guidelines. With the results being the following six aspects of consideration:
1. Multi-functionality: all the required institutional functions had to fit within one compact 4000-square-metre site located on Jozenji-dori Avenue in the heart of the city.
2. Art: not merely a large space to hold ongoing regional exhibitions, but also a workshop section with full-time curators, as well as a media center fully equipped to handle the demands of digital age multimedia.
3. Data media (books): in addition to present library functions, offering integrated services of audiovisual materials (ultimately inclusive of even artworks), as well as on-line networking capabilities. Not merely a space for looking at "books", but a place for searching out "data".
4. Operations: unification of previously separate operations in order to realize improved services, rational use of available space and reduced compartmentalization.
5. Urban role: key project in the shaping of the twenty-first century city, intended to put Sendai proudly on the world map. Also, conceived as a leavening agent to liven up

the existing district around the site.
6. Design competition: in order to make a clean sweep of various problems caused by lack of transparency in recent institutional projects initiated by administrations, the architect is to be selected by highly transparent and open methods. (From the Sendai Mediathèque Design Competition Records)
From this we can see that even prior to the launch of the competition, this was to be no conventional facility. Moreover, the choice of Arata Isozaki to chair the selection committee brought the proposal into clear focus. Isozaki urged the City to observe the following three points that might well serve as a model for future public architecture competitions:
1. Openness: the judging process shall be completely open to public scrutiny. The final stage will be broadcast live.
2. Specialization: judges shall be limited to specialists only. And, furthermore, specialists with direct citizen contact experience. Moreover, the architect in charge of implementation is to be decided by personal interview.
3. Vision: qualities sought in applicants, in addition to overall strength in design, are a social vision to substantially re-work plans. Especially with the mediathèque, a building type such as never existed in Japan, re-working the program as new ideas are needed must always be considered as a possibility, to which the administration side must also respond with flexibility. (From the Sendai Mediathèque Design Competition Records)
The part about "re-working the program" here is addressed toward the administration, as can be readily understood from Isozaki's text. That is, the administration must not stay fixed on their own program, but rather be receptive to attractive free proposals from the architect.

Likewise in the design competition application guidelines, the mediathèque is defined as "the image of a new urban function space for a new age, which together with collectively amassing and providing sensual media such as art, intellectual media such as books and other data sources, as well as new media such as electronic audiovisuals that are a fusion of these, will also support each individual citizen in realizing his or her imaginative potential to communicate". Thus, from the very top of the guidelines, the task is set at nothing less than the pursuit of an archetype.

The facility to be known as the mediathèque is not without precedents, albeit few, in the West. Particularly noteworthy are the German model, ZKM, Karlsruhe, dedicated to research fusing art and digital technology, as well as to the cultivation of media artists; and the French model Carré d'Art, Nîmes, centred on a library, yet aspiring to fuse art and data media.

The Sendai approach might seem close to the latter, though in any case it being no mere civic culture meeting hall, the call that went out under the rubric of mediathèque, inclusive of any programatic re-working, was to prove a decisive event for the developments to come.

The definition for the competition stage was

then re-phrased as follows by the project review committee established after the start of master planning and whose members included Koji Taki (writer), Masaki Fujihata (computer artist; Professor, Tokyo University of Art) and Eishi Katsura.

"A facility whose infrastructure of present-day information technology composes a sum intellectual mass, such as may also be used to create new emblematic ideas. Accordingly, while subsuming the functions of library and art museum into a new system, it will answer to the full diversity of citizen access needs."

The mediathèque in this definition thus became "a civic facility aimed at promoting arts and culture and lifelong learning, not by present standards of service, but by supporting participatory, self-expressive activities". The review committee report cited four means by which to realize these aims:

a. an "intelligent environment" equipped with information technologies to meet the demands of the times

b. mutual staff-user support of intellectual pursuits and imaginative activities, not fixed one-sided services

c. network sharing capable services to replace static in-building services

d. constant review of activity programming, study of methods by which to embrace new findings

The establishment of such basic concepts and activity goals at this very early stage was to take on even greater meaning in later discussions. While these goals have yet to filter out to the City and citizens at large, without such definitions the mediathèque would surely have succumbed long ago to the same old conventional model "concrete box" facility. Nor would there probably have been any round-table discussions or e-mail exchange or any other volunteer intellectual activities. The extremely realistic character of the discussions likewise traces back to these concepts. Thus, however great the gap between concept and reality, the above-stated aims and means have certainly already been set in motion throughout the mediathèque.

3. A "Place" Structured of Tubes and Plates

The aim of our proposal as selected was, in a sense, a simple prototypical building. By prototypical, I mean to say, not a specific form of building attuned to one set specific program, but rather a system capable of meeting any and all programatic conditions that might arise. Now that the construction is completed, the building does indeed embody such flexibility, yet is far different in character from the so-called twentieth-century ideal of "Universal Space".

The Sendai Mediathèque is comprised of basic architectural elements: plates (floors), tubes (columns), and skin (façade/exterior walls).

All buildings stripped of extraneous elements reduce down to the fundamental roof plus structure of walls, columns and floors. However, in most cases, these make up a specific compound volume designed to meet a given function, hence they remain ordinary particularized forms.

In the Sendai Mediathèque, however, from its very first conception, we pursued a structural system of only the three above elements, or to put it even more extremely, of only plates (floor slabs) and tubes (tube-columns). This is shown quite clearly in early sketches. Even in the competition-stage model, the proposed building was highly abstract, with all but these three elements pared away.

Of course, in order to make this a real building to be used it was necessary to add on many other elements. Exterior walls to separate inside from out, not to mention numerous partition walls, doors, elevators, stairways in the building as actually constructed. The additional elements are many, so perhaps the realized building is no longer prototypical and thus no different from other buildings. Certainly the building-in-the-making is not as abstract as the competion model.

Nonetheless, over the last five years our team has tirelessly continued to do studies based upon strictly abstract tube-and-plate models. These studies have, in other words, been an exercise on how to maintain the prototypical image even while adding on elements.

Modern architecture is said to have proposed two schemes of prototypical building: Mies van der Rohe's "universal space" and Le Corbusier's "Dom-ino" system. The former being an articulated space composed of a uniform three-dimensional gridwork of posts and beams, more or less adopted in all high-rise office buildings today, indefinitely extendible in principle both vertically and horizontally. Behind this principle lies Mies' belief that all human actions can be achieved within a uniform grid, with no need for any special spatial accommodation to specialized functions.

Instead Le Cobusier's "Dom-ino" solution is composed of columns and flat slabs without beams. If Mies's space is all glass and steel in image, Le Corbusier's is concrete. The "Dom-ino" was to be an image of universality and freedom, yet more than the free-standing homes or low-rise apartments on which it was first premised, it has since proven better suited to the factories of modern industrialization. And in fact, from the 1920s on into the 1930s Le Corbusier himself altered this scheme by freely introducing curved walls and other elements to create a series of beautiful houses.

The construction system we proposed for the Sendai Mediathèque perhaps resembles the "Dom-ino" in its use of flat slabs and columns; whereas Le Corbusier's chosen material was concrete, the Sendai floors are "honeycomb slabs", twin steel plates with ribbing spaced in between, which allows for a far broader span than concrete. Moreover, the columns are hollow bundles of steel pipes, each with its own tubular shape ranging in diameter from 2 to 9 metres. And while each of these tubes is circular in cross-section, the centers shift from top to bottom so that they thread between floors at an angle. By no means organic forms each yet tends toward its own individuated expression. These various hollow tubes serve for vertical transport and energy-core connec-tions, housing elevators, stairways, ducts and cables. Glass-covered tubes serve as-is for air supply and exhaust flues, while also conducting natural light down to the lower levels. Within this stratified man-made environment they function as conduits for the natural elements of light and air.

Another feature of our system is an almost random placement of the tubes in plan and the varying heights for each floor. The intent here is not necessarily toward an industrial productivity or spatial uniformity as with Le Corbusier or Mies, but rather toward a site-specific uniqueness as seen in the treatment of the tubes. In fact, we had originally envisioned running the ribs through the 50-square-metre honeycomb floor at regular 1-metre grid intervals, but as planning progressed it became clear that the distribution of force around the tubes and in middle of the floors differed too greatly, so the ribs were made to radiate out from the tubes. The result is that the distribution of force is not uniform throughout the slabs, so different spaces have different dynamics, a clear indication via structural analyses of the specification of the various spaces on each floor. Introducing the tubes made the floors non-uniform, causing a ripple effect, which brings a fluidity to the spaces.

The spatial experience is not unlike walking through the woods. The presence of trees creates different spaces among which people can choose where to do whatever, in much the same way as humans since ancient times have made places to live within the flux of nature. Long ago, the act of making a building consisted in creating relationships relative to that natural flux. However, architecture has long since cut itself off from such fluidity and turned into a labour of linking up closed rooms. But the body feels stifled sealed inside such static rooms.

Our greatest hope for a Sendai-scheme multilevel building such as this is to create "differentiated spatialities". Designating "room" spaces specific to functions is to limit free action, whereas human actions are originally complex in nature and should not be specified one particular action to one particular space. To assign such single-definition correspondences is modernist planification. Whereas with the Sendai Mediathèque, we do not unilaterally assign "room" spaces nor specify particular uses; rather we want the building to allow users to discover new places and new uses for themselves. A new public building truly ought to invite discovery and some little creativity, shouldn't it? Our efforts to make each tube different properly aspired to creating an architecture that would allow such "discovering places".

Even now as the opening draws imminent, activities to be conducted here at the Sendai Mediathèque are still open to discussion which we'd like to think has something to do with our all-out avoidance of "rooms". Of course, it goes without saying, there are spaces that must be enclosed in order to function. However, compared to the normal public building, Sendai has dramatically fewer closed-off "rooms", all made possible by the intervening tubes.

353

Over these five years, as each floor has continued to evolve, we've drawn up an incredible number of floor plans. All of them are quite abstract, square-framed diagrams on which the activities for each floor are indicated only in brief symbolic notation. They almost look like gameboards where the markings show a game being played. Unlike the typical floor plan completely constrained by established practices, these Sendai floor plans seem to function a bit more freely. Whether or not the game will continue past completion of the building is still anyone's guess.

The third element of the building, the skin forms a huge screen over three of the five outer surfaces (four walls plus roof). The main façade facing onto the Zelkova trees of Jozenji-dori Avenue is covered in a double-paned glass screen (double skin), affixed with a pattern of horizontal stripes as per the original design so as to create subtle visual effects between the exterior and interior and change the appearance of the building continuously throughout the day as light reflects or passes through the two layers of glass. The roof and west side are covered in a metal-louvered screen, both temporary-looking, almost like lightweight screens floating off the volume of the building itself. The east and north sides vary materials with each floor, the spaces between the slabs filled with transparent and semi-transparent glass or metal as expressions of the use-related treatment of the interiors extended outside, although unlike the other three sides this probably seems to directly expose the insides of the skin.

The appearance of these various skin surfaces gives the building an overall presence quite distinct from any previous architecture. The reason seems to be that we have tried to see the building in ways the diametric opposite to the usual single-volumetric expression based on a cosmology of architectural self-containment. Instead, using the given 50-metre-square site, we have cut away a 36-metre-high cube from the space of the city and exposed the volume in cross-section.

4. Blurring Architecture

From late autumn 1999 to the beginning of 2000, our exhibition "Blurring Architecture" was held simultaneously in Aachen, Germany and Tokyo (the Aachen exhibition at the Museum Sümondt Ludwig, 23 October 1999–23 January 2000; the Tokyo exhibition at TN Probe, 16 November–23 December 1999). At both venues we created an installation using computer graphic simulations of the Sendai Mediathèque.

"Blurring" was perhaps not the right word, at least not in the usual sense of haziness or indistinct vision. So why then this title for an exhibition about the Sendai Mediathèque? Simply put, it was because the facility aimed to be "barrier free", taken here in the broadest sense of the words. Not merely in terms of the physical problems faced by the handicapped (as in the mediathèque charter), but also in terms of problems of mutual interpenetrability between divergent programs, not to mention the barriers set up by architecture itself.

As we have already mentioned, public buildings today are typically a series of subdivided and self-contained "rooms", all the easier to control and maintain specialized functions for being closed-in. Opening up ambiguous thresholds only makes things that are much more difficult to manage. And not just "rooms", the same is true for "buildings" as units. As a result, the contemporary city is a line-up of sealed boxes with mutually unrelated contextless exteriors. Even the shapes of public spaces or residential environments are merely the result of ruthlessly cutting off independent enclosed interiors from the world outside. "Blurring" thus also referred to our attempts at a more loose and open ambiguity between inside and out.

In Sendai we had tubes penetrating the floors. Where in an ordinary office building there would be no relationship between up and down, the introduction of tubes gave visual intimations of other floors as well as serving to mutually connect vertical traffic spaces. They made for a degree of interpenetrability between floors, what we might term a "blurring" of levels.

In both exhibition spaces, computer graphic simulations of Sendai were shown in four large-screen video projections. These black and white CG images were "collages" of plans we'd drawn up over the last few years toward realizing the building, running studies that changed minutely over repetition forming a series of overlapping floor plans that could be projected sequentially. The study process was thus compressed in time and displayed as a kind of graphic sign notation. The forest of tubes cut into cross-section and elevation appeared in video projection to flow endlessly in both vertical and horizontal directions. All were abstractions of the spatial experience of the building, depicting the Sendai Mediathèque free of spatial and temporal thresholds, yet another sense of "blurring".

At the Tokyo exhibition, alongside these CG screens were monitors showing hundreds of digital images of the building site. The actual site was a raw struggle with "steel", the very antithesis of the clean exact world of abstract computer graphics. We'd recorded over a year's worth of these metalwork battle scenes. The labours of working the thick heavy metal, applying the heat of welding torches, beating bent steel plates, cutting and stripping, welding again, iron that would stop at nothing until it was covered with scars, virtually a time-lapse history of primitive civilization since the iron age in its fight with physical matter. Matter that can never be more than matter, almost pitiable for its very strength.

The Sendai Mediathèque was thus a space in which these two completely different visions existed: the slowly flowing abstracted sign-space of the huge wall screens, and the metal-grimed matter-scape of the monitors. The steel wars came to an end, but the signifier streams still flow on. The Sendai Mediathèque is soon to open as a facility. These two diametrically coexistent spaces or not, the "building" will start to be used and become part of society. Even though the mediathèque has already been "in use" for five years, the opening is merely a point of passage in the building's long history. For it still must continue to be created and must go on changing. The Sendai Mediathèque must always remain "under construction".

2000

Appendices

Biography

Toyo Ito was born in Japan in 1941.

He graduated from Tokyo University in 1965. From 1965 to 1969 he worked in the studio of Kiyonori Kikutake, a leading member of the Metabolism movement. In 1971 he opened his own studio in Tokyo, called Urban Robot (URBOT) until 1979 and subsequently Toyo Ito & Associates, Architects.

He commenced his career working predominantly on the design of residential buildings, culminating in that of his own home, Silver Hut (1986), after which he obtained his first public commissions and began to work on a large scale. He is currently engaged in the construction of the pavilions of the Hiroshima Trade Fair Centre and the design of Mahler 4, a high-rise office block in the city of Amsterdam.

Since 1990 he has been invited to take part in a number of major international competitions, including the ones for the Maison de la culture du Japon in Paris (1990), the Library of the University of Paris (1992), the extension of the Museum of Modern Art in New York (1997) and the Centre for the Contemporary Arts in Rome (1999).

Honorary professor at the University of North London, he has also been invited to teach at other major universities, including Columbia University in New York in the academic years 1991–92 and 1994–95; the Berlage Institute in Amsterdam in 1992; Harvard University in Cambridge, Mass., in the academic years 1994–95 and 1995–96.

He has participated in various seminars and conferences, including the seminar dedicated to Alvar Aalto at Helsinki in 1994, where he gave a lecture entitled "Architecture that Creates Its Context", conferences at the Centre Pompidou in Paris in 1997 and at the Milan Triennale in 2000 and the symposium "Japanese Architecture" at the Venice University of Architecture in the academic year 1999–2000.

He has received numerous prizes and awards: the prize of the Japanese Institute of Architecture for the Silver Hut in 1986; the prize of the city of Kumamoto for the Yatsushiro Museum in 1991 and the Yatsushiro Fire Station in 1996; the Interarch '97 prize, gold medal of the Bulgarian Union of Architects in 1997; the prize dedicated to Arnold W. Brunner by the American Academy of Fine Arts in 2000.

His has work has been in various exhibitions, including "A New Wave of Japanese Architecture" which travelled to a number of cities in the United States from 1978 to 1979; "Post

Metabolism", held at the Architectural Association of London in 1978; the travelling exhibition "Architecture International Series" which visited Sydney and Melbourne in 1987; "Transfiguration – Europe '89" at Brussels in 1989; the exhibition at the In. Arch. in Rome in 1990; "Japan Today '95, the Third Reality", at the Louisiana Museum in Copenhagen in 1995; "Today's Japan" in Toronto, in 1995; "Moving Cities", an exhibition travelling to the cities of Vienna, Bordeaux, New York, Copenhagen, London and Helsinki between 1997 and 2000; "At the End of the Century: a Hundred Years of Architecture", a travelling

exhibition organized by the MOCA in Los Angeles in 1999; he also participated in the Venice Biennali of 1996 and 2000.

A series of monographic exhibitions on his work have been staged, including: "Toyo Ito: Architecture for a Silver City", at Fiesole in 1986; "Toyo Ito", at the Tooricho Gallery in Yatsushiro, Kumamoto, in 1992; "Electronic Surface, Liquid Structure" at the O Museum in Tokyo in 1993; "Blurring Architecture", a travelling exhibition held at the Sümondt Ludwig Museum in Germany, the TN Probe Gallery in Tokyo and the DeSingel Museum in Antwerp from 1997 to 2000.

Bibliography

Writings by Toyo Ito

1978
"Collage and Superficiality in Architecture", in *A New Wave of Japanese Architecture*, catalogue of the exhibition at the Institute for Architecture and Urban Studies, catalogue no. 10, New York, p. 68.

1981
Editor of the Japanese edition of *The Mathematics of the Ideal Villa and Other Essays* by Colin Rowe, Tokyo.

1982
"In Search of a Context", 1971, in *Japan Architect*, April, p. 22.

1985
"Architecture of Wind", in *Kenchiku Bunka*, January (also in Toyo Ito, *Escritos*, Colección de Arquitectura 41, Colegio Oficial de Aparejadores y Arquitectos Técnicos, Libreria Yerba, Cajamurcia, Murcia 2000, pp. 21–43).
"The Primitive Hut in the Modern Town", in *Japan Architect*, May.

1986
"Cultural Center in Fujisawa", in *Space Design*, September, p. 29.
"Nomad Restaurant Project", in *Space Design*, September, p. 32.

1988
"Una arquitectura que pide un corpo androide", in Toyo Ito, *Escritos*, Colección de Arquitectura 41, Colegio Oficial de Aparejadores y Arquitectos Técnicos, Libreria Yerba, Cajamurcia, Murcia 2000, pp. 45–65).

1989
Kaze no Henyotai – Transfiguration of Winds, Seidosha, Tokyo.

1990
"Architecture in a Stream", in *Shinkenchiku*, October (also in Toyo Ito, *Escritos*, Colección de Arquitectura 41, Colegio Oficial de Aparejadores y Arquitectos Técnicos, Libreria Yerba, Cajamurcia, Murcia 2000, pp. 67–80).

1991
"Architecture as Metamorphosis", in *Jutaku Kenchiku*, February (also in Toyo Ito, *Escritos*, Colección de Arquitectura 41, Colegio Oficial de Aparejadores y Arquitectos Técnicos, Libreria Yerba, Cajamurcia, Murcia 2000, pp. 81–95).
"Architecture in a Simulated City", in *Kenchiku Bunka*, December (also in *El Croquis*, 71, 1995, pp. 6–15, and in Toyo Ito, *Escritos*, Colección de Arquitectura 41, Colegio Oficial de Aparejadores y Arquitectos Técnicos, Libreria Yerba, Cajamurcia, Murcia 2000, pp. 97–111).

1992
"A Travel for a Transparent Erotic Space", published in the special series of *Gendai Shiso, I: Ecology of the Landscape*, September (also in Toyo Ito, *Escritos*, Colección de Arquitectura 41, Colegio Oficial de Aparejadores y Arquitectos Técnicos, Libreria Yerba, Cajamurcia, Murcia 2000, pp. 113–30).
"Vortex and Current. On Architecture as Phenomenalism", in *A.D. Architectural Design*, nos. 9–10, September.
Yatsushiro Municipal Museum, Toto, Tokyo.

1993
"A Garden of Microchips", in *JA Library*, 2, July (also in Toyo Ito, *Escritos*, Colección de Arquitectura 41, Colegio Oficial de Aparejadores y Arquitectos Técnicos, Libreria Yerba, Cajamurcia, Murcia 2000, pp. 131–49).
"The Visual Image of the Microelectronic Age", in *JA Library*, 2, Shinkenchikusha, Tokyo, pp. 5–15.

1994
"Le Corbusier Rendered into Line Drawings", April (also in Toyo Ito, *Escritos*, Colección de Arquitectura 41, Colegio Oficial de Aparejadores y Arquitectos Técnicos, Libreria Yerba, Cajamurcia, Murcia 2000, pp. 151–160).

1995
"Bay Area. Landscape-thoughts on Two Projects", in *Shinkenchiku*, July (also in Toyo Ito, *Escritos*, Colección de Arquitectura 41, Colegio Oficial de Aparejadores y Arquitectos Técnicos, Libreria Yerba, Cajamurcia, Murcia 2000, pp. 161–174).
"The Image of Architecture in the Electronic Age", in *Kenchiku Zasshi*.

"Public Architecture as a Passage Point", in *Shinkenchiku*, July (also in Toyo Ito, *Escritos*, Colección de Arquitectura 41, Colegio Oficial de Aparejadores y Arquitectos Técnicos, Libreria Yerba, Cajamurcia, Murcia 2000, pp. 175–87).

1997
"Tarzans in the Media Forest", in *2G*, 2, 1997.
"Three Transparencies", in *Suké Suké*, Nuno Nuno Books, Tokyo, pp. 19–23.

1998
"A Body Image Beyond the Modern: Is There Residential Architecture Without Criticism?", in *Shinkenchiku*.
"Which is the Reality of Architecture in the Future City", December (also in Toyo Ito, *Escritos*, Colección de Arquitectura 41, Colegio Oficial de Aparejadores y Arquitectos Técnicos, Libreria Yerba, Cajamurcia, Murcia 2000, pp. 189–201).

1999
Blurring Architecture, Charta, Milan 1999.
"Changing the Concept about What Boundaries Are", December (also in Toyo Ito, *Escritos*, Colección de Arquitectura 41, Colegio Oficial de Aparejadores y Arquitectos Técnicos, Libreria Yerba, Cajamurcia, Murcia 2000, pp. 203–16).

2000
Escritos, Colección de Arquitectura 41, Colegio Oficial de Aparejadores y Arquitectos Técnicos, Libreria Yerba, Cajamurcia, Murcia.
Report on Mediathèque in Sendai (also in Toyo Ito, *Escritos*, Colección de Arquitectura 41, Colegio Oficial de Aparejadores y Arquitectos Técnicos, Libreria Yerba, Cajamurcia, Murcia 2000, pp. 217–38).

Writings on Toyo Ito

1986
Kenneth Frampton, "Ukiyo–e and the Art of Toyo Ito", in *Space Design*, September, p. 144.
Lynne Breslin, "Ito and Ecriture", in *Space Design*, September, p. 90.
Koji Taki, "Fragments and Noise, the Architectural Ideas of Kazuo Shinohara and Toyo Ito", in *Architectural Design*, May–June.

1988
Toyo Ito, monograph, Shinkenchikusha, Tokyo.

1991
Toyo Ito, Architecture Fluctuante, Institut Français d'Architecture, Paris.
S. Roulet, S. Soulie, *Toyo Ito*, monograph, Electa Moniteur, Paris.
Koji Taki, "Towards an Open Text. On the Work and Thought of Toyo Ito", in *Toyo Ito*, Electa Moniteur, Paris, pp. 6–18.
Patrice Goulet, "Möbius Bands", in *Toyo Ito*, Electa Moniteur, Paris, pp. 18–24.

1993
Yoshiharu Tsukamoto, "Toyo Ito: An Opaque 'Transparency'", in *JA Library*, 2, Shinkenchikusha, Tokyo, pp. 154–58.
Christian Hauvette, "The Path Between Abstraction and Metaphor", in *JA Library*, Shinkenchikusha, Tokyo, pp. 88–91.

1995
Koji Taki, "Una conversaciòn con Toyo Ito", in *El Croquis*, 71, Barcelona, pp. 16–32.
Inaki Abalos, Juan Herreros, "Toyo Ito. El tiempo ligero", in *El Croquis*, 71, Barcelona, pp. 32–48.
Toyo Ito, Architectural Monograph, 41, Academy Editions, London.

1997
Toyo Ito, in *2G*, 2, monographic issue, Barcelona.

1999
"Toyo Ito", in *Pro Architect*, 15, Archiworld, Seoul.

2000
A. Maffei, "La mediateca di Sendai: un organismo scomposto", in *Casabella*, 684–85, pp. 144–65.

Writings on His Works

Aluminium House, Kanagawa, 1970–71
Shinkenchiku, 10, 1971
JA, 2, 1972
Toshijutaku, 11, 1971; 3, 1976
Jutakukenchiku, 7, 1985
SD, 9, 1986
Bessatsu-Shinkenchiku, 1988

Cottage in Sengataki, Nagano, 1973–74
Kenchiku Bunka, 6, 1974
GA Houses, 4, 1978
Jutakukenchiku, 7, 1985
SD, 9, 1986

Black Recurrence, Tokyo, 1974–75
Shinkenchiku, 8, 1975
JA, 1, 1976; 10–11, 1977
GA Houses, 4, 1978
Jutakukenchiku, 7, 1985
SD, 9, 1986
Bessatsu-Shinkenchiku, 1988

Hotel D, Nagano, 1974–77
GA Houses, 4, 1978
Interior, 3, 1978
JA, 5, 1978
Kenchiku Bunka, 3, 1978
Shinkenchiku, 3, 1978
SD, 9, 1986
Bessatsu-Shinkenchiku, 1988

White U, Tokyo, 1975–76
Kenchiku Bunka, 11, 1976
Shinkenchiku, 11, 1976
Interior, 4, 1977
JA, 4; 10–11, 1977
Jutakukenchiku, 7, 1985
SD, 9, 1986
Bessatsu-Shinkenchiku, 1988
Shinkenchiku-rinjizokan

House in Kamiwada, Aichi, 1976
Interior, 4, 1977
JA, 12, 1977
Shinkenchiku, 6, 1977
GA Houses, 4, 1978
Jutakukenchiku, 7, 1985
SD, 9, 1986
Bessatsu-Shinkenchiku, 1988

PMT Building, Nagoya, Aichi, 1976–78
GA Houses, 4, 1978
JA, 7, 1978
Kenchiku Bunka, 6, 1978
Shinkenchiku, 6, 1978
SD, 3; 9, 1986

PMT Factory, Osaka, 1978–79
Kenchiku Bunka, 5, 1980
SD, 9, 1986

PMT Building, Fukuoka, 1979
Kenchiku Bunka, 5, 1980
SD, 9, 1986

House in Koganei, Tokyo, 1979
JA, 11–12, 1980
Kenchiku Bunka, 8, 1980
Shinkenchiku, 8, 1980
Jutakukenchiku, 7, 1985
SD, 9, 1986
Bessatsu-Shinkenchiku, 1988

House in Chuorinkan, Kanagawa, 1979
JA, 11–12, 1980
Shinkenchiku, 8, 1980
Jutakukenchiku, 7, 1985
SD, 9, 1986
Bessatsu-Shinkenchiku, 1988

House in Kasama, Ibaragi, 1980–81
JA, 11–12, 1982
Kenchiku Bunka, 4, 1982
Shinkenchiku, 4, 1982
Toshijutaku, 4, 1982
Jutakukenchiku, 7, 1985
SD, 9, 1986
Bessatsu-Shinkenchiku, 1988

House in Umegaoka, Tokyo, 1981–82
Jutakukenchiku, 7, 1985
SD, 9, 1986

House in Hanakoganei, Tokyo, 1982–83
Shinkenchiku, 12, 1983
JA, 3, 1984
Jutakukenchiku, 7, 1985
Kenchiku Bunka, 1, 1985
Toshijutaku, 1, 1985
SD, 9, 1986
Bessatsu-Shinkenchiku, 1988

House in Denenchofu, Tokyo, 1982–83
Jutakukenchiku, 7, 1985
SD, 9, 1986

Silver Hut, Tokyo, 1982–84
a+u, 11, 1985
Interior, 2, 1985
JA, 5, 1985
Jutakukenchiku, 7, 1985
Kenchiku Bunka, 1, 1985
Shinkenchiku, 1, 1985
Toshijutaku, 2, 1985
SD, 9, 1986
Bessatsu-Shinkenchiku, 1988

Pao I, Installation for "Pao: in Dwelling for Tokyo Nomad Women", 1985
Kenchiku Bunka, 12, 1985
Shinkenchiku, 12, 1985
JA, 12, 1985; 7, 1986
SD, 9, 1986
Toshijutaku, 1, 1986
Bessatsu-Shinkenchiku, 1988

Competition Project for the Sports Complex in Owani, Aomori, 1985
SD, 9, 1986
Bessatsu-Shinkenchiku, 1988

House in Magomezawa, Chiba, 1985–86
Jutakutokushu, 9, 1986
Kenchiku Bunka, 9, 1986
SD, 9, 1986
Toshijutaku, 9, 1986
Bessatsu-Shinkenchiku, 1988

Honda Automobile Showroom, Tokyo, 1985–86
SD, 9, 1986

Competition Project for the Fujisawa Municipal Cultural Complex, Kanagawa, 1985–86
Kenchiku Bunka, 4, 1986

SD, 9, 1986 (project)
Shinkenchiku, 4, 1986
Bessatsu-Shinkenchiku, 1988

M Building in Kanda, Tokyo, 1985–87
SD, 9, 1986 (project)
Kenchiku Bunka, 10, 1987
Shinkenchiku, 10, 1987
Bessatsu-Shinkenchiku, 1988

Exhibition: "Furniture for Tokyo Nomad Women", Tokyo, 1986
SD, 9, 1986 (project)
Bessatsu-Shinkenchiku, 1988

Nomad Restaurant, Tokyo, 1986
Icon, 11, 1986
Kenchiku Bunka, 10, 1986
SD, 9, 1986
Shitsunai, 11, 1986
Shotenkenchiku, 11, 1986
Bessatsu-Shinkenchiku, 1988

Tower of Winds, Kanagawa, 1986
SD, 9, 1986 (project)
Kenchiku Bunka, 2, 1987
Shinkenchiku, 2, 1987
Bessatsu-Shinkenchiku, 1988
Lotus International, 75, 1993

Project for House in Saijo, Hiroshima, 1986
SD, 9, 1986
Bessatsu-Shinkenchiku, 1988

House in Takagicho, Tokyo, 1986–88
Bessatsu-Shinkenchiku, 1988
Jutakutokushu, 7, 1988
Shitsunai, 7, 1988
Kenchiku Bunka, 5, 1989

Project for Noh Theatre, 1987
Bessatsu-Shinkenchiku, 1988

MAC Project, Tokyo, 1987
Bessatsu-Shinkenchiku, 1988

Roof-garden Project, Tokyo, 1988
Bessatsu-Shinkenchiku, 1988

I Building in Asakusabashi, Tokyo, 1988–89
Bessatsu-Shinkenchiku, 1988
Kenchiku Bunka, 10, 1990
Shinkenchiku, 10, 1990

Yatsushiro Municipal Museum, Kumamoto, 1988–91
Kenchiku Bunka, 12, 1991
Shinkenchiku, 11, 1991
GA Document, 33, 1992
JA Library, 2, 1993
El Croquis, 71, 1995

Amusement Complex H, Tokyo, 1988–92
GA Japan, 3, 1993
JA Library, 2, 1993
Kenchiku Bunka, 12, 1991 (project); 4, 1993
Shinkenchiku, 4, 1993

T Building in Nakameguro, Tokyo, 1989–90
Kenchiku Bunka, 10, 1990

Shinkenchiku, 10, 1990

Guest House for Sapporo Brewery, Hokkaido, 1989
Bessatsu-Shinkenchiku, 1988 (project)
Kenchiku Bunka, 11, 1989
Shinkenchiku, 11, 1989

Pastina Restaurant, Tokyo, 1989
Bessatsu-Shinkenchiku, 1988
Kenchiku Bunka, 11, 1989
Shinkenchiku, 11, 1989

Pao II, Exhibition Project for "Pao: a Dwelling for Tokyo Nomad Women", Brussels, 1989
Bessatsu-Shinkenchiku, 1988
Kenchiku Bunka, 10, 1990
Shinkenchiku, 10, 1990

Galleria U in Yugawara, Kanagawa, 1989–91
Kenchiku Bunka, 12, 1991
Shinkenchiku, 11, 1991
JA Library, 2, 1993
El Croquis, 71, 1995

F Building in Minami-Aoyama, Tokyo, 1989–91
Kenchiku Bunka, 12, 1991
Shinkenchiku, 12, 1991

Competition Project for the Maison de la culture du Japon, Paris, 1990
Shinkenchiku, 10, 1990

Gate of Okawabata River City 21 ("Egg of Winds"), Tokyo, 1990–91
Kenchiku Bunka, 12, 1991
Shinkenchiku, 12, 1991
Lotus International, 75, 1993

Shimosuwa Municipal Museum, Nagano, 1990–93
Kenchiku Bunka, 12, 1991 (project)
Shinkenchiku, 11, 1991 (project); 7, 1993
GA Japan, 4, 1993
JA Library, 2, 1993
El Croquis, 71, 1995

"Visions of Japan" Exhibition, London, 1991
Kenchiku Bunka, 12, 1991
Shinkenchiku, 11, 1991

Hotel P, Hokkaido, 1991–92
Kenchiku Bunka, 12, 1991 (project); 9, 1992
Shinkenchiku, 9, 1992
GA Japan, 2, 1993
Lotus International, 82, 1994
El Croquis, 71, 1995

ITM Building, Ehime, 1991–93
Kenchiku Bunka, 12, 1991 (project); 4, 1993
GA Japan, 3, 1993
JA Library, 2, 1993
Shinkenchiku, 3, 1993
El Croquis, 71, 1995

Tsukuba South Multi-storey Car Park, Ibaragi, 1991–94
JA Library, 2, 1993 (project)

Shinkenchiku, 6, 1994
El Croquis, 71, 1995
SD, 8, 1995

Planning and Urban Design for Luijazui Central Area, Shanghai, 1992
GA Japan, 3, 1993
JA Library, 2, 1993
El Croquis, 71, 1995

Competition Project for the University of Paris Library, Paris, 1992
GA Japan, 4, 1993
JA Library, 2, 1993
El Croquis, 71, 1995

Competition Project of Rejuvenation for Antwerp, Antwerp, 1992
Kenchiku Bunka, 12, 1991
GA Japan, 2, 1993
JA Library, 2, 1993
JA14, 2, 1994
El Croquis, 71, 1995

Old People's Home in Yatsushiro, Kumamoto, 1992–94
Kenchiku Bunka, 12, 1991 (project); 6, 1994
JA Library, 2, 1993 (project)
JA14, 2, 1994
Shinkenchiku, 6, 1994
Domus, 771, 1995
El Croquis, 71, 1995
2G, 2, 1997, Toyo Ito

Yatsushiro Fire Station, Kumamoto, 1992–95
JA Library, 2, 1993 (project)
JA14, 2, 1994 (project)
El Croquis, 71, 1995 (under construction)
GA Japan, 15, 1995
JA19, 3, 1995
Shinkenchiku, 7, 1995
2G, 2, 1997, Toyo Ito
Arquitectura Viva, 1, 1997

Eckenheim Municipal Kindergarten, Frankfurt am Main, 1993
Kenchiku Bunka, 12, 1991
JA Library, 2, 1993
Archis, 12, 1994
DBZ, 2, 1995

Competition Project for O Hall and Museum, Saitama, 1993
GA Japan, 7, 1994
JA14, 2, 1994
El Croquis, 71, 1995

Nagaoka Lyric Hall, Niigata, 1993–96
El Croquis, 71, 1994 (project); 88–89, 1998
JA14, 2, 1994 (project)
2G, 2, 1997
Architecture, April 1997
Shinkenchiku, 1, 1997
Domus, 800, 1998

Dome in Odate, Akita, 1993–97
JA14, 2, 1994 (project)
2G, 2, 1997 (under construction)
GA Japan, 28, 1997
Kenchiku Bunka, 9, 1997
Shinkenchiku, 9, 1997

359

Arquitectura Viva, 59, 1998
Domus, 800, 1998
Lotus International, 99, 1998

S House in Tateshina, Nagano, 1994–95
JA19, 3, 1995 (project)
GA Houses, 49, 1996
Jutakutokushu, 7, 1996

Community Activities & Senior Citizen's Day Care Centre in Yokohama, Kanagawa, 1994–97
JA19, 3, 1995 (project)
GA Japan, 22, 1996
Shinkenchiku, 7, 1997
Casabella, 657, 1998
Casabella, 676, 2000
TU Delft, *Plandocumentatie Kleine Woonhuizen*

S House in Oguni, Kumamoto, 1995–96
2G, 2, 1997 (Toyo Ito)
GA Japan, 25, 1997
Jutakutokushu, 3, 1997

Ota-ku Resort Complex in Nagano, Nagano, 1995–98
JA19, 3, 1995 (project)
GA Japan, 22, 1996 (project); 34, 1998
2G, 2, 1997 (project)
Lotus International, 97, 1998
Shinkenchiku, 9, 1998
Kenchiku Bunka, 6, 1999

Project for an Information Centre in Urayasu, Chiba, 1996
2G, 2, 1997

Notsuharu Town Hall, Oita, 1996–98
Kenchiku Bunka, 9, 1997 (project)
GA Japan, 36, 1999
Kenchiku Bunka, 6, 1999
Shinkenchiku, 1, 1999

T Hall in Taisha, Shimane, 1996–99
JA14, 2, 1994 (project)
GA Japan, 17, 1995 (project)
Lotus International, 99, 1998
Kenchiku Bunka, 6, 1999; 1, 2000
Architectural Record, 5, 2000
Axis, 3.4, 2000
Casabella, 682, 2000
Shinkenchiku, 1, 2000

MOMA 21, Competition Project for Extension of the Museum of Modern Art, New York, 1997
Lotus International, 95, 1997

Crystal Ballpark, Competition Project for the Seoul Dome, Seoul, 1997
GA Japan, 32, 1998
Kenchiku Bunka, 6, 1999

T House in Yutenji, Tokyo, 1997–99
JA34, summer 1999
Jutakutokushu, 6, 1999
Casabella, 676, 2000
GA Houses, 60

Aluminium House in Sakurajosui, Tokyo, 1997–2000
GA Japan, 38, 1999 (project)
JA37, spring 2000 (under construction)

Jutakutokushu, 4, 2000
Kenchiku Bunka, 4, 2000
Monument, 2000
Shitsunai, 11, 1999 (under construction); 3, 2000

Sendai Mediathèque, Miyagi, 1997–2000
JA14, 2, 1994 (project)
GA Document, 43, 1995 (project)
JA19, 3, 1995 (project)
Technique & Architecture, 422, 1995 (project)
Shinkenchiku, 11, 1996 (project)
Lotus International, 93, 1997 (project)
Shitsunai, 3, 1997 (project)
The Virtual Architecture, Tokyo University Digital Museum, Tokyo 1997 (project)
Domus, 800, 1998 (project)
El Croquis, 88–89, 1998
GA Japan, 36, 1999; 38, 1999; 39, 1999; 40, 1999; 41, 1999; 43, 2000 (report on the work in progress)
Kenchiku Bunka, 6, 1999
AMC, 104, 2000
Casabella, 684–85, 2000
Hunch, vol. 2, 2, 2000 (project)
Shinkenchiku, 2, 2000 (project)

Trade Fair Centre in Hiroshima, 1997–
GA Document, 2000

Competition Project for the Extension of the Bank of International Settlements, Basel, 1998
GA Japan, 40, 1999
Kenchiku Bunka, 6, 1999

"Health Future" Installation, Expo 2000 Hanover, 1998–2000
ARCH+, 149–50, 2000

Project for the Centre for the Contemporary Arts, Rome, 1999
GA Document, 58, 1999
Kenchiku Bunka, 6, 1999

Agricultural Park in Oita, 2000–01
Lotus International, 97, 1998 (project)

Photograph Credits

We would like to thank Toyo Ito & Associates, Architects, for supplying the illustrative material of this volume.

The photographs published in it are the work of:
000Studio, p. 235
Andrea Maffei, pp. 240 bottom, 251
Dana Buntrock, pp. 184, 325 centre
Hiro Sakaguchi, pp. 237, 238, 239, 240 top and centre, 241, 244, 245, 246–47, 250, 252, 253, 254, 255, 256, 257, 258, 259
Hiroyuki Hirai, pp. 272 bottom right, 274, 276, 329 bottom, 332 centre
Kaoru Mende, p. 319 centre
Katsuaki Furudate, p. 46
Kindai Kenchiku, p. 356
Koji Taki, pp. 33 top, 305 centre
Meyer und Kunz, p. 322 bottom
Mikio Kamaya, pp. 160, 161, 162 bottom, 164–5, 323 bottom

Nàcasa & Partners, pp. 248, 324 bottom
Naoya Hatakeyama, pp. 212, 114, 115, 117, 118–19, 122–23, 127, 129, 131, 135, 139 top, 140, 141, 142–43, 145, 147, 148, 174, 176, 318 bottom, 320 top, 321 top, 322 centre, 325 top
Sadamu Saito, p. 320 centre
Skinkenchiku-sha, pp. 15, 17, 20, 37, 38, 41, 42–43, 62, 70, 71 left, 84–5, 181, 185 bottom, 223, 225, 285, 288, 304 top and bottom, 305 bottom, 309 centre, 310 centre, 313 bottom, 321 centre
Shuji Yamada, pp. 36, 306 top
Tomio Ohashi, pp. 11 bottom, 12, 14, 16 bottom, 22, 32, 39, 45, 47, 48, 49, 52, 53, 54, 56, 57, 58, 58–59, 63, 64–65, 67, 71 right, 72–73, 75, 76, 78, 79, 87, 88, 90–91, 93, 95, 97, 100, 101, 103, 104–05, 106, 108, 110, 111, 121, 124, 125, 128, 134, 136, 137, 139 bottom, 150–51, 152–53, 154, 156, 158, 167, 169, 170, 172, 173, 187, 188, 191, 192, 193, 195, 196–97, 197, 199, 200, 202, 203, 204, 205, 208–09, 216–17, 218, 220–21, 227, 228, 230, 231, 267, 278, 281, 292, 293, 294, 295, 296, 306 bottom, 307 top, centre and bottom, 308 top and bottom, 309 top, 311 top and bottom, 312 bottom, 313 centre, 314 top, centre and bottom, 315 top, centre and bottom, 316 top and bottom, 317 centre and bottom, 318 top and centre, 319 bottom, 320 bottom, 321 centre and bottom, 322 top, 323 top and centre, 324 centre, 325 bottom, 326 top and centre, 327 centre, 328 top, 329 top, 330 centre
Tohru Waki (Shokokusha), pp. 162 top, 304 centre
Yu Suzaki, pp. 28, 29
Yutaka Suzuki, pp. 28, 29

The publisher is at the disposal of any copyright holders of illustrations that have not been identified.